PAPERS OF THE
YUGOSLAV-AMERICAN SEMINAR
ON MUSIC

Papers of the Yugoslav-American Seminar on Music

Edited by
MALCOLM H. BROWN

School of Music
Russian and East European Institute

INDIANA UNIVERSITY
BLOOMINGTON

School of Music
Russian and East European Institute

INDIANA UNIVERSITY

Copyright © 1970 by Indiana University

No part of this book may be reproduced in
any form, by print, photoprint, microfilm,
or any other means without the permission
of the publishers

Distributed by:
SLAVICA PUBLISHERS, INC.
Post Office Box 312
Cambridge, Mass. 02139

Two staff members of the Union of Yugoslav Composers were victims of a tragic automobile accident while on a trip to conclude arrangements for the Seminar on Music. With deepest respect, the Papers of the Yugoslav-American Seminar on Music are dedicated to

the memory of
Mrs. BRANKA TASIĆ
who lost her life

and

Mrs. MIRELA STABLOVIĆ
*who will ever bear a reminder
of that senseless tragedy.*

EDITOR'S FOREWORD

The papers contained in this volume represent the rich yield of opinions, ideas, and factual information shared at the Yugoslav-American Seminar on Music in Sveti Stefan, Yugoslavia, July 6-14, 1968. During seven days of intensive interchange, the Yugoslav and American participants discussed many of the fundamental issues that concern music and musicians everywhere, irrespective of nationality. By approaching these issues in the context of an international exchange, new ideas and fresh insights inevitably emerged.

The Seminar was unique in two respects. First, never before had Yugoslav and American musicians confronted each other in formal session to share and compare common interests. Second, and more surprising, never before had a group of American musicians of such *diverse* interests met together to attempt an overview of those interests. Not only did the Yugoslavs and the Americans learn from each other — that was, after all, expected — American experts found themselves faced with the necessity of trying to explain and justify to fellow Americans aspects of their particular area which they had earlier taken for granted as self-evident. Thus, Americans learned from other Americans as much as they learned from their Yugoslav colleagues.

Doubtless, the Yugoslav participants also learned from each other, as well as from the encounter across international frontiers. The fact is that not many opportunities occur in any country for a dynamic confrontation between music school administrators, composers, music librarians, specialists in music financing, historical musicologists, music critics and commentators, music folklorists and estheticians!

These papers naturally reflect divergent approaches and disparate viewpoints. Some appear concerned essentially with factual data; others seem more engaged in the exposition and interpretation of ideas. The subjects range wide, spanning so broad an area and dealing with such varied issues that the reader may need reminding from time to time that the theme of all the "variations" is MUSIC.

The Yugoslav-American Seminar on Music was the eighth annual summer seminar sponsored jointly by Yugoslav and American institutions. The Seminar on Music was made possible through the co-operation of the Union of Yugoslav Composers and Indiana University, with the financial assistance of the United States Department of State and the Ford Foundation.

Ronald Gottesman, at that time chairman of the Advisory Committee to the American-Yugoslav Exchange Program, conceived the idea of a seminar on music in the fall of 1966 and invited the editor of the present volume to prepare a list of topics and outline a program. At my request, Miloš Velimirović of Yale University (now of the University of Wisconsin at Madison) joined me in this undertaking and contributed much thoughtful advice in formulating the final program.

A year later — following the American-Yugoslav Seminar on Federalism held in Bloomington during the summer of 1967 — the proposed seminar on music was sent to the Union of Yugoslav Composers. Vojislav Kostić, the imaginative and energetic Secretary General of the Union, persuaded his colleagues that the proposal held the promise of mutual profit and international benefit far beyond the immediate rewards to the participants in the seminar. The executive board of the Union voted not only to accept the proposal, but to assume the extraordinary expense and responsibility of having the Union of Yugoslav Composers act as host for the Seminar.

The Seminar on Music is now history. But its contribution to international musical culture has extended beyond the limits of space and time in Sveti Stefan during July of 1968. The papers printed here demonstrate a part of that contribution and provide a substantial source for its continuation.

The editor thanks Ronald Gottesman for his idea and initiative, and for his unmatched administrative acumen in carrying the venture forward; Vojislav Kostić for recognizing the rich potential of a seminar on music, and for his determination and executive virtuosity in bringing it to realization; and Carol Greene and Ivan Tasić for their unflagging energy and unfailing dedication to the details of day-to-day administration.

Without Andrej Rijavec to encourage a number of his dilatory countrymen, the editor might be waiting yet for some of the revised versions of the Yugoslav papers. Barbara Krader verified the correctness of the English translation of Cvjetko Rihtman's paper. Miloš Velimirović assumed the heroic task of translating into English Enriko Josif's fanciful and highly personal Serbian. The editor, however, prepared the final English texts of all the Yugoslav papers.

The bibliographic notes and references that accompany a number of the papers, both Yugoslav and American, appear as their authors prepared them. Because of severe time limitations, the editor could not accept the responsibility for verifying their accuracy and completeness.

Dan Morgenstern, the American specialist designated to speak on the subject "Light and Popular Music in the United States," not only failed to

Editor's Foreword

appear at the Seminar sessions, but lacked the courtesy to explain his absence or to apologize to the other participants for his profound disregard of common consideration. The paper he wrote and submitted in advance of the Seminar has not been included in this publication.

Without the generous material and moral support of the Union of Yugoslav Composers, the Seminar would never have been possible.

Appreciation is also due the Indiana University Office of Research and Advanced Studies for funds in support of the Seminar and for publication of the papers.

Finally, I warmly and most sincerely thank the Yugoslav and American participants who took our program outline and from it shaped the true meaning and substance of the Yugoslav-American Seminar on Music.

Malcolm H. Brown

Bloomington, Indiana
August, 1969

CONTENTS

	Editor's Foreword	*Malcolm Brown*	vii
I	Financing Music in Yugoslavia	*Vojislav Kostić*	1
II	Support for Music in the United States	*Nancy Hanks*	9
III	Schooling the Young Composer in Yugoslavia	*Milo Cipra*	20
IV	The Schooling of Young Composers in the United States	*Charles Wuorinen*	26
V	The Scope of Music Studies in Yugoslav Music Institutions	*Predrag Milošević*	35
VI	The Scope of Music Studies in American Music Institutions	*Wilfred C. Bain*	43
VII	Contemporary Trends in Yugoslav Music	*Enriko Josif*	52
VIII	Notes on American Music in the 1960's	*Lukas Foss*	58
IX	Music and the Mass Audience in Yugoslavia Today	*Ivo Supičić*	62
X	Music Today and the Mass Audience in the United States	*Howard Taubman*	67
XI	Musicological Studies in Yugoslavia	*Dragotin Cvetko*	73
XII	Musicological Studies in the United States	*Miloš Velimirović*	80
XIII	Problems of Music Bibliography In Yugoslavia	*Ivan Klemenčić*	86
XIV	Problems of Music Bibliography in the United States	*Edward N. Waters*	95
XV	Light and Popular Music in Yugoslavia	*Milivoj Koerbler*	113
XVI	Applications of Modern Technology in Musicology and Music Theory in Yugoslavia	*Andrej Rijavec*	119

XVII	Applications of Modern Technology in Musicology, Music Theory, and Composition in the United States	*Vladimir Ussachevsky*	123
XVIII	The Philosophy of Folk and Traditional Music Study in Yugoslavia	*Cvjetko Rihtman*	143
XIX	The Philosophy of Folk and Traditional Music Study in the United States	*Barbara Krader*	149
XX	The Place of Ethnomusicology in Yugoslav Music Study	*Radmila Petrović*	164
XXI	Ethnomusicology in American Music Education	*Bruno Nettl*	173
XXII	Folk Music as an Influence on Art Music in Yugoslavia	*Zija Kučukalić*	179
XXIII	Folk and Popular Music as Sources in the Development of National Schools of Composition in the Americas	*Juan Orrego-Salas*	185
XXIV	Nationalism in Textbooks, Articles, and General Studies in the History of Music in Yugoslavia	*Krešimir Kovačević*	194
XXV	Nationalism and Anti-Nationalism In American Music Histories	*H. Wiley Hitchcock*	199

Vojislav Kostić

FINANCING MUSIC IN YUGOSLAVIA

Introduction

The financing of art requires the mobilization of vast financial resources, and music is certainly one of the most expensive forms of art in this respect. The fact that financing music means financing schools and academies of music, music-theatrical institutions, music ensembles, music competitions, music festivals, music creativity, and so on, may suggest the extent of the financial commitment necessary to foster the continued development of this art which we consider so essential to the spiritual welfare of mankind.

The post-war development of cultural activities in Yugoslavia has been extremely rapid and intense. This is all the more remarkable when one bears in mind that despite the extraordinary financial burden of reconstruction after World War II, society never failed to earmark considerable funds for cultural affairs, including music. Often, however, there is a gap between needs and possibilities, and we must sometimes content ourselves with what at first sight appears modest and even insufficient in relation to real needs.

Culture Funds

Cultural activities in Yugoslavia are generally financed through Culture Funds established in the six constituent Socialist Republics (Bosnia and Herzegovina, Montenegro, Croatia, Macedonia, Slovenia, and Serbia), the two Autonomous Provinces (Vojvodina and Kosovo-Metohija), and the communes (municipalities). The adoption of the new Constitution of Yugoslavia, the decentralization of numerous activities, and the transference of some of the Federation's responsibilities to the republics obviated the *raison d'être* of the Federal Culture Fund, so it was dissolved several years ago.

Republican funds for the promotion of cultural activities are generally raised through:

1. Taxes levied by the republics on authors' royalties.
2. Republican budgets.
3. Interest on investments of the Culture Fund's monies.
4. Donations, gifts, endowments, etc.

These funds are used to promote the more important cultural undertakings in the country and abroad, to finance the activities of cultural institutions of various types, to support advanced training in cultural fields, and to provide for prizes and awards, social security insurance for free-lance artists, construction of studios and apartments for artists, publishing activities, etc.

The bulk of a republic's Culture Fund is at present drawn from budgetary commitments. A specific case will illustrate the sources of support from which a particular Culture Fund draws — the Culture Fund of the Socialist Republic of Serbia for the year 1967 will serve as an example:

Republican budget	17 per cent
Budgets of the Autonomous Provinces	19 per cent
County budgets	3 per cent
Belgrade city budget	22 per cent
Municipal budgets	39 per cent

It is readily apparent that the investments of the city of Belgrade and the municipalities considerably exceed those of the Republic and the counties. The reason for this is that Belgrade and the other municipalities support the regular activities of all the schools and cultural institutions established by them. Thus, it becomes clear that the percentage contributed by the Republic is actually the largest, since it is designated exclusively for cultural activities.

Unfortunately, the funds allocated for music fall below those for the theater or the visual arts. In Serbia, for example, out of the total granted for cultural activities in 1967, music received 8.34 per cent, the visual arts 11.7 per cent, and the theater 12.83 per cent.

Financing Schools and Academies of Music and Musical Institutions

Primary and intermediate schools of music and the academies of music are financed by the several Republican Education Committees and the municipalities. It should be pointed out, however, that part of the revenue for supporting the primary music schools comes from tuition fees. Schooling at the intermediate and academy level is free.

Musical institutions and establishments, such as orchestras, ensembles, operas, musical theaters, etc., are supported by towns and municipal communes. Town and municipal assemblies always include a Culture Council; each year the Council decides on the allotments to be made to the various musical establishments under its jurisdiction. The musical establishments are obliged to submit their annual budget requests, with line by line justifications, in good time. In addition to this source of regular support, which is expected to meet the establishment's routine maintenance costs, possibilities exist for partial self-support through monies earned by professional activities, or for extraordinary funds from the Administrative Committee in support of musical events of special significance.

The distribution of funds within a given musical institution is decided on solely by the artists employed there. The Constitution guarantees their right to self-administration.

Naturally, musicians who are professionally active outside of the institutions where they are employed on a regular basis receive separate fees for performing, arranging, composing, or performing other services. All such fees, and royalties, are subject to taxation. Of course, expenses related to professional activities are deductible. As has already been mentioned, the revenue from these taxes goes to republican culture funds.

Financing Musical Creativity

Fees payable to musicians for the public performance of their works constitute a significant means of financial support for musical creativity in Yugoslavia. The Union of Yugoslav Composers is responsible for the copyright protection of all Yugoslav composers and has established a system which provides maximum protection of a composer's interest within limits determined by law and other pertinent regulations.

The most vital issues in overseeing copyright protection, ones of paramount importance for the financing of musical creativity, are (1) the amount of copyright fees to be paid by the users of musical works and (2) the manner of distributing the monies so obtained.

The obligation to pay copyright fees is regulated in Yugoslavia by the Copyright Law, while the actual amount of such fees — under the new draft Copyright Law — will be determined by organizations of authors acting independently from any other agency. Up until now, the amount of copyright fees, on which many musicians depend for livelihood, was set by the supreme government agency charged with education and culture. This method of determining the amount is anachronistic for two reasons: (1) it does not fit into the general system of self-administration, which is the basis of Yugoslavia's entire legal and political system, since it prevents the ones who create from setting the prices of their own creations; and (2) the amount of the fees, which was fixed by a regulation dating back to 1952, is much too small under present economic conditions.

At present, fees for public performances of musical works are collected in the following manner:

A. Radio and television broadcasting stations.
   1. Stations collecting license fees are obliged to pay
      a. 4 per cent of their gross proceeds from license fees for broadcasting pure music (music not associated with any type of musical theater);
      b. 0.50 dinars per minute of broadcast time for broadcasting theatrical works which include music continuously performed.
   2. Stations not collecting license fees (local stations and "Muzak"-type systems) pay a fixed amount of 3,000 dinars per year.
B. Motion picture theaters pay a monthly fee ranging from 3 to 30 dinars for playing recordings of musical works during intermissions.
C. Public performances.
   1. Performances of works in concert are figured at 4 per cent of the gross ticket sales;
   2. Dances, dancing schools, sports stadiums, etc., pay 3 dinars per performance.
D. Restaurants, nightclubs, and the like, pay between 3 and 120 dinars per month, depending on the season of the year and the category of the establishment.

Fees are not charged if performances are given for educational or charitable purposes.

The capital cities of the republics (Belgrade, Zagreb, Ljubljana, Skopje, Sarajevo, and Titograd) have radio and television stations, and payments from them account for the majority of revenue from public performance fees. Add to this the radio stations in the remaining larger towns, the local stations and the "Muzak"-type systems, and one can begin to appreciate the scope of the broadcast medium and to understand why it provides the largest single contribution of monies from performance fees.

These royalties paid on contract by radio and television stations are received more or less automatically. Fees from other sources (shows, concerts, performances in restaurants, etc.) are collected by agents located in all the major Yugoslav cities. This service is maintained by an organization concerned exclusively with collecting royalties; it remits to the Union of Yugoslav Composers monthly sums for individual breakdown and payment to the designated composers.

The Copyright Law protects all copyright interests of Yugoslav citizens throughout the territory of Yugoslavia. Also protected under the law are first performances of foreign works in Yugoslavia; this protection is guaranteed by Yugoslavia under the terms of reciprocal international agreements.

All foreign authors are paid royalties for works published or performed in Yugoslavia, as Yugoslavia is a signatory of the Bern and Universal Conventions. The Union of Yugoslav Composers has thus far concluded reciprocal copyright protection contracts with twenty-two foreign copyright organizations, including the American organization ASCAP.

Royalties due Yugoslav and foreign composers are computed by deducting from the total amount the cost of copyright protection and the royalty tax (its rate changes almost every year). A further ten per cent deduction is then made, which goes to a fund for financing the several unions of composers and their activities. The remainder is then paid to the composer.

Financing Associations of Music Creators

As mentioned above, the funds for financing associations come primarily from the ten per cent deduction on the net royalty payments to Yugoslav and foreign composers. The deduction is reciprocal, on the basis of contractual agreement with foreign copyright organizations. These funds constitute the main source for the support of musical creativity, for they are used to finance the several republican unions of composers — those of Bosnia and Herzegovina, Croatia, Macedonia, Slovenia, and Serbia — as well as the federal Union of Yugoslav Composers. (Perhaps it should be pointed out here that music scholars as well as composers are affiliated with the unions of composers.) The republican unions act jointly as a single body in the federal Union of Yugoslav Composers, which is concerned with the promotion of musical creativity and musical culture throughout the country as a whole. Through the Union, arrangements can be made for composers and music scholars to take study trips abroad (with expenses paid by the Union), to spend their holidays in the resort owned by the Union, to have their works published, to receive commissions for works, etc. The numerous services provided by the Union for its members more than justify its existence.

Income of Composers from Royalties

The fee for public performance of non-theatrical works (mentioned above) is now decidedly outdated. Nevertheless, the total of royalties paid has been increasing with each passing year. The following table shows the *net* amount of money paid to Yugoslavia composers in royalties for non-theatrical works from 1963 to 1966:

>1963 . . . . 1,326,278.48 dinars
>1964 . . . . 1,909,962.29 dinars
>1965 . . . . 2,177,754.99 dinars
>1966 . . . . 3,357,082.77 dinars

These figures do not include royalties due from Yugoslav television stations, as these have not actually been paid due to certain administrative and legal questions still unsettled.

The continual increase in the earnings of Yugoslav composers results primarily from those royalties paid on a percentage basis (radio and concerts). Some increase may also have resulted from more efficient collection of the fees, especially in provincial areas. Also, the number of users of musical works unquestionably increases all the time.

The Union of Yugoslav Composers is presently protecting the copyright interests of approximately 3,000 Yugoslav and 10,000 foreign composers. The Union also protects those interests of Yugoslav composers abroad.

Despite all that has been done, analysis shows that the average earnings of Yugoslav composers are far from commensurate with the talent and creative work invested. For the sake of illustration, here are data on earnings in 1967 of Yugoslav composers:

> 1. Copyright fees for non-theatrical related works,
>   collected in Yugoslavia 2,816,605.31
> 2. Copyright fees for mechanically reproduced music
>   (principally phonograph recordings), collected
>   in Yugoslavia 2,020,521.82
> 3. Copyright fees for non-theatrical related works,
>   collected abroad 1,147,253.82
> 4. Copyright fees for mechanically reproduced music,
>   collected abroad 131,576.54
>   TOTAL PAID 6,115,957.49

If this total is divided by the number of Yugoslav composers protected by the Union of Yugoslav Composers (2,788 in 1967), the average income from this source is seen to amount to less than 2,200 dinars a year, or about 183 dinars a month.

True, such a generalized fact cannot be taken as an accurate reflection of the earnings of a Yugoslav composer, since individual incomes differ. What this fact does demonstrate, however, is that musical creativity in Yugoslavia is not in a position to finance itself; composers cannot earn their living only by composing. At this moment, composing music does not command a financial return equivalent to the talent and work invested. This is especially true in the case of composers of serious music.

Free-Lance Composers

The comparatively small earnings from composing music have resulted in a state of affairs that is practically a rule: a composer does not count on composing as a livelihood. He is generally employed, usually at a job connected with music in one way or the other (music teacher, music editor, musical adviser, etc.); more often than not, however, the job does not entail any creative work.

We have a few composer-enthusiasts who free-lance, composing being their only source of income. As we have seen, the royalties from serious creativity do not suffice, so these free-lancers are compelled to compose on commission from various commercial enterprises – radio, television, theater, motion picture, etc.

Being free-lancers, these composers can count on no regular monthly income. Nevertheless, society has taken it on itself to provide social security insurance for them, at present financed by republican Cultural Activities Promotion Funds. Thus, the free-lance composer does not have to worry about his retirement or health insurance.

In conclusion, it should be emphasized that regardless of the expense of financing music, regardless of the insufficiency of funds for certain musical activities, regardless of occasional lacks in even the most elementary conditions for promoting music, the art of music continues to develop in Yugoslavia with every passing day. Music has become a recognized spiritual need of the Yugoslav people, who grow increasingly less chary of the high cost when they realize it is necessary to finance the art form they love.

Nancy Hanks

SUPPORT FOR MUSIC IN THE UNITED STATES

To explain fully the patterns of support for music in the United States, one should really begin with a description of the social, political, and economic context in which the patterns of support for all the arts have developed. To do so, however, is a task far beyond our present limitations of time and space. Let me say only that the size and diversity of our country, together with the rapid sociological and technological changes that have taken place, have had tremendous effect not only on the development of the arts themselves, but on the so-called "structure" of the arts.

The lack of firm facts and figures and up-to-date knowledge in the field of the arts is appalling. There has been little fact-gathering and less research. Nonetheless, I have prepared a most rudimentary chart of the structure of the arts in America to serve as a guide in our discussion of support. I will limit myself to a consideration of the nonprofit, live, professional performing arts, *omitting* reference to commercial theater or music, to radio, television, or film, and to the tremendous amateur movement in the arts.

One must keep in mind that every figure included in this chart is at best an approximation. One should also be aware that an "organization chart" for the arts is in many respects "impossible"; some would say that it is "undesirable." I use it here as a short-cut to our discussion.

An Organization Chart of the Arts

The "structure" of the arts in the United States is vastly different from a decade ago; the next thirty years may hold even more drastic changes, but it is important to understand the basic framework from which these changes may emerge. Its components are the artists, the arts organizations, the audience, the service organizations, and the fund sources.

In terms of sheer numbers, it is interesting to note that some three hundred new arts organizations were given tax-exempt status in 1966 alone. In our country, "tax exempt" means that you are operating an educational or

THE VISUAL & PERFORMING ARTS

PROFESSIONAL ARTISTS

Dancers & singers:	2,000	Actors: 2,800
Symphony musicians:	7,500	Playwrights: 500
Painters & sculptors:	5,000	Composers: 1,200
Choreographers: 550		

— Commercial Managers
— Noncommercial Managers
— Critics
— Unions

FUND SOURCES

Individual
$200–300 million

Foundation
$20–30 million

Corporate
$16–21 million

Municipal and Community Agencies
$25–35 million

ARTS ORGANIZATIONS

Museums: $400 million
Performing: $100 million

ART MUSEUMS
620

SERVICE ORGANIZATIONS

Associated Councils of the Arts
500 members
$330,000 budget; $265,000 contributions

Arts Research Program
$400,000 budget; $400,000 contributions

Business Committee for the Arts
$250,000 budget; $250,000 contributions

American Association of Museums
4,200 members
$159,000 budget; $13,000 contributions

American Federation of Arts
3,680 members
$700,000 budget; $475,000 contributions

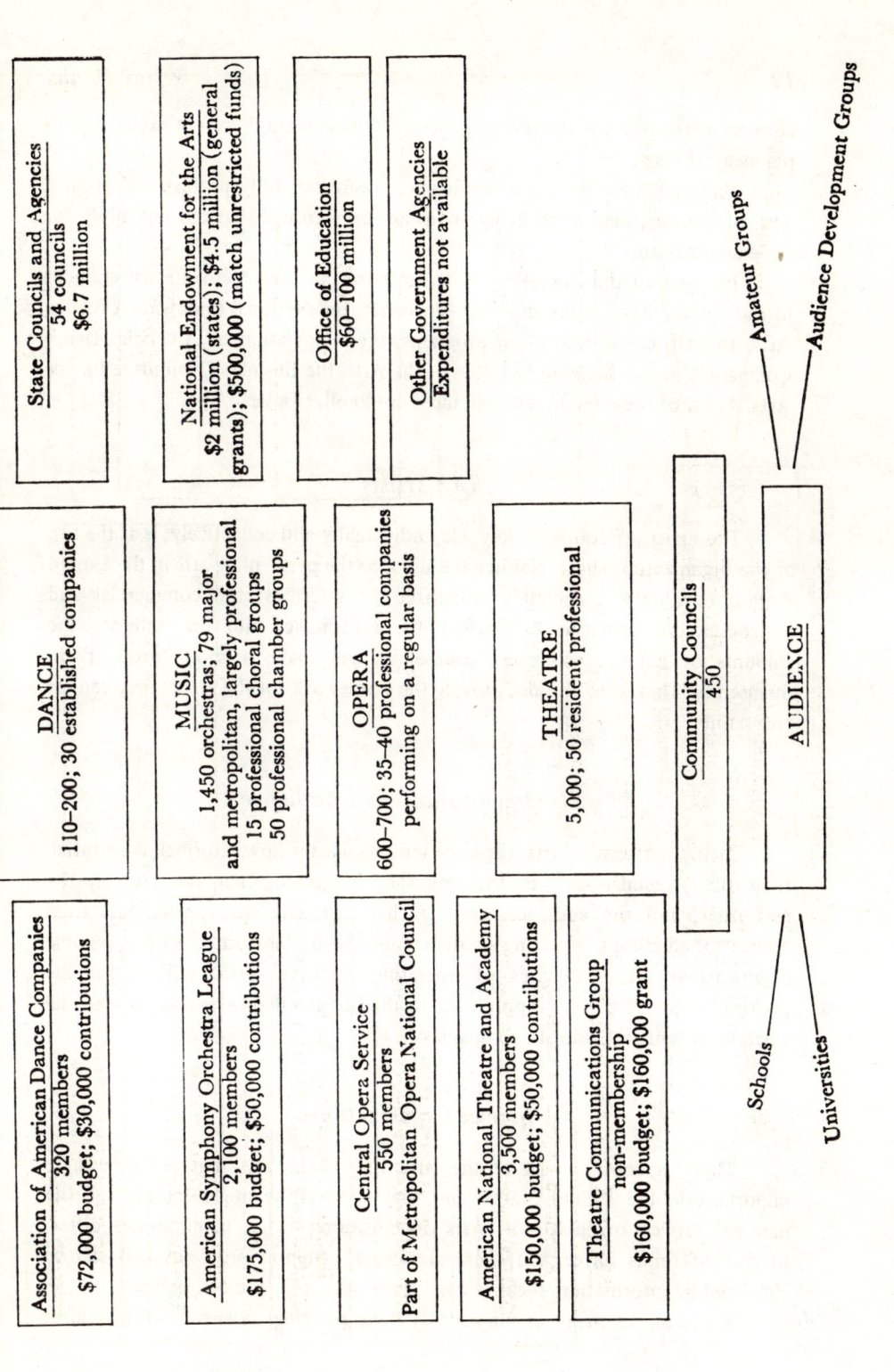

cultural institution for the public good and that you are therefore excused from payment of taxes.

Many of these new arts organizations were not fully professional groups, and, of course, there were many more amateur groups that did not apply for tax-exempt status.

In terms of the changed pattern, note on the chart the state arts councils in each of the fifty states and four territories, the National Endowment for the Arts, the Office of Education programs, the Association of American Dance Companies, the Associated Councils of the Arts, the Business Committee for the Arts. A few of these barely existed, most not at all, five years ago.

The Artists

The artist, of course, is key. He, individually and collectively, is at the top of the organization chart. Neither the unions (the performing arts in the United States are almost completely unionized), the critics, the commercial and noncommercial managers that affect his performance, nor the audience, the amounts of money, or expert counseling, can make a good "product" in themselves. They can, and do, provide the framework for the artist; they cannot create one.

Arts Organizations and Audience

In the performing arts, organization, no matter how informal, is essential. It is the "organization" in the arts that brings together the creator, the performer, and the audience. On the chart, we give the approximate total number of all groups, including amateur; followed by the number of professional organizations. The estimates of operating costs of $100 million for the performing arts, however, apply only to the nonprofit professional, not to the amateur or semiprofessional, companies.

Service Organizations

There is another part of the structure in the arts that is increasingly important in the United States, and that is what we might loosely call the national service organizations. Arts organizations differ, communities differ, sources of funds differ, but there are many common problems that can be alleviated by information, technical assistance, research, and counseling.

There are as many as nineteen of these privately financed organizations.

There are almost ninety if you add the education groups with some interest in the arts. The chart lists only nine.

The objective and purposes of these organizations are numerous and diverse. In the field of music, their concerns range from assisting orchestras to strengthen their work, stabilize their financial base, and expand their cultural services within their communities to advancing the cause of music education generally. Their role is essentially advisory.

Fund Sources

Almost all "public" aspects of our life are financed by a "pluralism" of support — earned income, government subsidy, philanthropic contributions from foundations, corporations, and individuals.

Our "attitude" in the United States toward support for the arts has changed within the last decade. The arts have often been considered ornamental, peripheral to the main-stream of American life, essentially "private" in character. Today, as clearly reflected in the new funds from all sources, the arts are increasingly considered to be "public"; a central element of a good society. (I wish to stress that by "public" I do not mean "government.")

Individuals

Historically, the arts in the United States have been almost totally financed by individuals. Although the nonprofit performing arts do not come close to meeting their expenses at the box office, the individual who buys the ticket for the performing arts is paying more than half the cost. And, in contributed funds to make up the box office deficits, individual support for the arts composes far and away the single largest source of funds. Although there is increasing support from foundations, corporations, and governments, it is essential to note that the arts are today largely financed by the individual through his purchase of tickets and through his generous contribution of funds. Total giving to all the arts by individuals, including support for museums, is estimated at between $200 and $300 million annually. This figure does not include bequests.

Philanthropy is not a recent, nor an American, invention. It should be noted, however that

> philanthropy expresses certain postulates of American life, notably decentralized responsibility and voluntary action.... [It reflects] an acceptance of responsibility by private citizens.[1]

Foundations

Philanthropic foundations are comparatively new institutions in the United States, having existed in significant numbers only within the last fifty years. The majority of foundations are established with a sizeable gift from a single donor or family and grants are made from the income derived, although some spend their capital as well. The foundations are incorporated under the laws of a state and usually are managed by a board of trustees.

[They are] ... established to maintain or aid social, educational, charitable, religious, or other activities serving the common welfare;[2]

but they are diverse in size, purpose, and program within this general framework.

There are approximately 18,000 foundations in the United States, one-third of which have assets of more than $200,000 or make annual grants totaling $10,000. Only thirteen report assets of over $200 million.

Unfortunately, not all foundations are interested in the arts. However, on an average foundations are now giving between 3 and 4 per cent of their total philanthropic dollar to the arts, with total giving estimated from $20 to $30 million each year. Music actually is a comparatively new and growing area of foundation interest. Evidence of an increase in interest is shown by a comparison of reports in *Foundation News*. In September 1960, eight music grants were reported. In March 1968, fifty-seven grants of $10,000 or over from thirty-six foundations were reported. The total of these 1968 grants amounted to $6,495,492.

Among the large foundations, the Ford Foundation initiated a long-range program of aid to the arts and humanities in 1957. It has established a program of pilot projects

> to aid talented individuals, strengthen the institutions which are their outlets, and develop musical resources at various levels throughout the nation.[3]

In the ten years since the first grant was given, approximately $174,798,807 has been awarded by the Division of Humanities and Arts, $105,150,993 for support of music.

The bulk of this total was made up in a series of grants amounting to nearly $85 million for support of the larger professional symphony orchestras. Announced in 1966, these grants exceeded any previous allocation made by a foundation to a single art form by nearly ten times.

Most foundations, at least the large national ones, direct their grants to institutions, not individuals. There are several, however, that have significant programs for the individual artist. The John Simon Guggenheim Memorial Foundation, for example, was established

> to further the development of scholars and artists by assisting them to engage in research in any field of knowledge and artistic creation in any of the fine arts, including music. . . .[4]

Since the year 1925, $769,200 has been expended on 136 Guggenheim Fellowships in music composition, with the highest individual award of $12,000 being given in 1968.

Another example is the Martha Baird Rockefeller Fund for Music which gave a total of $1,622,858 to 569 individuals in the field of music during the years from 1957 to 1967. The grants ranged from a low of $290 to a vocal artist for a one-year period to $17,000 to an accompanist during the ten-year period. The largest amount given to an individual in one year was $6,000 and three persons received this amount. The size of the grant is related to the need of the individual and not based on competitive auditions. The fund also makes grants to service organizations that give assistance to individuals in the fields.

Other foundations that have made it a practice to provide support for the individual, rather than the institution, include the Fromm Foundation, the Koussevitsky Foundation, the Thorne Foundation, and the Leventritt Foundation.

In addition to its major programs of assistance in the arts, the Rockefeller Foundation also has a program of grants for young composers or to a composer engaged in a specific type of work. Its "composers-in-residence" program has a fixed stipend of $7,500. A composer in residence at an educational institution may be asked by a conductor to work with him on a particular composition. The grants in music usually are in the range of $5,000 to $10,000.

Some foundations hold periodic competitions with prizes of cash, study scholarships, and opportunities for performances for the winning individual. A few well-known artists and musicians have established foundations and offer fellowships to assist the young musician. Other foundations also assist composers through commissions, sponsoring music concerts, recordings and publications, as well as lecture tours.

Corporations

A relatively recent source of support for the arts has come from business firms and now totals between $16 and $21 million annually. However, as well as we know, only one-half the corporations give anything to the arts; and the percentage of total giving going to the arts is about 3 to 4 per cent.

Not surprisingly, major corporate contributions have been less venturesome, less innovative, than some recent examples of foundation philanthropy or government activity in the arts. But support is on the increase, and the interest of business in the arts will unquestionably become of increasing importance in the years ahead.

Among the more recent grants made by business to the arts was a $250,000 contribution made by the Bristol-Myers Company — a manufacturer of soap products — to New York City's educational television station to underwrite a series of twelve programs on the performing and fine arts. Even more widely publicized was a grant of $500,000 from Eastern Airlines to the Metropolitan Opera Association to meet the cost of production of Wagner's *Ring* cycle from the 1967 through the 1970 seasons.

Contributions from business have been extremely helpful in the capital development of performing arts facilities. In 1965, Henry Bessire, director of development at New York's new Lincoln Center for the Performing Arts, reported contributions totaling $9 million from some 361 corporations. The experience of the John F. Kennedy Center in Washington, D.C., and the Los Angeles Music Center has been comparable.

Corporate support for the arts at the present time is generally hesitant and is often directed to a single highly visible project. But the trend is changing. The formation of a Business Committee for the Arts in October 1967 is a very significant development. Patterned on the highly successful Council for Financial Aid to Education, which stimulated business to give in that field, the major aim of the organization is to stimulate support for the arts.

As Governor Nelson Rockefeller stated,

> By helping to bring about a steady and significant increase in corporate support of the arts, the Business Committee can play a crucial role in achieving the balanced participation of every sector of American society in the high adventure of the arts, those products of man's genius that so illuminate and enhance the lives of us all.

GOVERNMENTS

Municipal and State

A major new development in the United States is the increased interest of government in the arts. Municipal governments, which actually have a long history of financing museums, are supporting the arts on the order of $25 to $35 million a year. (Private united fund raising councils in sixteen cities contribute an additional $4 million.) There are fifty state and four territorial agencies for the arts. State funds on the order of $6.7 million are now going into the arts directly through these councils. New York alone accounts for $1.9 million of this figure; and Puerto Rico is over $1 million. This year, ten councils have $100,000 or more in operative funds, and the amounts are growing, if slowly.

Federal

As long ago as 1877, a federal government council on the arts was proposed in Congress. But it was not until 1962, when President Kennedy appointed a Special Consultant on the Arts and asked him to examine programs and policies within the federal government and make recommendations for raising standards and encouraging the full use of the available opportunities for the arts that the National Council actually began to take shape. In 1965 Congress passed the law establishing the National Foundation on the Arts and the Humanities. The National Council on the Arts, composed of private citizens who are broadly knowledgeable and experienced in the arts, must advise the Chairman of the National Endowment for the Arts on policy and procedures, and must make recommendations on applications for assistance.

> The National Endowment for the Arts was authorized
> to establish and carry out a program of grants-in-aid to groups or, in appropriate cases, to individuals engaged in or concerned with the arts, for the purpose of enabling them to provide or support in the United States — 1) productions which have substantial artistic and cultural significance, giving emphasis to American creativity and the maintenance and encouragement of professional excellent; 2) productions, meeting professional standards or standards of authenticity, irrespective of origin which are of significant merit and which, without such assistance, would otherwise be unavailable to our citizens in many areas of the country; 3) projects that will encourage and assist artists and enable them to achieve standards of professional excellence; 4) workshops that will encourage and develop the appreciation and enjoyment of the arts by our citizens; 5) other relevant projects, including surveys, research, and planning in the arts.[5]

The funds from the National Endowment for the Arts by any standard of measure are peanuts. This year's appropriations included $2 million to be apportioned among the state arts agencies (approximately $37-40,000 for each), which have to be matched; $4.5 million for general grants; and $500,000 to match any unrestricted grants that might be received. The National Endowment has made modest funds go further in encouraging the arts than even its staunchest supporters would have hoped. The funds are extremely small given our total federal expenditures, but in my view *any* direct support of the arts by the federal government is a very hopeful sign.

Office of Education. The largest amount of money available for the arts within the federal government is not in the National Endowment for the Arts, but in the Office of Education. The Elementary and Secondary Education Act of 1965 made specific provision for funding innovative educational programs in the arts within our educational system. While actual dollar amounts expended on such programs across the country can only be guessed at, some knowledgeable estimates put the figure as high as $50 to $60 million annually. These programs, funded by the federal government through local educational agencies, have made extensive use of professional musicians and other performing artists. Although this is not a form of direct subsidy, it has great importance in terms both of providing additional employment opportunities for the professional artists and of developing future artists and audiences for the arts.

Through various other programs, the Office of Education has provided funds for educational research in the arts, for the development of facilities (particularly on college campuses), and for bringing the arts into a more central position in our educational system generally.

Department of State. The programs of cultural exchange, administered through the Department of State, are widely known both within the United States and abroad. At one time, they constituted virtually the only involvement of the federal government in the field of the arts.

The Fulbright Program of scholarships for a two-way exchange of students has been very important to young artists and musicians in providing grants for study abroad. Nearly 20 per cent of all grants to American students were awarded in the arts. Well over 1,000 scholarships have been given to young American musicians — composers, conductors, pianists, singers — under the Fulbright Program.

The American Specialists Program, also administered through the Department of State, has sent abroad for periods of up to a year a substantial number of established musicians and other artists for the purpose of working with their peers throughout the world.

Summary

In sum, music, like all the arts, is supported by a variety of sources under the American system. While a patronage system based on the interests of a few wealthy families or individuals was typical at one period of American history, the base of support for the arts is far broader today than it has been at any time in the past. The individual still provides the lion's share of support, and the number of individuals actively committed to support of the arts has grown dramatically. Private foundations have made a major commitment to the arts.

Business corporations are coming to recognize their responsibilities to the arts. And, perhaps most significantly, government at all levels is moving into the area of direct support in a way that would have seemed inconceivable even a few short years ago.

Editor's note: Because of unexpected and undeferrable professional obligations, Nancy Hanks was unable to attend the Seminar. She designated an able deputy, Stephen Benedict (also of the Rockefeller Brothers Fund), who presented a summary of her paper and participated in her behalf in all the Seminar sessions.

NOTES

[1] Warren Weaver, *U.S. Philanthropic Foundations, Their History, Structure, Management and Record* (New York: Harper & Row, 1967), p. vii.

[2] *The Foundation Directory* (2nd ed.; The Foundation Library Center, Russell Sage Foundation, 1964), p. 9.

[3] Weaver, *op. cit.*, p. 331.

[4] John Simon Guggenheim Memorial Foundation brochure (undated).

[5] *Public Law 89-209,* 89th Congress, S. 1483 (September 29, 1965), pp. 2-3.

Milo Cipra

SCHOOLING THE YOUNG COMPOSER IN YUGOSLAVIA

> "Ein jeder lernt nur, was er lernen kann." Goethe: FAUST, I.

At the time I agreed to write on this subject, the approach I would take came to me of its own accord: I would cover the essence of the problem in several key questions and direct those to the most renowned of our composer-educators at the four Academies of Music in Yugoslavia. Of the eight people contacted, seven replied, providing most interesting answers. It became apparent immediately that the ways of teaching composition varied greatly, in contrast to the decision at the Bled Conference some twenty years ago that a *single* curriculum be instituted for all of the Academies of Music (only three existed then) as well as for all the primary and intermediate music schools in the country. The desire to achieve unity — understandable only in view of the social and political situation at that time — soon proved to be futile and quite unacceptable in its rigidity. Things soon took the natural course of liberalization, quite in line with the main principles underlying the development of Yugoslav society as a whole.

It goes without saying that the professional formation of a young composer in Yugoslavia is not confined to the academy — to formal schooling. The musical frontiers in our country have long been thrown wide open, so the young composer is subject to all of the currents in contemporary musical thought. But to measure and evaluate the nature of this sort of "schooling" poses problems that exceed the scope of my paper. I have thought, however, that it would be interesting to examine the real role of "academic" education in the making of a composer. The poll I have taken was in fact designed to determine that "academic" role, or to put it more simply, to find an answer to the question: "What do the academies provide the young prospective composer in his search for artistic identity?"

Art academies have always been known, in a certain sense, as guardians of tradition. Not that such a role is unjustified, for the academy can thus facilitate the student's effort to fit into the established world and to do so with a minimum of meandering. The danger lies in the tendency to turn toward the past and insist on ossified formulae in support of the allegedly eternal laws of the beautiful, and thereby to shut one's eyes (or ears!) to the undeferrable demands of the present — and the present, it goes without saying, is the time to which one is most closely attached.

Here now is a summary of the answers to the first question in my poll, namely: "What are the places of classic harmony and classic counterpoint in the teaching of composition?"

All of the answers had one thing in common: the systems of classic harmony are indispensable *as a basis!* There were differences of opinion as to the manner of application, resulting mainly from the fact that the homophonic and polyphonic styles are taught as separate subjects (and by different professors) at some academies, while at others both styles are incorporated into the composition course (taught by a single professor). The historical range of the subjects as covered in the instruction also differs from place to place: in some, the students work within the limits of a single historical style period, while in others, they may go as far as Debussy (in harmony) and the masters of dodecaphony (in counterpoint). Bach's *Kunst der Fuge* and *Das wohltemperierte Klavier* are the object of particular attention. Exercises in composing motets and madrigals (in Latin, Old Slavonic, and the national languages), as well as fugues of all kinds, are required. Although some of the professors do not exceed the limits of four-part writing in their teaching of harmony, others go much farther, giving particular attention to exercises in the instrumental style as well, as recommended by most authors of modern textbooks. The exercises include performance on the piano, and in some academies examinations include (in addition to the written tests) performance *prima vista* on the piano by the candidates. Unfortunately, exercises in improvisation do not accompany the study of polyphonic styles, and are prescribed only for organists. Harmonic analysis is tied in with the study of part-writing, with particular emphasis on the organic and functional inter-relationship between form and harmony. Written papers are also required, based on the analytical methods of Husserl, Mersmann, Halm, and others.

The second question — "What textbooks do you use in teaching composition?" — elicited exhaustive answers. The best and most to the point, in my opinion, was one stating that long years of teaching constituted the best textbook.

A comprehensive list of all the authors and textbooks named would be superfluous, but some should be mentioned for the sake of general orientation:

Harmony: The Yugoslav authors Živković and Devčić, and the foreign ones Thuille and Koechlin, plus the didactically excellent Russian and Oxford textbooks.

Counterpoint and fugue: The Yugoslavs Lučić and Škerjanc, in addition to Kurth, Jeppesen, and Hindemith.

Composition and form: The Yugoslav Peričić-Skovran, and Vincent d'Indy, Albert Bertelin, and Spossobin.

Orchestration: Berlioz in the Strauss revision, Rimsky-Korsakov, Koechlin (the most thorough!), and Piston.

In addition to basic textbooks, studies, essays, and analyses appearing in both Yugoslav and foreign publications are often used. These are particularly important in the study of contemporary movements. Some of the authors' names mentioned in this regard were Leibowitz, Jelinek, Krenek, Rufer, and Boulez.

I should comment that perhaps the third question in my poll was framed because of particular conditions in Yugoslavia: "Is the teaching of composition determined to a certain extent by a knowledge of folklore?" While the answers were mainly negative, the question itself seems worthy of some additional statements.

Between the two world wars, the Music Academy in Zagreb laid special stress on the necessity of orienting composition toward the nationalistic side, arguing that only this way might Yugoslav music assert itself as something distinctive in contemporary European music. The freshly awakened nationalistic forces that had emerged on the eve of World War I, and later, demanded expression in music no less than in the political sphere. Stravinsky (in his Russian phase), Bartók, Kodály, Janaček, and the rediscovered nineteenth century Russian nationalists (particularly Musorgsky, Borodin, and Rimsky-Korsakov) became paragons to be emulated. This belated burst of Romanticism was felt less in Belgrade and Ljubljana, because the Serbs and Slovenes were more inclined toward the international music centers (Prague, Vienna, and Paris) where they had received their musical education. Moreover, in Belgrade and Ljubljana, even the tendencies considered extremist at that time appeared (influenced by Hába's and Schoenberg's ideas). We know now that this "destiny-marked historical moment" of nationalist music in Yugoslavia was limited both in time and space. We deny neither its significance nor certain of its positive results; but for all that, it was merely a passing period in the history of Yugoslav contemporary music. The present generation of composers has resolutely adopted other ideas: it thinks in internationalist terms, or perhaps in "extra-nationalist" terms. The present generation is simply *contemporary!* And, what is perhaps most surprising, we now seem to understand one another better than we could earlier, when we endeavored to speak our national musical languages.

The fourth question read: "From what periods do you draw samples and models for your analyses?"

Here again, the historical span of the material chosen varied considerably. The earliest period ranged from Palestrina (or Gallus-Petelin in Slovenia) to Bach, and the latest from the "modern classics" (Schoenberg and his circle, Stravinsky, and Bartók, among others) to the "avant-garde" (Messiaen and Boulez). Some professors went only so far as Debussy. The particular choice seems to be determined not only by the teacher's taste, but by the student's inclination. Good choice at the right moment means a great deal! The suggestion that a whole semester be devoted periodically to a thorough study of a single composer seems very appropriate. This should be a separate course, with papers written, and it should be co-ordinated with a parallel course in composition. Study scores complete with recordings, which are now so easily accessible, would make this approach interesting for non-composition majors as well.

The fifth question in the poll asked: "What importance do you attach to the study of contemporary compositional techniques (from dodecaphony to aleatorics)?"

The opinion prevails that the study of the latest techniques should be undertaken only after the student has mastered the "classic" ones. The five years devoted to composition (from which the first two are concerned primarily with harmony and counterpoint) do not suffice for a truly satisfactory study of the new styles. I should like to quote some excerpts from the answers to this fifth question:

> Regarding contemporary movements, I choose those which I myself have been able to master and understand (ethically, esthetically, and technically). I submit my personal judgment — which itself is subject to change — to the student, and he is free to accept or reject it.
>
> I think that the student should, at least in the beginning, compose in a tonal style and only later introduce contemporary innovations. Since I myself am outside these contemporary practices, I do not aim the student in their direction; I did not do so, even when my assistant X had completed a course in dodecaphony in Vienna under Jelinek.
>
> While I do not deny the new doctrines (new ones appear with every passing day), I believe that all these movements — beginning roughly at the turn of the century — are mostly experiments and should therefore be considered as phenomena rather than as finished products. They may be studied in separate courses, outside the curricular framework for composition studies.

As far as I know, no professor at a Yugoslav music academy teaches his own system of composition (as do Messiaen, Boulez, and Leibowitz, or as did Hindemith and Hába). There is also a noticeable difference between what the professor teaches (and expects his students to know for examination) and what he actually composes. Curricula based on certain principles are still too much adhered to. Today, they obviously hamper both the teacher and the student and cause crises with subtle consequences. Which brings us to the sixth question: "In teaching composition, do you follow a system of your own, and to what extent do you take into account the individual talent (and inclination) of a student or a group of students?"

The answers indicated that a student's personal preference was allowed more or less free play only in the preparation of his graduation piece. In the earlier stages of study, he is generally expected to follow the prescribed curriculum. Certainly, the acquisition of technical skill is only one side of the coin, the other being the development of a mature artistic personality (as the ultimate, post-academic goal). Both sides complement each other. The teacher should also be something of a psychologist (even a psychiatrist!).

The seventh question explored the problem of co-operation between teachers of orchestration and composition where the two are taught as separate subjects by separate teachers. The answers pointed out the need to abolish such artificial division where it is still practiced. But then another very real question arises: "Where and how are future *conductors* to learn instrumentation?"

I wish to digress for a moment to mention something not unrelated to the primary subject at hand. I should like to pay tribute to my esteemed teacher, the composer Blagoje Bersa (1873-1934). As a professor at the Zagreb Academy of Music, he worked out (some fifty years ago!) an original method by fusing the two subjects into an indivisible whole. He resolutely opposed orchestrating piano pieces and refused to teach by that method, even though he had himself been taught it at the Vienna Conservatory in the 1890's. He used to say:

> The piano style is so peculiar and different from that of the orchestra as to be nearly untransferable. Or, rather, the task imposed is so demanding that it can be carried out well only by someone who already has a good knowledge of the orchestra. You'll never learn the living language of the orchestra if you keep struggling with "transferring." Why, the spoken languages are also taught now by this direct method, rather than through translation!

And thus, he led us, through three years of carefully graduated tasks, to complete mastery of even the very complex problems of orchestration. The tasks consisted of providing us with an instrumental "skeleton," in which the roles of individual instruments or groups of instruments were indicated. We were to be "inspired" by the structure and fill it in with living music. Even a few bars would do. Studying the results, Bersa would roundly condemn a mechanical approach. He wanted "expression." He profoundly respected the personal inclinations of his students, however; thus it happened that Bersa, whose ideals were Wagner,

Mahler, Strauss, and above all Rimsky-Korsakov (as an orchestrator) — Bersa, who was a music cosmopolite, raised a generation of markedly nationalist composers. Yet, he lived in a mistaken belief: he thought the orchestra of his time a structure definite, absolute, and accomplished. He thought, with Mahler, that Beethoven orchestrated poorly and that there was nothing for us to learn there — which, in a way, was methodologically true. Bersa was an optimist, an idealist, deeply inspired with the idea of progress. He failed to see, however, the profound crisis that engulfed music at that time, above all the so-called modern orchestra with its hypertrophied sound.

And this brings us almost to the end. In the last, eighth question, I inquired about the general requirements for graduation examinations and criteria for grading.

Naturally, there is a prescribed curriculum for each year. Generally speaking, it is not overly rigid, although some think — I among them — that it should be made more flexible. Finally, there is the diploma requirement, under which the student is obliged to submit a largish orchestral composition, with or without a vocal part. This composition is worked on during the last year of study under a professor's supervision and submitted to a board of examiners for evaluation. It is also evaluated by the public, for public performance is obligatory. Our thanks are due to symphonic and radio orchestras which perform and record such pieces free of charge when the academy orchestras are not in a position to do so.

During the past few years, experimental tendencies have been increasingly present in these graduation works, and the boards of examiners have encountered some very audacious solutions, often backed by the supervising professors. This frequently leads to misunderstanding and disapproval, even to heated dispute. How then is one to establish grading criteria?

Let us now ask ourselves what it is that our schooling has given to us and what it is that we have made for ourselves afterwards. Without our schooling, we certainly would not have been what we are. But what would we have been with it *alone?* Man's development is miraculous: it is a road full of perilous and precipitous curves; following it, one is exposed to influences from all sides, swayed by unforeseen circumstances.... We learn, as Romain Rolland said somewhere, to know what to forget. "Stirb und werde!" as Goethe put it. One must know how to die in order to be able to live. To resist being captured by one's heritage. To turn both to one's own self and to the time in which one lives. To sense the demand of the moment. To feel its irretrievability. To pit freedom against the law of necessity! And thus to accomplish the mission of art in a world where everything is soon to become determined. To escape from that determination. To risk the adventure of escape. To live in danger!

Charles Wuorinen

THE SCHOOLING OF YOUNG COMPOSERS IN THE UNITED STATES

The size of the United States makes it difficult to generalize about the education of its young composers. Nevertheless, one can assert the American university as the primary institution for almost every young American composer's schooling. While there are still a few self-taught composers in the U.S. (peripheral figures such as professionals from other fields who dabble in composition: engineers, painters, happening specialists), and a fair number who receive old-fashioned conservatory training, the vast majority of young American composers receive their significant training in universities. For this reason, although they are generally able to take their place in the "concert-world" aspect of the profession, their university provenance is so influential that it has largely redefined the profession itself. Since by far the most characteristic livelihood for U.S. composers is now university teaching, a large part of their training also necessarily goes toward preparation for that role. That this is of great significance is seen from the fact that because thousands of composers have taught hundreds of thousands of undergraduates in American universities since World War II, an impressive new public has developed for new music — university trained, of young to middle years — and ignored by both music publishers and press — but not entirely by U.S. record companies. The most influential aspect of the university scene, however, is that U.S. composers have been thrown perforce into contact with other disciplines at just the time in the general compositional development when such contacts are most urgently needed, and have made contact with a new life style at just the point when the old professional musical scene is most in need of revision. Thus we have recently seen not merely an impressive expansion of compositional sophistication and resource in the U.S., but also some of the most important music-theoretical work of the century. Particularly impressive advances (regrettably almost unknown outside the U.S.) have been made in understanding the structural implications of the 12-tone system, and its profound divergences from previous musical systems.

It is important to understand the above, however, in a context that adequately defines the American university itself: a diversified catchall for many non-self-supporting activities for which U.S. society has never bothered to find adequate governmental or private subsidy. Thus we find that those arts requiring large sums for their survival, and which cannot be successfully merchandized to the mass public, tend to gravitate toward the university (while, for example, painting, which *has* been merchandized, is not so strongly connected). Certainly this is most strikingly true of music. It must also be recognized that the mere fact of university training and environment seems to have no effect favoring any specific set of compositional attitudes. In a period of justified criticism of U.S. universities for their lack of responsiveness to social issues, and their passive complicity in the realization and execution of controversial government policies, it is remarkable that their basic validity and strength in substantive matters should be shown in the impressive range and diversity of compositional attitudes manifested by university composers.

In urban universities (or those near urban centers) such as Columbia, Princeton, Yale, Harvard, and the University of California at Los Angeles, the environment is enriched by its location within a larger context of professional musical activity. Thus at Columbia, for example, the new music activities on the campus co-exist with the general proliferation of concerts of contemporary music in New York City — and the contact which Columbia students have with their teachers is complemented by those they make with the hundreds of other practicing professional composers in New York. The same is true of other urban universities. A reverse phenomenon takes place, particularly in the midwest, in less populated areas where the university (usually state supported) tends to be the major cultural institution itself and hence is directly concerned with sponsoring concerts of new music. (Three-fourths of all, including the most commercial concerts in the U.S., now take place under university auspices.) This preponderance often leads to the university's generating its own opposition. Thus at the University of Michigan, for example, where an active program in composition and performance is in operation, the milieu it has created has given rise to a non-university-affiliated extremist group (the Once Festival) opposed to the more centric position of the university composers. The university environment tends to generate and gather many relevant but usually conflicting points of view; and in this as in many other respects, the university compositional scene is part of the present decade's larger awakening from the caution, self-censorship and passivity that characterized U.S. university life immediately after World War II.

What do university composers study? I would admit at once that the superiority of the university to the conservatory usually does not lie in a superior curriculum. Most university music departments and schools of music (the latter involving more emphasis on performance than the former) offer no more imaginative or up-to-date fare than can be found at most conservatories: the routines of harmony and counterpoint, taught mainly as they were a half-century ago, still claiming to constitute the relevant musical intellection, accompanied by equally routine music-historical studies. These offerings are still widely regarded as the "basic" curriculum. Indeed, so laggard are so many music departments that I predict a violent upheaval during the next few years, since most students and young faculty find these disciplines — as they are taught, not as they are — largely irrelevant to their concerns. But it is with material traditionally considered peripheral to the "basic curriculum" that the university emerges as the best, indeed the only source for the enlightenment of the student composer. These allegedly marginal but actually central areas may be divided into the study of composition itself, the study of media, and the confrontation of relevant non-musical disciplines.

Under the first heading: The teaching of composition is of course fundamental to all other aspects of a composer's educational career, but here I refer only to direct contact between teacher and student. Naturally one cannot generalize meaningfully about such confrontations, but there are two points about the university scene: First, that it is the healthy fashion for the teacher not to assert any one compositional approach as "correct," but rather to seek the student's own predilections and identify them for him, to enable his own compositional choice. (This attitude contrasts with more doctrinaire approaches characteristically found in conservatories.) Second, that in sharp contrast to the situation a generation ago, most composition teachers in American universities are professionally active composers. (Indeed, this is more often the case than with their colleagues in conservatories.)

Since composition teaching must be devoted to direct consideration of the student's work itself, there is little time for instruction in essential but more general contemporary matters. Since few teachers make any attempt to promulgate general compositional approaches, the student must acquire the general knowledge of recent developments elsewhere. Since the curriculum to which he is subjected has little to do with contemporary issues or with preparing him for professional life, it is difficult for him independently to absorb such essential information.

Under the second heading: the study of the "media" through which compositional relations are projected has traditionally been limited to "orchestration." Naturally, any divorcement of "compositional relations" from the sound-medium by which they are to be projected creates a falsification of the compositional process itself, since the meaning of any, say, pitch/rhythmic configuration is totally dependent on its timbral, articulative, and dynamic context and its own embodiment. Here lies the major point of attack on the traditional separation of the investigation of instrumental/vocal resources from composition itself; and therefore the idea that "orchestration" can reasonably be taught by a non-composer is highly suspect, for what does a non-composer know about the relations to be "orchestrated"?

But here we are concerned with investigation of the *properties* of musical media. Thus, we include not merely traditional instrumental resources, but also considerations of newer (particularly electrically amplified) instruments, and, especially electronic media. The universities have taken the unquestioned lead in developing electronic music studios, and it is only recently that any U.S. conservatories have interested themselves in the provision of such resources for their composers. (A recent example is the Juilliard School, which has been forced into a progressive compositional stance by the pressure of events at nearby universities.) The university is thus the most logical place for the teaching of electronic synthesis. From the classic analogue studios (the first of which was established at Columbia in 1952) to other more recent methods of synthesis (often making use of the universities' computing facilities for sound generation and analysis), university composers have achieved a primacy in both production and teaching which is unlikely to be challenged by either conservatories or private studios in the foreseeable future. From formal courses to extra-curricular experimentation, a wide range of instructional electronic facilities is available to young composers. We must remember that the establishment of electronic music studios is but one reflection of the fact that composers, originally entering academic confines for economic reasons, found in the U.S. university a reasonable field for the development of a redefined compositional profession. In the university, the composer has tended increasingly to resume his rightful position at the center of the musical scene — and the studios, like the university-based performing groups which I shall mention next, were established mainly to enable the composer to reassert his authority over the actualization in sound of his ideas and over the circumstances in which the actualization is carried out and presented to the public.

While most universities still offer courses in manipulating the traditional orchestra, most students find them useless and ludicrously out of date — especially when delivered by teachers having no understanding of the relation of instruments to compositions. (Even more misguided are the occasional attempts of their composition teachers to force them actually to *write* works for orchestra.) The massive failure of American orchestras to discharge their responsibilities, not merely to U.S. composers but to seminal twentieth century literature as well, has made the study of the "orchestra" largely pointless in the life of the young composer. Since student composers cannot look forward to a professional position from which their works will be solicited by large orchestras (such solicitation having recently been put off at least a generation by the disastrous Ford Foundation orchestra subsidy program), there is little (save historical) reason for them to concern themselves with the orchestra as a relevant medium. But on the other hand, the last decade has seen the establishment on many campuses of professional performing groups, varying in size from a handful of performers to small chamber orchestras, usually directed by a composer, primarily designed to perform twentieth century music. Such groups are now in operation at Columbia, Mills College, Rutgers, Sarah Lawrence, the State University of New York at Buffalo, the University of Chicago, the University of Colorado, the University of Illinois, the University of Iowa, the University of Michigan, the University of Pennsylvania, the University of Washington, and on many other campuses. *These* are the relevant ensembles in the lives of student composers, and it is from them that they learn about instrumental resources. Moreover, if the orchestra remains a relevant force at all, it is through the accomplishment of *university* orchestras, which during the past few years have in many instances changed from predominantly student affairs to serious concert-producing organizations (the Universities of Iowa, Illinois, and Indiana are particularly outstanding cases). Naturally, these reasons impress student composers, and it is safe to say that though the first six to eight years of the university performance movement have as yet produced little formal educational result, the informal benefits are already incalculable, and the formal picture will soon change. Even now, the students' informal contacts with the campus performers are far more instructive than their formal memorization of "facts" about "orchestration."

Under the third heading: Contact with non-musical disciplines can only occur in an environment where diverse forms of intellectual activity operate in close contiguity. Perhaps even more than their teachers, therefore, student composers in U.S. universities are constantly exposed to a host of insights and methodologies far removed from the old-fashioned vagaries of the musicology/music-theory complex: disciplines which, because of their penchant for clarity and reason, encourage the tendencies in contemporary composition that lead to coherence and understanding rather than to metaphysics. Thus, paradoxically, they open the way for profound consideration of artistic and human issues, since they attempt to make the *surface* of such issues as penetrable as possible. Recent developments (largely unknown not merely outside the U.S. but *in* U.S. public musical circles as well) in theory and criticism are particular evidence for this assertion, and the responsiveness of students to such developments is most encouraging to those who value them. It is the other side of the coin from the musical nihilism which, common throughout the U.S. (and Europe), receives so much publicity. Inevitably, contacts with non-musical intellectuals greatly enrich the students' professional contacts with composers and performers.

The university degrees available are an important indication of the quality of educational life for the young composer. The Masters degree is universal, and generally considered an essential professional certification, especially for teaching. But there is increasing concern for more advanced degrees, and therefore many universities are currently awarding doctorates, and such degrees under various names are becoming increasingly available. The education of young composers in the U.S. thus follows the same unhealthy trend found elsewhere in the American educational picture: emphasis on ever more elitist degrees, the achieving of which is primarily a matter of knowing correct academic behavior rather than a reflection of mastery. But encouragement of mediocrity has long been characteristic of academia, and it is probably a less formidable obstacle to the establishment of professional standards than are the vulgarities forced upon those who would be serious composers wholly outside the university milieu.

It is not within my scope to comment generally on the U.S. musical scene, but I feel constrained to speak to one particular because of its environmental effect on young composers: the conduct of the major U.S. institutions responsible for disseminating music and information about it — the publishers, recording companies, broadcasters, and press. Here is a dismal picture indeed, especially of press and publisher. The ignorance and prejudice of the majority of critics and publishers; the irrelevance of what they do print or talk about; their often deliberate omissions and distortions: all make it almost impossible for students to use them for any reasonable informational purpose. And of course, while the meaninglessness of these institutions is a byword among educated professionals, the student is without the protection of experience, and his innocence is therefore violated. But it is some consolation that the record companies, at least, appear to be at the start of an awareness of their responsibilities to contemporary music; and their awareness is more important than that of any other disseminator, since they are now the most significant distributors of music in the U.S., and through their output determine conduct of broadcasters.

In my view, the educational picture is essentially sound, because there are so many gifted people at work within it. But its institutions desperately need revision. The problems are many: within, they emerge from the condition of universities themselves and the endemic, specific problems they pose to the education of the young composer; without, they emerge from the still massive indifference of U.S. society to cultural concerns, specifically manifested by the unenlightened behavior of the publishing, recording, and journalizing industries.

What of possible changes? Improvements may be considered under two headings, reform of curriculum and revision of the educational format; but I shall group them together.

While there is widespread agreement that traditional training is outmoded, it is amazing to what degree the old curricula for composers still hold sway in the U.S. It is still a general conceit that harmony and counterpoint should be studied as "preparation" for composition, that matters of musical intellection (historical or theoretical) are best handled by non-composers, and so forth. Clearly, it is essential to introduce changes that take account of the revolutionary compositional developments of the past seventy years. That more reflection of these by now historic changes has not occurred is particularly appalling in the university context. Of course, a major cause of the situation lies in the fact that until the post-World War II era, while most other academicians were in universities because their *professions* were traditionally practiced there, the rule usually was that musicians sought university positions to escape the pressures of professional competition. But the scene has now changed: the compositional profession in the U.S. is almost wholly practiced within universities. Obviously, curricular changes that reflect this new condition must be introduced.

First, I suggest that composition be made the beginning of any intended composer's undergraduate curriculum, instead of being deferred until he is thought "ready." All his other training must proceed from and relate directly to the specific needs revealed in his work. Second, since the encouragement of compositional skill and maturity requires a different approach with every student, the total scheme in which the student learns to compose must be tutorial. Mass-education pressure must not be allowed to intervene. Third, it follows that a course of study cannot be invented to suit the "general" needs of student composers. There *are* no general needs: only arrays of individuals, each with an array of specific needs, lacks, skills, and experience. Thus (fourth) under a tutorial approach, the matters to be investigated by each student beyond specific training in composition must be individually worked out: in each case, no doubt, such a program will combine course work in the traditional music department with direct professional experience. Fifth, the presence on so many campuses of professional performing groups suggests that all students be given a formal opportunity to work with these groups, both in order to test empirically their compositional efforts and to gain experience in performing new music. (The restoration of performance activity as an essential component of professional compositional training is one of the most dramatic results of the recent transfer of U.S. compositional life to universities.) Sixth, the electronic resources now increasingly available must be made a basic part of all composers' education. Particularly important, beyond basic instruction in the synthesis and generation of electronic sound, is the valuable ear-training that occurs naturally in the course of work in the electronic medium. Activity in electronic studios is a far more effective means of developing aural sensitivity than is traditional ear training. Under carefully controlled and electronically stable conditions, the manipulation of those sound materials which are themselves to become the piece forces on the composer the necessity to make aural decisions and distinctions that have been traditionally ceded to live performers. One who has not worked in the electronic medium cannot appreciate the significance of these influences. Seventh, it is necessary to train composers in the use of computers. Compositionally, of course, computers have a triple function: as sound synthesizers, as generators of systematic compositional processes, and as analyzers of conditions of theoretical interest. All must be included.

Last, what should be retained from the old curriculum? It is never a question of *eliminating* what presently exists, only of reordering priorities. My private view, for instance, is that compositional calisthenics are essential, and I therefore advocate early study of species counterpoint, since its constrained and easily definable world allows the testing of compositional ingenuity under very unambiguous conditions. On the other hand, I am against the early study of harmony, since I think its disciplinary importance is minimal, and its use ought to lie mainly in explicating the structure of the tonal system. Therefore, I recommend the abandonment of harmony in undergraduate days and its relegation to graduate seminars in the historical investigation of theoretical systems. But none of what I have said should be taken as more than the *advice* I would give an inquiring student. The whole point of the tutorial approach is that such generalities are *not* applied to every student. My attitude toward historical musicology should also be clear: the historical work undertaken by any composition student must be determined by the literature he already knows and by those gaps in his experience that are widest, not by generalities about what "everyone ought to know." (Even so, however, since our lack of knowledge about non-western music systems is so general, I would advise every student composer to avail himself of the expanding resources for ethnomusicological study in U.S. universities.) Moreover, the conceit that musicologists are the sole proprietors of musical intellection and the guardians in the university environment of intellectual values must be categorically rejected.

These proposals may be unrealistic. But I can only say that if we cannot find means to restore the dignity of individual students, to identify and respond to their needs as human beings, rather than as objects for processing, we may as well abandon all concern about what they learn. It is the environment, not the subject matter, and the values rather than the mouthings of their teachers, that most deeply affect the students. A professional community of composers never will develop until the youngest student is presented from the earliest time with examples from his elders of responsible, disinterested support of the values of the compositional profession. If he is not, he will never have a compelling reason to subject himself to the rigors of mastering what is, after all, one of the highest forms of human thought.

Predrag Milošević

THE SCOPE OF MUSIC STUDIES IN YUGOSLAV MUSIC INSTITUTIONS

The information related here is valid for Yugoslavia as a whole, though each of the federal republics is fully independent regarding regulations on the type and content of musical schooling. Notable differences and occasional divergencies from the common structure will be pointed out. Minor deviations will be ignored as they are irrelevant to the subject, and an attempt to enumerate and explain them would be a sheer waste of time.

Before dealing directly with the subject, I should like to make a brief survey of music instruction as a part of general education, so that one can understand how the art of music is promoted in Yugoslavia from the earliest grades to graduation from the secondary school.

Compulsory elementary education in Yugoslavia lasts eight years (before World War II it lasted four). Music education is curricular and continues throughout the eight years, starting with basic instruction by the classroom teacher, but later with a specialist in music education. The goal of this instruction is to develop an appreciation for music in the student, to give him elementary training in the rudiments of music, to build up in him a feeling for rhythmic and melodic movement, and finally to give him an understanding of the idea of music. The child's voice is developed and his taste improved. By listening to music of different types, live and recorded, he becomes acquainted with basic musical forms, instruments, instrumental and vocal combinations, orchestras and choirs.

The children are encouraged to try to play an instrument. Notation is also taught: the children read notes and attempt to sing the intervals. They are also given the opportunity to try their own creative capacities, though mostly in group activity and with given, simple strophic texts. In the upper grades, they learn about the musical life of their region and their country, about the more important musical institutions (music schools, academies, opera companies, philharmonic societies, and professional groups), and about the more important musicians of home and abroad, past and present. Hopefully, their interest in and love of music will continue once out of school, so that they will keep in touch with the musical life of their community and perhaps participate in it to a degree. In other words, the students are educated to be future consumers of music – a good public. Of course, certain exceptionally gifted individuals are encouraged to play instruments (usually violin or piano), and they thus acquire a professional orientation. They are advised to enroll in a music school where their abilities can be cultivated. In the eight-year (elementary) school, a choir is formed of selected students for the performance of music suited to their vocal and technical levels. Such choirs frequently engage in contests. Orchestras are organized as an extracurricular activity.

In all cases, instruction begins with the practice of simply playing and listening to music; the theory of music, explanation and interpretation, is introduced later. Music education in the eight-year elementary school is conducted by the teacher in so-called "class instruction," while later, a special instructor gives what is called "subject instruction." The elementary school teacher is qualified for the former at pedagogical schools, while the specialized music teacher is certified either at a music or a pedagogical academy.

In the gymnasium (high school), which is not compulsory and lasts for four years, a place is also made for music, but from a different aspect. As the students generally range in age from fourteen to eighteen and possess some maturity in understanding and thinking, music is presented to them at a more sophisticated level. More complicated and longer musical forms are presented, including some of the very modern ones. The importance of music in the history of mankind is pointed out. Its relationship to the theater, movies, or even sports is explained. Not infrequently, students choose some musical subject for their final graduation paper, often treating the life and work of an outstanding musician or a period in the history of music. Recently the formation of choirs in the gymnasium was resumed. Participation is not obligatory, but once a student decides to join and is accepted, he also assumes the obligation to attend rehearsals and performances. The music instruction in the gymnasium is conducted by teachers who have graduated from a music academy, or at least who have completed the "first grade" of such an academy (the first two years). The specialized gymnasia (medical, technical, commercial, etc.) also offer music education, but in a somewhat more limited amount.

All schools are closely linked with an organization called *La jeunesse musicale* which has developed in our country into an activity rich in imagination and resourcefulness. *La jeunesse musicale* arranges for special concerts and opera performances for students (usually on Sunday mornings). In conjunction with school administrations, the organization plans musical excursions to the city for students in more remote areas where concert life is limited. Appropriate information is provided the students about the composer and his work in advance of performances. This system of "trains to operas" or "busses to concerts" has produced excellent results in extracurricular musical instruction for youths between six and eighteen.

Greater importance is given to music in the curriculum of the teachers' training school (the professional school of education), because the elementary school teacher trained in such a school will also be the first music teacher for many children. During five years of study, the future teachers take courses which prepare them fully for work in a class where they will teach all subjects. The program in music includes theoretical instruction, solfeggio (up to three accidentals), musical forms, music appreciation, and recognition of instruments. In other words, all those things the teachers themselves will have to teach in the elemtnary schools. Methods and a knowledge of child psychology are stressed. The future teacher learns how to play the accordion, the mandolin, and the guitar. These are instruments the students in the teachers' training school can easily afford to buy. Moreover, these instruments prove very useful in work with children. The choirs in the teachers' training schools in Yugoslavia have always had a fair artistic standard; competitions between them have always been very interesting if not exciting. Graduates of music academies generally instruct the future teachers in their musical activities. Pedagogical institutes (a higher type of professional school of education) have special departments of music where future music instructors in elementary schools are trained.

In the category of specialized music schools, I shall discuss first the School for Elementary Music Education, known also as the Primary Music School. The period of instruction lasts six years, and only children of seven, eight, and nine are admitted, since the children must be able to read and write. At this age, the selection of instruments is limited; the students generally have piano and violin lessons, and rarely 'cello. Besides applied music lessons, which are the major emphasis, the students study solfeggio and music theory, and sometimes play in a string orchestra. Parents often send their children to this school just to see if they have a gift for music. As one would expect, a percentage of the children stop attending sometime during the six years, thus, the Primary Music School tends to weed out the less gifted and diligent. Graduation may be taken as the basis for a possible final commitment to music as a profession.

Students of the Primary Music School also attend the normal eight-year elementary school for their general education. Since student choirs already constitute a regular part of the general education curriculum, the Primary Music School does not insist on choirs. All the instructors in a Primary Music School must be graduates of a music academy. The Primary Music School is attached to an Intermediate Music School if there is one in the township; otherwise, it is independent. Such an independent school has proven less efficient than one linked to an Intermediate School.

The Intermediate Music School provides the next higher level in professional music schooling. It embraces all the applied fields and theoretical disciplines in a four-year curriculum. For admission, a student must pass a test from the level of the Primary Music School. Selection is extremely rigorous. Two programs of study are offered, (1) vocal-instrumental and (2) theoretical.

To suggest the content and level of the work done at the Intermediate Music School, it should be known that a voice student must sing for his final examination (after four years of study) two arias by seventeenth and eighteenth century composers, a coloratura aria, and an aria from the current operatic repertory. A pianist must play the Chopin Études, the Bach Partitas, some of the early Beethoven sonatas, and one of the easier concertos with orchestra. The theoretical program offers harmonic analysis, including enharmonic modulation, and vocal and instrumental counterpoint. Composition of a two-part invention is required. The student in this program also does exercises in composition as preparation for the possible continuation of his studies in a music academy. Courses are also given in pedagogy, psychology, and logic. The studies include practical classroom exercises.

All students in the Intermediate Music School must study solfeggio, music history, recognition of instruments, and choral singing, and they must participate in rehearsals, orchestral concerts, and solo performances. A choir and an orchestra are organized within the school's program; their concerts frequently attain high quality. The students may attend the gymnasium at the same time, but if they do not, they may study their national language, geography, a foreign language, history, and elementary sociology in the music school itself. These subjects are taught on the level of the gymnasium. It is worth noting that seventy per cent of the students prefer to study these subjects in the music school, rather than at the gymnasium, which may show their definite commitment to music.

Recently, courses in accordion have been introduced in some Intermediate Music Schools, because of the pressure of practical (if not profane!) reasons.

The Intermediate Music School prepares teachers for general elementary schools, as well as instructing musicians for vocal and instrumental companies and preparing candidates for more advanced professional training in a music academy. Thus, the teaching must be on a high level, consequently the instructors themselves are thoroughly trained academically and are graduates of a music academy.

Both the Primary and the Intermediate Music Schools are financed by municipal budgets. As in the other schools of Yugoslavia, tuition is not required.*
Instruction is free to all who are admitted.

*Editor's note: According to Mr. Kostić, tuition is paid at the Primary Music School (Cf. above, p. 2).

The Music Academy represents the highest level of musical training in Yugoslav education. Five music academies have been established, in Belgrade (Republic of Serbia), Ljubljana (Republic of Slovenia), Sarajevo (Republic of Bosnia and Herzegovina), Skopje (Republic of Macedonia), and Zagreb (Republic of Croatia). In Skopje, the designation *Visoka Muzička Škola* is used instead of Music Academy (this institution was established only in 1966). All the academies have the rank of a college in a university; their teachers are given the same titles as university faculty: *redovni profesor* (professor), *vanredni profesor* (associate professor), *docent* (assistant professor), as well as lecturer, assistant, and "artistic" or "technical" associate. The majority of eminent musicians, composers, conductors, singers, instrumentalists, and music scholars in Yugoslavia work as teachers in music academies. Their involvement in the academy assures a high level of professionalism. Only in cases where there are no national experts in a discipline are temporary, or permanent, jobs offered to foreign experts.

To be admitted to the Music Academy, a candidate must be graduated from an Intermediate Music School, and he must also pass examination in his major field. In certain disciplines, e.g., composition, conducting, and music theory, the candidate must prove his ability at the piano as well. Candidates without an Intermediate Music School education may also be admitted, but they must prove their ability in all the supplemental subjects taught in the last year of intermediate schooling as well as pass examination in their major.

The Music Academy trains professional musicians of the highest quality — composers, conductors, singers, all sorts of instrumentalists, music scholars, music folklorists, theorists — and, after some four or five years of study, awards them the highest certifications. Along with its instructional function, the Academy also engages in artistic and scholarly activities involving its apprentice artists and scholars in the methods of creative work.

The structure of the several music academies in Yugoslavia is very similar, but not identical. All are divided into departments or sections for the study of the respective disciplines: piano, organ, harp, composition, conducting, voice, strings, wind and brass instruments, music scholarship (music history and folklore), and music theory. In some departments the course of study continues four years, in some five. Composition, as a rule, requires five.

All Yugoslav music academies have introduced so-called "Graded Instruction." The *Prvi stepen* or "First Grade" comprises the first two years of study, when the schedule includes those subjects which qualify a student to teach in schools of general education. If for any reason the student shows insufficient progress and is not deemed qualified to continue to the *Drugi stepen* or "Second Grade," he is given a "First Grade" diploma and the title *nastavnik muzike* (instructor of music). More auditions and examinations are required for admission to the "Second Grade," which comprises the final two or three years of study in the academy. Upon the successful conclusion of these studies, the student is given a "Second Grade" diploma and the title *akademski muzičar* (academic musician).

During the first two years of study, students in composition widen their knowledge of harmony to include the newest theories and problems (the crisis of romantic harmony, the 12-tone system, serialism). The study of polyphony is based on a detailed examination of the works of Palestrina, Orlando di Lasso, and J. S. Bach (especially the Well Tempered Clavier and the Art of Fugue). Students begin individual work in composition with the simpler instrumental and vocal forms and continue through variations and sonatas to chamber music, finally presenting as their graduation work a composition in a more complex form, such as a symphony, symphonic poem, instrumental concerto with orchestra, or a cantata for choir and orchestra. For general orientation only, the young composers take as their models Bartók, Prokofiev, Hindemith, or Stravinsky. However, in searching for new means of expression, they go much further, even to aleatoric procedures or to works for prepared instruments. The inclusion of electronic music studies has been considered, but it remains a matter for the future because of the sizable financial investment required. The young composers' works are performed at their final examinations, either live or recorded, so that members of the committee are not limited to mere visual perusal of a score. At some of the academies, arrangements are made to enable students to visit national and international festivals of modern music (e.g., at Zagreb or Opatija). Once graduated, the young composers most frequently work as teachers of music theory in the primary and intermediate music schools, or as program editors at radio stations.

The conducting students acquire their technical skill with a choir or an orchestra. They study works initially with a professor in the classroom, advance to conducting the choir of the Music Academy, perhaps a hired group of professional singers, or on their examinations, a full professional choir. They may also have the opportunity to conduct the Academy's orchestra (full or chamber) or a local professional orchestra. Here, as in composition, special emphasis is placed on playing the piano. The final examination consists of conducting either a large Beethoven symphony, a symphony by Franck, Tchaikovsky, Dvořák, or Shostakovich, or a symphonic poem.

Young singers refine their technique in the study of scheduled programs of works which range from those of seventeenth and eighteenth century masters to those of today's composers. During opera study, portions or entire acts are occasionally performed and, less often, complete operas in some local theater. In the latter case, one of the technically more simple operas which requires only a small ensemble is selected (Mozart, Gluck, Rossini, or Pergolesi).

All of the instrumentalists in order to graduate must perform outstanding works of national and world literature, both in solo recital and, at least once, with orchestra.

The Musicology Department offers two programs of study, one in the history of music, the other in folklore. In the history program, besides detailed study of world music, particular importance is placed on the study of the history of national music in all of the Yugoslav republics. The folklore program also treats the whole territory of Yugoslavia. Field work in the collection of folksongs is carried out in the region of a particular music academy.

Perhaps it should be mentioned here that in Ljubljana, the Musicology Department has been transferred to the College of Arts in the University (Faculty of Philosophy) as an independent discipline. Ljubljana for the time being is the only place in Yugoslavia where one can earn a Ph.D. in musicology.

The Department of Music Theory (pedagogical section) is the most crowded one in all the academies, perhaps because no special talent must be shown for admission. This section supplies instructors for the schools of general education, and quite a number are needed since a great many schools have been established in Yugoslavia since World War II (not to mention the increase in the number of pupils). No matter how hard the academies try, no solution to the problem of the teacher shortage appears in the near future. In Zagreb, the Music Academy tried to alleviate the shortage by establishing special sections with two-year courses of study. Graduates have no difficulty finding jobs, especially if they relinquish the ambition to live in the larger towns. These young people have a sound and varied knowledge of theory, classroom methods, conducting a school choir or orchestra, as well as command of elementary instrumentation. Thus, they satisfy fully the requirements of any elementary or secondary school.

The Music Academy has its own orchestra and choir. The students from the various orchestral instrument departments play in the orchestra, while the students from all the other departments sing in the choir. Public concerts of the musical masterworks are given, thus the Academy participates in the musical life of the community. Sometimes more gifted students play solo programs. All the instrumentalists must take a course in chamber music.

After graduation from the Academy (i.e., from its "Second Grade"), a young musician may attend yet a "Third Grade" or *Treći stepen* course of studies. Since this highest grade is a sort of *Meisterschule,* only the very best are accepted. Only the major is studied, without supplemental subjects. The graduate from the "Third Grade" is given the title *magister muzike* and is considered a full-fledged artist with great expectations. Frequently he is taken as an assistant to his old professor, with good possibilities for an important teaching career.

Though essentially alike, the music academies of Yugoslavia have some traditional differences. One is noted for excellent pianists, another for wind players, a third for an excellent choir or orchestra. Though the academies are not formally united, annual interacademic festivals are held with alternate academies acting as host. These are not contests — no prizes are awarded. Rather, these festivals provide a review of the activity of each academy, including performances by soloists, student orchestras with student conductors, student composition recitals, and meetings of young musicologists where papers are read on diverse musicological problems in history, esthetics, and folklore. During the festivals, the deans and faculty of the various academies also meet to discuss issues of common interest. A number of the Yugoslav music academies maintain lively contact with other advanced music schools in Europe and, among other things, exchange student concert groups. All of the Yugoslav academies belong to the *Sociétée européenne des académies de musique, des conservatoires et des Hochschulen für Musik.*

Wilfred C. Bain

THE SCOPE OF MUSIC STUDIES
IN AMERICAN MUSIC INSTITUTIONS

Every phase of music in the United States is receiving major attention on the part of the general public. The fourteenth revised edition of *Concert Music USA*[1] compiled by Broadcast Music, Inc., cites some interesting statistics. In 1939 there were approximately 600 symphonic orchestras. Twenty-eight years later there are 1,436. Currently there are 918 opera-producing groups as compared with 752 last year. The American Music Conference estimates that more than 15 million young Americans play musical instruments and receive musical instructions in the schools of the nation or with private teachers.

More than 68,000 instrumental music organizations are found in the schools of the United States. These include 7,000 orchestras, 50,000 bands, and 11,000 so-called stage or jazz bands. All told, there appear to be not less than 41 million amateur musicians in the country, according to figures available in 1966. This represents an increase of six per cent over the previous year and a growth rate more than four times that of the overall population.

Almost a billion dollars were spent by the American public on musical instruments, sheet music, and musical accessories in 1966. This is an increase of 960 per cent over similar expenditures in 1950, twice the rate of growth of the country's gross national product during the same period of time.

The sale of recordings in all categories during 1966 represents 57 per cent of the world's total sales; since 1940 recording sales in the United States have increased by 1,758 per cent. Fifteen per cent of all American LP record sales are in the classical music category.

These statistics are cited to serve as a background for our inquiry into the scope of music study in the United States. This paper will focus primarily on the study of music in preparation for a professional career, either as a performer, teacher, or worker in some area of music.

One of the most reliable sources of information on the scope and extent of music study in the United States is the statistical information gathered by the National Association of Schools of Music — the N.A.S.M. The N.A.S.M. is a non-governmental, private organization, whose membership consists of several types of institutions, all at the college or university level. Included are private and tax-supported colleges, independent schools of music, junior colleges, and theological seminaries. The Association was organized to encourage excellence in the education of musical performers, composers, researchers, and teachers. It also serves as a forum for the discussion and dissemination of information on developments in the field of education for musicians. Membership is gained through formal application and subsequent evaluation of the applicant institution by a team of examiners. The evaluation team considers an institution's adherence to its stated purposes, the appropriateness of those purposes, and their relation to the nationally accepted standards. To be accepted into N.A.S.M., an institution must first be accredited by the regional educational accrediting agency, of which there are six covering the United States. The largest of these is the North Central Association which has jurisdiction in nineteen states.

An institution desiring membership in the N.A.S.M. must offer a curriculum in music or music education leading to a formal degree, and it must have graduated at least one class prior to the application for membership. Of the 3,000 institutions of higher education in the United States, more than half offer instruction in music. However, not all those who have music departments are institutional members of the N.A.S.M. As of January 1967, only 279 colleges and universities held such institutional membership. The total student enrollment of music majors, undergraduate and graduate, in these 279 schools was 44,005 during the fall term of 1966. Total enrollment during the summer session, graduate and undergraduate, usually amounts to about forty per cent of the enrollment for the academic year.

The total number of undergraduate music degrees awarded in the U.S. during the academic year 1965-66 and the summer 1966 amounted to 5,314; 2,177 of these were from tax-supported universities.

At the undergraduate level, twice as many music majors elect a curriculum that trains them as elementary and secondary school teachers than those who train for a career as performers.

Since so few opportunities exist for young singers to make a living in opera in the United States and since, until recently, the musician in a professional symphony orchestra was not employed on a twelve-month contract, many music students have looked to the professional security offered by teaching positions in elementary and secondary schools and in institutions of higher education. Those wishing to brave the hazards of making a living in the commercial music field frequently earn an excellent income as performers. Such employment, however, offers little continuity, stability, or security. It is no small wonder that the young graduate of a four-year curriculum, faced with the necessity of making a living, chooses security rather than subjection to the capriciousness of half-year employment, sporadic income, year to year contracts, etc.

It might be argued that since the U.S. is preparing twice as many music teachers as performers, the standards of instruction and level of student performance tend to be lowered. According to our experience, this does not necessarily result. Evidence of the high standard of American music instruction is seen in the fact that 600 American singers currently hold contracts in German opera theaters and, as foreigners, meet the international competition for employment.

In examining in greater detail the instructional system for the education of musicians at the higher education level, I wish to use as an example the School of Music at Indiana University whose enrollment of music students at all levels — baccalaureate, master's, and doctoral — is the largest in the United States. The educational practices at Indiana University School of Music are not unusual and, in general, correspond to the national norm as expressed in the regulations and standards of achievement set forth by the National Association of Schools of Music.

At Indiana University a student wishing to major in music must first be admitted to the University on the basis of his academic record in secondary school and the grades received on the Student Achievement Test, a national examination used as a qualitative standard. If he resides outside the United States or has attended a secondary school not approved by a national accrediting agency, he must pass entrance examinations in general subject matter in order to qualify for admission to the University.

Admission to the University does not imply acceptance into a specific curriculum or major. A student wishing to major in music must further qualify by audition in a major and minor applied music field, and by examination in the grammar, syntax, and vocabulary of music. The latter is verified by tests in oral and written harmony, counterpoint, sightsinging, and keyboard harmony. A student preparing to teach at the elementary and secondary school levels must use one field of applied music as a principal performing medium. Certain minimum standards of competence are specified in the School of Music publications.

At the end of the second or sophomore year the educational objective of the individual student is reviewed before the faculty of his discipline. This consists of an examination in which the student's academic record is reviewed, his performance auditioned, and his progress evaluated. On the basis of this review the student is either (1) allowed to proceed with his educational objective, (2) warned that he may have to be enrolled for a longer period than normally is required for the degree, or (3) denied further opportunity to work on the curriculum of his choice. All undergraduate students, regardless of curriculum, must present a public graduation recital. Those working toward the

Bachelor of Music degree present full recitals during the third and fourth years. Those working on teaching degrees, or degrees in which applied music is not the principal interest, perform the recital during the fourth year. An undergraduate may choose any of seventeen undergraduate curricula leading to a bachelor's degree. These include curricula leading to competence as an opera stage director, an opera scenic designer and technician, or a music therapist who is qualified to work with the emotionally disturbed.

To complete a degree at the undergraduate level a student must achieve an overall accumulative grade average of 2.0 (C) on a 4.0 declining scale (A-4, B-3, C-2, D-1, F-0). To be admitted to graduate studies a student must have achieved not less than a 3.0 (B) average. At the graduate degree level he must maintain a 3.0 average in his studies. The same grade level is required for those seeking admission to the doctoral curricula.

Since degrees are recognized principally in educational institutions they may be considered primarily as credentials for teaching. Concert artists or those wishing to make a career as performers are seldom if ever asked to present credentials or diplomas attesting to completion of courses of study at any level. Performers are engaged primarily if not solely on a demonstration of their performance ability.

Students wishing to obtain a permanent license to teach in the elementary and secondary schools in any state must complete either the master's degree or its equivalent in graduate studies in specific courses before being awarded a permanent certificate or license.

Institutions of higher education, private or public, may not require the doctor's degree of the beginning teacher. There are no state or national laws requiring faculty at the higher education level to hold the doctorate. However, reputable institutions require that those who are to be a permanent part of the instructional faculty complete all curricular offerings leading to a doctor's degree.

A fully qualified student may earn the master's degree in one academic year at Indiana University. The master's is offered in all applied music fields, as well as in voice pedagogy, string instruments as a group, woodwind instruments as a group, composition, music theory, musicology, church music, choral conducting, instrumental conducting, and music education. Master's degrees related to the music major are offered in music therapy, concert management, and music theater scenic techniques.

Only recently has the doctor's degree in music been offered in American universities in other than a few traditional fields, such as musicology and composition. Over the past twenty-five years, the content of the doctor's degree in music has undergone almost continuous re-evaluation and reinterpretation.

More and more the attempt has been made to combine theory and practice, historical and critical studies, creative composition and demonstrable competence in performance. Thus, new educational objectives have been defined, and new degree titles and curricula have emerged.

The traditional Doctor of Philosophy degree has also responded to the pressure of contemporary needs, and it now includes as legitimate subject matter music education, music theory, music therapy, and ethnomusicology.

One new concept in the evaluation of student competence has resulted in the development of a degree program at the doctoral level which requires that a student be able publicly through performance to demonstrate his understanding and control of the stylistic elements of the music he studies. With this in mind, the National Association of Schools of Music has approved a degree title known as the Doctor of Musical Arts with course work leading to a major in the music literature for performance. The student seeking this degree studies extensively and intensively the repertory of his specific field, approaching the material in much the same scholarly fashion as the musicologist, but with performance in mind. He seeks to analyze in detail the musical style of the composer as it relates to the performer and performance. While the musicologist writes critically concerning the work of the composer, the performer attempts through the study of performance practice and styles analysis to isolate those elements which facilitate communication with his audience and in so doing to set forth fully in performance the musical ideas of the composer.

An artist may intuitively interpret music with a high artistic sense; however, formal study in interpretation at the university level aims at setting forth systematically principles applicable to the discovery and understanding of the artistic elements in music. Such study requires a careful and ordered approach, especially in view of the fact that the music studied is finally to be performed in public by the student himself.

The period of residence for doctoral study at the university varies with the individual. Three academic years or six semesters is the usual minimum. One of these academic years may be devoted to completing work for the master's degree.

After a student is admitted to a doctoral degree program, an advisory committee is appointed. The committee consists of three representatives from the major field, one from each minor area, and a representative of the administrative office. The committee (1) administers the qualifying and final examinations, (2) supervises the writing and final approval of documents or dissertations, (3) approves and grades any required recitals or performances, and (4) certifies to the appropriate dean the completion of the curriculum, examinations, and degree requirements. The chairman of the advisory committee is usually the professor under whom the dissertation is to be written or, if the student is in a performance area, his applied music teacher.

Candidates for the doctor's degree who expect to do research in highly specialized areas or whose particular field of inquiry demands specialized techniques beyond those normally required must either already possess the requisite skills and techniques or else acquire them in addition to the regular requirements. A specific course of study is recommended for each candidate on the basis of his entrance examinations, his degree choice, and his area of particular interest. The candidate may elect to challenge the recommended course of study by requesting special examinations in specific areas, or else he may accept the course of study as prescribed.

Candidates for the Doctor of Philosophy degree are expected to have a reading knowledge of two foreign languages. These are usually French and German. Candidates for the Doctor of Music degree with a major in music literature and its performance will have tool subject requirements according to the nature of their degree plans. For example, tool subject requirements may be foreign languages, score reading, or keyboard skills.

The essential difference between the traditional Doctor of Philosophy degree with a major in historical and critical research (musicology) and the Doctor of Music degree with a major in music literature and its performance is the difference between writing critically about musical style and using performance to demonstrate understanding of musical style. In the first instance, the student shows control of the subject by writing critically about it, while in the second, he shows control of the subject by recreating it in performance. The candidate for the Doctor of Music degree in performance is also required to demonstrate in written form his concept of musical style and his insight into performance practice through documents of more limited scope than a thesis or dissertation.

At Indiana University the doctor's degree is awarded through curricula leading to the Doctor of Philosophy degree, the Doctor of Music Education degree, and the Doctor of Music degree. A Doctor of Philosophy degree represents breadth of training and experience in the arts and sciences, and it is recommended for persons planning to enter research and scholarly writing, as well as college or university teaching. The dissertation required for the Ph.D. must result from original research and must represent a contribution to knowledge of sufficient value to warrant publication. Instead of a dissertation the Ph.D. in composition requires a major composition together with a tape recording of its performance.

The Doctor of Music Education degree has a broader curricular pattern and more educational implications, involving the psychological principles of learning and teaching, than the Doctor of Philosophy. It represents preparation for teaching at all levels, but particularly at the level of higher education in its administrative and teacher training aspects.

The Doctor of Music degree represents accomplishments in performance attained only by those candidates endowed with a combination of talents – musical, scholarly, and technical. It follows the tradition of all doctoral degrees in that the same order of inquiry and research is required. Such a philosophy discounts the intuitive virtuoso and requires a systematic approach to the study of music through high technical competence in performance, pedagogy, or composition, through scholarly insight into musical styles, and through native musical ability coupled with systematic development of musical intelligence.

The Doctor of Philosophy degree is offered in music education, musicology, and theory. The Doctor of Music Education is a generalist degree for the individual who might be teaching several fields. The Doctor of Music degree with a major in music literature and its performance is offered at Indiana University in violin, viola, cello, piano, organ, voice, woodwind instruments as a group, piano pedagogy as a field, brass instrument pedagogy as a field, composition, opera performance (literature, conducting, and coaching), instrumental conducting as a field, and choral conducting as a field. The combining of performance and scholarly studies is now a generally accepted practice in the United States. In developing this new pattern it was believed that the musicologist need not be inadequately prepared in the field of performance nor should the performer be merely a musical athlete parroting the traditions handed down by an authoritarian teacher.

My survey has attempted to cover all aspects of music study at the college or university level in the United States. Obviously, smaller institutions with limited enrollment cannot carry out such a complete program as I have outlined because of limited human resources; however, a number of major institutions offer broad programs similar to that which has been described in citing the example of the Indiana University School of Music.

The resident music student body at Indiana University in the first semester of 1967-68 numbered 1,507. If this is taken as a representative group, the following generalizations may be made. Approximately two-thirds of the total number are undergraduate students. The undergraduates are divided almost equally between those preparing for the performance fields and those wishing to become certified to teach in the elementary and secondary schools. The graduate division of the School of Music numbers approximately 500. Two-thirds of that group are seeking the master's degree. At least eighty per cent of those seeking the master's degree are preparing for the performance fields. If they are not successful in making a career as performers, they will in all probability eventually become teachers of their particular musical art at the college or university level.

Those graduate students working on the doctor's degree — about one-third of the graduate student body — have had for the most part a number of years of teaching experience, usually in colleges and universities in the United States, and have returned to the university for further enrichment and to complete the doctorate. The most intellectually and artistically mature students in the School of Music belong to this group.

The attempt in American institutions to co-ordinate theory, history, and practice has evolved a concept of the music laboratory, i.e., an ensemble in which the student can experience at first hand the masterworks of ensemble literature. All music students below the doctor's degree level must participate in a laboratory ensemble. These ensembles constitute the choral groups, orchestras, and small ensembles which present public concerts throughout the year under School of Music auspices.

A relatively recent innovation in music study in the United States is the teaching of jazz as a formal discipline. While a student does not usually major in jazz, he may participate in a jazz band as his principal ensemble during his tenure as a student.

The public performance program of the Indiana University School of Music may provide additional insight into the scope of music activity during a typical year. During the 1966-67 academic year, 524 public performances were given for which the School of Music printed programs. Extra copies of these have been bound and are available upon request. All performances are tape recorded, and the recordings are held in the Music Library archives.

Both student and faculty solo and ensemble performances are included in these concerts. For example, 114 piano recitals were given by students and 10 by faculty, for a total of 124 piano recitals; 90 student voice recitals and 3 by faculty members made a total of 93. Other totals might be of interest: organ, 24; brass, 39; woodwinds, 49; strings, 44; conducting, 8; percussion, 4; harpsichord, 2; harp, 2. Group and ensemble recitals totalled 23.

The School of Music has 11 choral organizations which performed throughout the year. Three ballets were mounted. From October to May, 9 different operas were staged in weekly performances. The opera workshop produced 4 operatic scenes or full acts, with piano accompaniment and limited scenery and costuming. The Indiana University Philharmonic presented 6 concerts; the Indiana University Symphony Orchestra, 5; and the Indiana University Concert Orchestra, 4. *Avant-garde* music was featured at 7 concerts, and 23 chamber music concerts were given. Guest soloists and groups accounted for 10 events. A total of 196 performances, including 6 by the opera theater, were given off campus by School of Music personnel.

Opera is performed each Saturday evening from the first week in October until mid-May and then again during a four-week period in the summer session. All performances are fully mounted, performed with orchestra, and sold to the public. During the 1966-67 season there was a repertory of nine operas with multiple performances of each, with the exception of the nineteenth annual performance of Wagner's *Parsifal.*

Both students and faculty are used for leads in the opera. Faculty, however, are used only when leading roles cannot be sung adequately by students. The fact that the School of Music has approximately 175 doctoral students in voice, many of whom are twenty-five years of age or older, gives the casting committee an opportunity to select students of maturity. Thus, the younger singers are not cast in demanding roles before they are sufficiently mature.

Some idea of the physical scope of music study at Indiana University should be suggested. The music library contains more than 70,000 titles, including 425 sets of periodicals and 2,500 opera scores. The record library has collected approximately 32,000 recordings and 1,000 miniature scores for use in class assignments and applied music study. Library facilities are administered by 11 full-time staff members, including a musicologist and 3 professional librarians. For practice and teaching, the School of Music requires 173 grand pianos and 203 upright pianos, which are maintained by 4 resident piano technicians. A total faculty of 132 is divided into departments, representing the various disciplines, such as piano, voice, musicology, and music education.

Other divisions of the School of Music include the Latin American Music Center, which was established under the joint sponsorship of the Rockefeller Foundation and Indiana University to promote research in and performance of Latin American music. The Institute for Vocal Research was organized to investigate the teaching processes in voice. Folk and primitive music courses are offered through the Department of Anthropology and Folklore. The largest archive of recorded folk and primitive music in the United States has been developed in connection with this program at Indiana University.

Here then is one example representative of the scope of music study in the United States.

---

[1]1968 *Concert Music USA,* 14th Revised Edition, first compiled in 1951 (New York: Broadcast Music, Inc., 1968), unpaged.

Enriko Josif

CONTEMPORARY TRENDS IN YUGOSLAV MUSIC

I am departing from the assumption, from the conviction, that any writing about the problem of the contemporary — about contemporary trends in the arts — is a confession. A confession of one's belief in Art and in the future of Art. Finally, a confession of one's possible illusion.

With this in mind, I shall try to sketch — through my intuition, my vision, and my thought — the path along which contemporary Yugoslav music is moving as an entity compounded of varied elements (differing from each other in a highly complex manner) in this era so crisscrossed by differences that all values negate each other, in this spiritual age of Man's existence and of Man's coming into new existence.

As one of many with an humble grain of creativity who participates in the ever evolving World of Structured Tone, my outlook shall of necessity differ from that of a more objective viewer — one who certainly may be more qualified to pass judgment about the creative events of our time — one who does not participate directly, actively in the elusive flux which is the ordering of tones into a viable entity fed by Truth.

Since I suspect that my conception will differ as well from that of the more passionate participants in the artistically Progressive (I used to belong and in part still do belong to that happy company), I want to mention at the outset the possibility of a total cleavage between my non-apologetic attitude toward some of the current happenings in the Art of Music and the attitude of the ardent apologists, those neo-rhapsodists and hymnists of new hope who trod the path which leads to a re-ordered tonal cosmos. If this cleavage comes, it could set fire — in a burst of verbal sparks — to a discussion of a whole range of new and newly resurgent questions in need of vital answers.

Before proceeding with the subject of my paper, I must define "contemporary." Two understandings of the word, as it applies to music, may be proposed. One, extreme in its formal, sterile logic, states that in any Art the contemporary is that which is created by contemporaries of an age. Such a definition, however much it simplifies the issue, is not acceptable to me. A second understanding, also extreme, maintains that *the contemporary* in the music of the present is *only* that which derives from searching in the unexplored tonal spaces being opened in the realm of the electronically formed tonal world.

This ultra-enthusiasm, though I myself am a kind of determined enthusiast, is equally unacceptable to me.

I shall myself postulate a third extreme understanding: In every age the *contemporary in essence* is that and only that which is not merely of its own time, but timeless. This understanding is based on the conviction that the only measure of a work's contemporaneity is its lasting value. Such an understanding is free from possible temporary delusions as to what is lasting and what is ephemeral.

It goes without saying that these three extreme understandings, and I suppose that they truly *are* extreme, may be exposed to abuse, especially the last one. Nevertheless, each in its way delineates or limits an area of artistic creativity. If one feels the greatest comfort in the first, the greatest power and lack of scruples in the second, in the third one feels helpless and uneasy. Yet I have chosen this third, my own understanding of the contemporary, and I shall follow it in my efforts here.

It may appear that by my understanding of the contemporary I have burnt all the bridges across which I might continue further. I shall try to deny this by means of a private delusion which may sound strange, but in which I firmly believe.

I consider the era of Romanticism one of transient value. I view it as a great and epochal *alteration* in the development of tonal thinking (the concept of "alteration" is used here figuratively, analogous to the chromatic passing tone in the purely musical theoretic sense), an era whose innate value is not self-sustaining as are the lasting values found in the Renaissance, Baroque, and Classic eras.

I admit that this conviction of mine may be absurd. I have no intention of justifying or defending it here. I wish only to state that it is not forced. It is a deep, non-rational, personal conviction, and I present it here to facilitate understanding of my concept of the *contemporary in essence*.

My point of departure in this subjective definition of the contemporary, as I see it, is found at that moment when the creative Tonal World became separated from the powerful, passionately painful forces of Late Romanticism. That moment may be identified by reference to the composers who made it occur: Musorgsky, Debussy, Ravel, Hindemith, Stravinsky, and Bartók.

The first surprise is that not a single representative of the Viennese school is included. As incompatible as it may seem with the generally accepted norms, Schoenberg and Berg are not involved in creating the point of departure for my concept of the *contemporary in essence.* I consider their works only as factually contemporary events — not insignificant ones for the development of a path which will transfer us from the realm of music into a non-musical realm enunciated by tones.

My reasons for believing as I do are derived from yet another possible delusion, which I embrace, like the first one, as a deep personal conviction.

In the polarization of the Tonal World into the diatonic and chromatic extremes, I consider the diatonic principle the only genuine, natural reflection of the Cosmic Musical Being.

It should be understood here that the term "diatonic" is not confined to the major and minor scales or the old modal scales. It embraces a wide area including the possibility of open chromatic movement which does not distort the character of a diatonically shaped line. I should like to cite as an example the well-known opening motif of Debussy's *Prelude to the Afternoon of a Faun*. A more penetrating analysis of this concept would take me too far, therefore I shall confine myself to the single example above in the hope that it will clarify my understanding of "diatonic."

The chromatic I consider an inferior abstract, a deviation, a weakening of diatonic sturdiness and purity. I feel it, viewed by ascetic ethical standards, as an aching wound in the Diatonic Being of Music. Undoubtedly, chromatic expression reflects our human expressive nature, but only that part which is transient in us. This is one reason why Romanticism touches our hearts and senses so tenderly, so painfully, and so tearfully. (I profoundly respect the wounds, tears, and pain of Man, but I consider them transient when compared to the timeless qualities of ennobled power, wisdom, and love in Man.)

In its evolving expression, music attained for the first time that pain, those tears, that sentiment in its Romantic phase. Chromaticism, as a transient, secondary and subordinate power in comparison with diatonicism, spilled itself on the romantics — especially on the late romantics — in tonally charged tensions which led to utter harmonic super-saturation. That great epoch of Man's transient wound has had its say — it had to have its say — it has passed away, although the pain and the wound did not go away! That epoch implanted itself in us, where it now withers, filling us with grief for its so very human traits, with tears for its irrevocable passing.

It should now be possible to grasp, if not to understand, my reasons for leaving out the representatives of the Viennese school in establishing the point of departure for my concept of the contemporary. Even if Schoenberg in his theoretical thought managed to break with Romanticism (and I question that he did), he failed to do so in his work.

I think that it is of more immediate impact to express the links which connect Yugoslav music with contemporary trends by referring directly to creative personalities without recourse to the dubious and restrictive labels which are often applied to current creative movements. I intend to mention here only those composers who have directly or indirectly influenced the development of Yugoslav musical art, and I shall begin by identifying those with a nationalistic orientation.

The fundamental source for our musical development throughout our existence as a community of several nationalities has been undoubtedly the inexhaustible wealth of the Folk Sung Word. This rich tonal ore, preserved in some parts of our country in its pure, unadulterated ancient form, naturally exerted a profound influence on our musical development, especially in the period between the two world wars. Treated at first with the ingredients of the Romantic heritage by composers who had been trained abroad, it has subsequently been developed in more creative ways by inspired composers who rejected the chromatic admixtures of Romanticism and sculpted from the intrinsic melodic patterns of the Folk Sung Word works of art much closer to the natural idiom of our language. This development took place under the influence of musical Realism, especially that of Musorgsky, Janaček, Stravinsky in his Russian primitive period, and Bartók with his inspired linguistic folklore. Significant artistic achievement within our Yugoslav domain has been accomplished in the works of our classics: Stevan Mokranjac, Josip Slavenski, Petar Konjović, and Krešimir Baranović, as well as Boris Papandopulo, Marko Tajčević, Ivan Brakanović, and others.

Hindemith, Schoenberg, the Prague school, and also the French "moderne" composers of the 1920's, influenced the development of a number of Yugoslav composers who did not follow the nationalistic direction, or who were even radically opposed to it. The most radical of the latter are Slavko Osterc and Marij Kogoj, while the more moderate group includes Danilo Švara, Matija Bravničar, Mihovil Logar, Stanojlo Rajičić, Bruno Bjelinski, Krsto Odak, Predrag Milošević, and others. Nevertheless, viewed as an entity, one may conclude that in the period between the two world wars, the nationalistic orientation in our country prevailed over all other trends.

Already this incomplete list of creators who have contributed to our musical development and the references to their ties with important foreign composers and trends show that in the period after World War II our music was to face all the problems and all the turbulence in which the age abounded. In some of our republics, which had very young art music histories, an extraordinary flourishing and sudden surge of development occurred. Within less than twenty-five years as much was accomplished creatively as would have taken an entire century in the not so distant past. This applies particularly to Macedonia, and to Bosnia and Herzegovina.

After World War II, a general separation from the nationalistic orientation, from the natural Folk Sung Word, took place, so that today we Yugoslav composers mirror all of those upheavals which occur in the international realm of the Tonal Research Storm. We live in a time when the attempt at a totally new way of expression is valued above the exploration of unknown depths in the process of tonal thinking. We find ourselves in a period when the *developmental value* of a work is prized over its *artistic value,* in the creative sense. Indeed, the developmental value of a work is often *identified* as the artistic value, and it seems to me this grave mis-identification has confused our understanding of the difference between the creator and the maker, the creator and his work, and, finally, between Art and its relationship to the non-artists who have need of it.

Let me first discuss those trends in Yugoslavia which, as I see them, have a *developmental value,* or which will perhaps have a developmental value when viewed from a future perspective. This includes those approaches to the Structure of Tone which I consider not necessarily essential but factual for the present time. These trends take as their point of departure the 12-tone system in all its aspects. Undoubtedly some of the works which have emerged from this orientation *do* possess artistic value in addition to developmental value, regardless of my own attitudes and convictions. I should mention first Ivo Malec and Milko Kelemen, whose works are distinguished by high technical refinement; Primož Ramovš, who brings to his present work a connoisseur's expertise from an earlier period of traditional writing; Natko Devčić, who has perhaps passed along the longest path in his stylistic span from the nationalistic to the avant-garde; Ruben Radica, whose works are characterized by stratified, dense structures of concentrated tension; Branimir Sakač, who has been engaged in a tireless and spontaneous search for his own individual expression in the shaping process that all too often threatens to depersonalize a composer's individual physiognomy; and Ivo Petričić, who has developed his tonal searchings on a mosaic-arabesque-like process. The composers named above exemplify the avant-garde trends in Yugoslavia. The more moderate adherents of the avant-garde include Stanko Horvat, Ivan Globokar, Darijan Božić, Lojze Lebić, Darko Obradović, Tomo Prošev, Vojin Komadina, and Zoran Hristić; their works betray certain traditional elements which they deliberately attempt to suppress. Petar Ozgijan and Rajko Maksimović have achieved in their work a more natural reconciliation of the inherited and the researched. But it is in the creation of Vladan Radovanović that I feel an organic synthesis of the two incompatible — philosophically as well as theoretically, in my view — elements: the nuclear tonal, that most actively functioning principle in the Musical Being, and the denuclearized non-tonal which contains the threat of Musical Non-Being. Is this that creative moment which has reconciled the irreconcilable? I wonder. To me, it appears entirely possible that in this case it happened; if so, it constitutes an artistic event of supreme significance.

I shall now consider the ties between Yugoslav music and contemporary musical trends in general — those which do not seem to contain the anxieties and fears with which I cloaked my observations of the trends discussed earlier. The representatives here express themselves individually by means of creative links with the classics of modern music and, at this moment, are contributing more of value to Yugoslav contemporary music. I shall mention only those composers who, in my opinion, represent this area of creativity most characteristically: Ljubica Marić's gift springs from the inspired union of archaic folk melos and a thoroughly sophisticated technique; Milan Ristić is a symphonist of neo-classical purity, balanced and masterly; Milo Cipra has mastered a subtle neo-impressionism rarely found in Yugoslavia; Uroš Krek has achieved a spontaneous, mature, thoughtful, and dynamic expression; Dušan Radić's finely shaped expression of dramatic lyricism emerges from a concentrated, high-tension lyrical essence of an original sort; Rudolf Bruči, Vasilije Mokranjac, Alojz Srebotnjak, Petar Bergamo, and of the youngest group, Tomislav Zografski, also belong in this creative category.

In keeping with my definition of the *contemporary in essence,* I have necessarily omitted the names of some composers who are producing artistically valuable works. I believe their creativity, by virtue of its importance, belongs to the history of Yugoslav music in the twentieth century, but that it is not and need not be closely connected with the problems treated here.

Lukas Foss

NOTES ON AMERICAN MUSIC IN THE 1960'S

For the sake of clarity, we might divide American music in the 1960's into four groups:

1. Traditional music   a. American (folk or jazz influenced)
                                           b. neo-classic

2. Serial music   a. classic 12-tone
                                           b. post Webernian (bad term)

3. Electronic music   a. computer
                                           b. all other electronic means and methods

4. Chance music   a. those who want to control the result
                                           b. those who don't want to control the result

A good composer does not fit into any one of these groups. John Cage is writing a computer piece. He is using tapes and harpsichords. He is also using Mozart and elements of indeterminate notation. In short, he belongs to group 1b, 3a, and 4b. How would I classify my own work? I suppose 1b, 2b, and 4a. My above mentioned groups are the schools. Schools are analytical abstractions. Individuals make the music. Composers don't belong to schools. Schools belong to composers.

Around 1960 or '61, we can detect a definite shift in the composer's attitude: In the 1950's the forward looking American composer was desperate for a new sound. Today he is desperate to break out of the world of sound, to incorporate other worlds (mixed media). He no longer wants to be a mere composer, but a poet, a prophet, a guru. He has little patience for "notes." He is rarely alone, often in the company of disciples. He thinks of himself as a catalyst in the revolution. Gone is the ivory tower. He tries to help save the world.

Notes on Things Remembered

From Schoenberg I learned that tradition is a home we must love and forego. Everything he discovered is a substitute for everything he loved. No, he didn't say it. It's in his music. He *did* say: "Talent is the ability to learn, genius is the ability to develop." Wherein lies the difference? I think developing means to take your past, as it were, take it by the hand and lead it into your future.

....

Stockhausen once told me that he identified with the fairytale knight who had to leave home, who went to seek — whatever it is that knights seek (the Holy Grail?). But one command the knight had to obey: "Don't look back." For this command to have any meaning, the knight must have something to not look back to — a home, a love, a past. Too many of our knights have little or nothing to not look back to.

....

I had a long drawn-out love affair with the past. Never thought of venturing out into something new. In 1956-57 at UCLA I became dissatisfied with the training of our young instrumentalists. They seemed forever tied to the printed note. I decided to make up a game of ensemble improvisation. Thus I began what was to be a mere pedagogic experiment. Gradually I became increasingly involved. Soon my students and I spent many hours a week practicing a kind of "controlled improvisation." Unwittingly I had opened a door which I had not intended to open and which changed me, eventually, more than it changed my students. When, after five years, I decided to leave ensemble improvisation to others who had more time to do it consistently, my composition and my whole attitude toward composition had undergone a change. I found myself, for better or for worse, in a no-man's land of unending possibilities — "Don't look back."

....

If one has nothing to not look back to, one plunges headlong into a would-be future. Anarchism, bookburning. One can hide in a would-be future, a cardboard future, even better than one can hide in the past. What Boulez so aptly called *"la fuite en avant"* — an escape forward. Many of us who belong to that club with the nasty military name *avant-garde* are "forward-escapists."

....

In a lecture "Beethoven's big feet" (march toward God) I quoted Pound: "All the angels have big feet." Did you know that he lifted that from an advertisement: "All the angels have big feet and buy their shoes at Rogers Peet." Pop poetry, forty years ahead of schedule. Those were the days when a few, a very few, were ahead of their time. Now we are all ahead of our time.

....

I *did* look back (commands — taboos not for me). As I advance — no escape forward this, rather, as I once put it, an advance rear first — I see in the distance a ghost: tonality. I wave. Like a dream. Tonality, children's tunes, Bach.

From a new vantage point everything is again possible: beat, melody, harmony . . . Bring the past in through the back door.

Notes on "Anonymous" Music

When, in 1956, I began making up charts for ensemble improvisation pieces, I thought I had invented a new kind of improvisation. I now know that I was merely the first not to sign my name.

. . . .

Signed or unsigned, a piece of music is anonymous only when not listened to. The minute it is performed, someone will be held responsible.

. . . .

For a "composed" piece, that is, one I have notated in every detail, I will, of course, take the blame and the credit; it's mine. When I devise a situation to be realized by the performer I offer it as a gift. I want it to be his.

. . . .

One of my illustrious friends said that he presents the camera; the performer takes the picture. Agreed. But does the inventor of the camera sign the photo? The one who snaps the picture does.

. . . .

Masterpiece = monument = composition: suspect today, it probably will endure. (That's what it is about — nonperishability.) I would not want to dismiss the possibility of new monuments.

. . . .

Whenever monument building becomes unbearable there is this more fragile, perishable art: performer's music = composition become performance = a kind of "instant composition" (only one step removed from improvisation). Its virtue its fragility. A music born and dying with each performance. Perhaps all music using "chance" or "indeterminacy" belongs to this frail, peculiarly attractive artform.

. . . .

I named a recent piece "Non-Improvisation": tasks so clearly defined that improvisation is ruled out. It is also a "non-composition" because it is not committed on paper. Hence it is also unsigned.

. . . .

On the whole it would appear that the composer's signature is hanging on — at least for the time being. Says one colleague who proclaims his music to be free of all personal touches: "I sign my name so that the people who know my work can tell in advance that they are in for an anonymous musical experience."

Personal Notes

Wherever we turn safeness lurks.

To take refuge in the past is to play safe. *avoidance of truth*

To burn the past is to play safe. *avoidance of knowledge*

Chance music can be the safest music of all namely if we accept any result as "nature having its way." To control the result is also to play safe: freedom, choice handed to the performer because it doesn't matter what he does; the given entities control the music, neutralizing the performer's personal additions.

"Shocking" music is safe music because shock is always effective. *cringe benefits*

Improvisation that works is improvisation made safe. One plays what one can play, i. e., what one knows. One invents traffic controls against disorder.

Electronic music is safe. *escape from the most dangerous element in music: performance*

Program notes, articles, are safe when couched in a pseudo-scientific jargon. *language used to conceal rather than reveal*

Silence is safe, even virtuous.

. . . .

Show me dangerous music. Music precise like tightrope walking. Music that will stop wars.

"Art is a weapon against the enemy." Picasso.

"He who understands my music is set free." Beethoven.

Ivo Supičić

MUSIC AND THE MASS AUDIENCE IN
YUGOSLAVIA TODAY

Yugoslavia is a country of several languages and cultures. The Yugoslav peoples and their cultures developed throughout the centuries separated from each other by frontiers that were often drawn according to the interests of foreign conquerors or of neighboring political powers. Thus, the variety and individuality of these cultures must be taken into account.

During the last twenty years, musical culture in Yugoslavia has risen in many respects to the level of the most highly developed countries in Europe and the world. This development is especially apparent in the achievements of musical pedagogy, in the creative works of Yugoslav composers, and in the quality of performing artists, both individuals and groups, who are well known and appreciated abroad. For example, the *Soloisti di Zagreb,* which was founded in 1954, performed in the first ten years of its activity in more than three hundred musical centers throughout the world, made more than twenty major tours, and participated in twenty-five festivals, securing world fame and unanimous acclaim as a first-rate chamber string ensemble. Such a high level of excellence can only be found in the major cultural centers of Yugoslavia, of course. This fact points up an important characteristic of musical life in our country: a few principal centers dominate the musical and artistic life of the nation. The most important centers are Zagreb, Belgrade, and Ljubljana; less prominent are Sarajevo, Skopje, Dubrovnik, Maribor, Novi Sad, Osijek, Rijeka, and Split. These cities possess opera theaters or symphony orchestras or both, and some are the seats of internationally known festivals.

Those cities or areas that have a richer musical tradition naturally have better audiences as well, quantitatively and qualitatively. I exclude here radio and television audiences, as well as the audience that comes into contact with musical life only on rare occasions, as for example when it is attracted by a particularly interesting or renowned musical personality or event. The reason for excluding these groups relates to the fact that they cannot be dealt with in a scholarly manner, as modern sociological and statistical analyses and surveys have yet to be made of this area. In my definition, the "mass audience" is that in attendance at concert halls and opera theaters and oriented for the most part to the so-called standard repertory. In qualitative terms, this audience is more or less integrated in musical culture. Indeed, music appears to be the most widespread, most vital, and most varied cultural activity in Yugoslavia, and its audience is — with the exception of the television and motion picture audience — the most numerous.

Music in Yugoslavia is integrated in the general culture almost in the same way as it is in countries which have the most highly developed musical culture. This statement is true primarily, though not exclusively, of the musical centers named above and of the musically cultivated stratum of the population who acquire their culture either through formal education or through prolonged residence in one of these centers. Yet this integration is far from embracing the vast potential audience.

The mass audience in Yugoslavia in the past two decades has grown importantly. The number of professional musicians has also increased, new concert halls opened, new ensembles have been created and old ones enlarged. The largest percentage of the increase in the mass audience comes from young people, and in the future further increases will certainly come almost exclusively from the ranks of youth.

The mass audience in the major musical centers represents an unorganized but actual sociological group, which assures more or less a steady "market" for music. This audience is a relatively compact body that does not show any particular fluctuations or oscillations; however, in spite of its homogeneity and stability, it is not organized like the audience in some countries. I must exclude from this generalization a considerable part of the adolescent audience, which is organized in the society *La jeunesse musicale*. This organization provides information, incentive, and opportunities for hearing music through special lectures, discussions, recitals, and concerts. A large part of the membership of *La jeunesse musicale* naturally belongs to today's "mass audience."

When I speak of the "unorganized" audience in Yugoslavia, I not only mean that it is not organized in music associations or listeners' clubs, but that few people view it as an entity. Consequently, communication with the audience is notably lacking. Of course, the more important musical events, festivals and the like, are reported in the daily press, and the principal newspapers carry critical reviews. But there is a lack of publications addressed especially to the mass music audience — publications which could maintain a permanent contact with that audience, inform it and cultivate it systematically. No tradition exists for this type of publication, and to establish one will not be easy. Yet communication must be effected if the mass audience is to continue drawing from the ranks of youth. (The review *Pro Musica* fulfills this type of function, at least partially, in Serbia.)

Radio broadcasts help to compensate for the lack of music publications for the mass audience. Many are highly informative, aimed at familiarizing a wide audience with music and composers (including interpretation and commentary) and informing them about major musical events. Radio stations thus play an important pedagogical role. By means of radio broadcasts, a wide audience can find informative and varied programs which cover all styles, historical periods, and genres, from folk and popular music to the traditional classics, as well as the works of today's serious composers.

Is it possible to speak of one definite general trend in the mass music audience in Yugoslavia with respect to taste, demand, and the frequency of attending musical performances?

Although general trends similar to those in most other European musical centers may be detected, certain differences distinguish one place from another. An indisputable trait of the musical audience in this country — and a very positive characteristic — is its receptive attitude toward the whole of musical culture, both traditional and modern, especially European (performances of Oriental music and of works by American composers are less frequent). This attitude is seen most clearly in the lively interest and spontaneous receptivity shown new and still unknown works. It is also evident in the successful appearances of foreign composers, soloists, conductors, and ensembles. I should stress here the high criteria of selection in contracting for the appearance of foreign artists.

The greatest attendance of the mass audience is probably at symphony concerts, then solo recitals, and finally concerts of chamber music. However, performances by particularly prominent chamber ensembles, and especially those by renowned soloists, excite great interest which perhaps exceeds that shown in symphony concerts. Tickets for these concerts, and for most others, are sold by subscription for the entire season. Most series are sold out.

According to data for 1962, Norway had three symphony orchestras, Belgium four, Hungary five, Austria seven, and the Netherlands eleven. Yugoslavia had thirteen (not counting opera orchestras and chamber ensembles). Today, Belgrade has three orchestras, Zagreb and Ljubljana two each, and the cities of Sarajevo, Skopje, Maribor, Novi Sad, Dubrovnik, and Rijeka one each.

The concert in its "classical" form is the event which plays the central role in communication with the mass audience. Concerts in Yugoslavia as a rule show strict standards of selection, both of works in regard to their artistic merit and of performing artists. A work of a native composer or else a contemporary work (if the concert is not exclusively dedicated to such works) is frequently included in programs which otherwise consist of the traditional standard repertory.

It is difficult to speak today about an audience in the singular, just as about music in the singular. There is no single audience, whether a mass audience or a specialized audience, i.e., one that is small in number and interested in a given field, movement, genre, style, or period of music. Moreover, in Yugoslavia, unlike in some other countries, the specialized audience seems to constitute a portion of the mass audience. From the information I have, there seem to be audiences in some countries that are almost exclusively oriented toward special areas, e.g., toward contemporary music, without being interested in the repertory that attracts the mass audience; but in Yugoslavia, this differentiation seems not to exist. Instead, many segments within the mass audience have special interests, yet their special interests do not lead to a separation from the general interests of the mass audience.

Opera seems to be gradually losing the important role it once played as the favored genre of the mass audience. The process can be observed in other countries as well, even in Italy, where opera has been for many years the main musical genre of the mass audience. The cause of this change may be found in general trends in the modern world, the widespread developments in television, and also in the migration of the best Yugoslav singing talents who are in great demand by opera theaters abroad. Nevertheless, ten or so permanent and very active opera theaters continue to survive in Yugoslavia. Four of these are located in Croatia (Zagreb, Osijek, Split, and Rijeka). Serbia and Slovenia each have two permanent operas (respectively in Belgrade and Novi Sad, and in Ljubljana and Maribor); Bosnia and Herzegovina, and Macedonia have one each (Sarajevo and Skopje).

Music festivals have certainly contributed to the development of the musical culture of the mass audience and to a general increased interest in music. In the course of the seasons of 1966-67 and 1967-68, for example, about thirty music festivals (including festivals of pop and folk music) have been held. Worth special mention are the Festival of Yugoslav Opera in Belgrade, the Ljubljana Festival, the Biennial Festival of Modern Music in Zagreb, the Dubrovnik Summer Festival of Drama and Music, the Festival of Chamber and Choral Music at Ohrid, the Festival of Contemproary Chamber Music at Slatina Radenci, and the Yugoslav Musical Tribunal in Opatija. Film music is represented at the Cinematographic Festival in Pula (founded in 1954), while the "Summer Plays" in Split (also founded in 1954) devotes more attention to opera. The Ljubljana Festival (founded in 1953) is concerned with both opera and ballet (along with drama, concert music, and folklore). The Zagreb Biennial Festival of Modern Music (founded in 1961) has already become world famous for its comprehensive surveys of contemporary music from East and West. The Dubrovnik Summer Festival (founded in 1959) encompasses virtually all of the arts, and its fame attracts visitors from all over the world. The program includes drama, opera, ballet, symphony concerts (up to sixty in a season), chamber music, solo recitals, and folk music concerts. The performers are mostly Yugoslav, but some foreign artists participate. The staging of the Dubrovnik Festival in natural settings around the ancient walled city (on the battlements, in parks, and in the squares before historic palaces and churches) adds a special charm.

My survey of the mass audience in Yugoslavia would not be complete without mention of a type of mass audience quite different from the traditional one – the audience for phonograph records. This audience is less extensive in Yugoslavia than in some other European countries, and as yet no popular publications specialize in communicating with this audience.

The problem of how to make music of the highest quality reach the greatest number of listeners must be viewed not only from technological and financial aspects, but from cultural, educational, and psychological ones as well. The problem grows especially acute in relation to contemporary music, because the mass audience is generally disinclined to accept radical departures from its standard musical fare. But with education, the mass audience develops greater flexibility in taste. This is evident in the countries which have a highly developed musical culture, and it also grows increasingly evident in the principal Yugoslav musical centers.

The vast developments in the musical life of Yugoslavia during the past twenty or so years have manifested themselves in the creation of new orchestras and ensembles, in the increased number of concerts, in the opening of new opera theaters and radio stations, in the energetic activities of new music schools and academies, and in the greatly increased number of professional musicians and music students. Problems remain, of course, and our principal task now is to strengthen the successful results and to expand them as much as possible.

Howard Taubman

MUSIC TODAY AND THE MASS AUDIENCE IN THE UNITED STATES

To speak of audiences in the United States without further definition or discrimination is not only to be brave but foolhardy and inaccurate. We are a huge nation and we have, like our landscape with its plains, mountains, and oceans, a great diversity. There is a staggering abundance of music of all sorts, and each kind has its audiences. Indeed, in each field of music there is a remarkable variety of audiences.

One might well argue that in some respects the United States has an excess of music. It is available on the radio, on television, in restaurants, in shops, on airplanes and trains, on the lifts in tall buildings, and in motorcars where nowadays one can have either a radio constantly tuned to a station broadcasting music or a system for playing tapes.

When we speak of audiences, therefore, we must be careful to differentiate. I shall do so, with the caveat that even in my effort to make distinctions, I cannot succeed in making enough of them. By approaching the question from the viewpoint of audiences and their differences in tastes and habits, I hope I shall also be able to sketch the variety and quality of music at the disposal and pleasure of Americans.

First, then, let me speak of the Captive Audience. This is the audience that must listen whether it wishes to or not, the audience that cannot escape the instrumental and vocal sounds that fill the American air, save in the remotest places where one can at last be shielded from the incessant playing and singing. For the great majority in this audience, of course, the never-ending melange of musical noises is not a hardship at all. There are many people — more than I care to admit — who regard music of some sort as an indispensable accompaniment to whatever they are doing. Thus one often walks into an intelligent American home for an evening's visit, hoping for good talk and cheerful companionship, only to find that the host has turned on his record player or radio to provide a background of music. In some homes one finds great, noble music serving as a distant background to conversation; in other homes light, popular music is employed. In either case the person who likes to give all his attention to any music he happens to listen to, like myself, finds that he is irritated and frustrated.

I live part of the time in a New York City apartment. In the summer, should I open the window, I often hear a young man across the street, with his window open, playing his guitar and singing. Even when it gets colder, he plays regularly. Then there is another chap, whom I've never seen but whom I can hear, who pounds away on a set of drums. That is a sound that can really get to you. And if neighbors don't provide uninvited entertainment, I can at times be regaled by my own sons, playing away at their guitars.

The Captive Audience, like myself, is privy not only to folk music, jazz, rock, and all the other popular forms, which, of course, are most numerous on the ever-present airwaves, it also hears a variety of other things from Strauss waltzes to Beethoven symphonies to Schoenberg pieces. Even for the mass audience, it seems to me, there is too much music. Some silence on occasion and some attentive listening to what one wishes to hear would be a gain. But I have little hope that we shall ever be able to screen out the waves of sound that inundate our lives, and I venture to guess that other lands, advanced or developing, will soon be in the same situation, if they are not there now.

My second category: The Faithful and Fashionable Audience. This is the audience for which most of the old, established institutions function. Let us look at some of these institutions:

The Symphony Orchestra. In the United States it is still king, though how long it will continue to be dominant is a question. There are almost thirty major symphony orchestras, scores of ensembles with smaller budgets and shorter seasons but still professional in makeup and standards, and hundreds upon hundreds of amateur groups. Among the major orchestras the finest are the New York, Boston, Philadelphia, Cleveland, Chicago, Pittsburgh, Minneapolis, San Francisco, and Los Angeles. Most of these play throughout the year. For the most part they appear in their home cities and in the surrounding territory. Occasionally they make far-ranging tours, including visits abroad. In the summer, some take part in festivals in pleasant, rural areas. In addition, they record, their recordings are played frequently on the radio, and they appear live on radio and, though rarely, on television.

The size of the American symphonic audience, counting only the patrons who attend the concerts in person, is enormous, running into the hundreds of thousands and millions. When one thinks of the New York Philharmonic's concerts in the parks of New York City in the summer, with as many as 75,000 men, women, and children filling a vast meadow in mid-Manhattan, one has some notion of the enormity of this audience.

The symphonic repertory is based largely on the classics, mostly in the range from Bach and Handel to mid-twentieth century, with such established figures as Stravinsky and Prokofiev and Britten appearing with moderate frequency. For the most part, the programs are made up of Beethoven, Brahms, Mozart, Schubert, and Tchaikovsky. Increasingly an effort is made to present the music of more recent times — not only by Americans but also by composers from other lands. Reaction is not always enthusiastic to the new and problematic. One might well ask, "Does the new and problematic always deserve attention, let alone enthusiasm?"

In the view of the comfortable, Faithful and Fashionable Audience of this category, the answer is, "Very rarely." This audience, by and large, is conservative. But even here one must be careful to differentiate. There are concertgoers who, though happier with the familiar greats of music, are willing on occasion to take a chance on something different and novel. There are others who resent any intrusion on the comfortable old procedures.

Among these concertgoers, one must confess, are patrons who have only a mild interest in music. These are the people who subscribe and attend for reasons of fashion. They want to go where their friends go; they want something to do that is cultural. They are a minority, and in my view, they are scarcely touched by what they hear.

Managers and conductors of orchestras are often attacked for their failure to be more adventurous in programming. And it is true that some managers are poorly informed and that some conductors are lazy or inclined to play it safe or both. But even forward-looking managers and conductors have their problems in moving against the wishes of their conservative patrons.

For example, Leonard Bernstein as conductor of the New York Philharmonic sought to introduce a representation of contemporary music. Much of it was listened to with the barest tolerance; some was hardly listened to at all. I remember that one year he decided to invite the critics to the second of the week's subscription series on Friday afternoons, rather than the first on Thursday evenings. The explanation was that in this way the orchestra would have the program, the same on both occasions, better in hand. As music critic of the New York Times at the time, I found myself at Carnegie Hall on Friday afternoons, in an audience made up largely of women. It was a trying experience. There were women around me, many from the affluent suburbs, who were doing what they thought was right and fashionable culturally by attending. But they listened with half an ear. If the music was in the least problematic, they would arrive late and leave early, clanking their charm bracelets as they came and went. They were, to say the least, unadventurous in listening tastes and habits.

But these patrons, and many like them all over the country, purchase expensive tickets, and without the sale of these tickets the orchestras would have even larger deficits than they now have. The result is that the orchestras are faced with a Hobson's choice — to alienate the conservative patrons by playing programs too far off the beaten path or to hold them and alienate a different and newer audience that wants to explore the musical, creative world of our time.

While I am still speaking of the orchestral situation, I must raise the questions that are on thoughtful American minds: If the repertory is to be renewed, how can this feat be accomplished in the face of the resistance of the old, established audience? If the repertory is not refreshed, how can the established orchestras attract new audiences and what will be their chances of survival? What will happen when the old, Faithful and Fashionable Audience begins to disappear? Will it mean attrition among the established, expensive orchestras?

The Opera: What I have been saying about the orchestras applies to our major opera companies. Their audiences are largely similar to those of the major orchestras. They like the safe, comfortable, and familiar.

The operatic situation is different in that there are only a few major companies. The biggest, most famous and most glamorous is the Metropolitan in New York. Others that aspire to similar reclame are the Chicago Lyric and the San Francisco Opera. In a few cities, like San Antonio in Texas, the local orchestra, using its own instrumental ensemble, also supplies a modest season of opera, usually several works that are reasonably familiar, with stars from major opera houses in the leading roles. On several large university campuses, brave music schools undertake ambitious opera projects.

These companies and the various odd ventures rely almost entirely on the operatic staples of Verdi, Puccini, Mozart, Strauss, and Wagner. Alban Berg's *Wozzeck* reached the Metropolitan more than thirty years after it was written, and even then it was a trying, novel experience for many listeners.

There are other avenues of some importance for opera. Consider two examples like the New York City Opera — a company of good, occasionally high accomplishment, which not only presents staples, but regularly offers new operas by Americans and authors of other countries — and the Santa Fe Company, which functions in a distant section of the Rocky Mountains in a small town, but which has made a reputation for its youth, eagerness, and curiosity — presenting old works, with unusual staging, as well as new or neglected ones.

When one considers these two companies, one must begin to make distinctions in the examination of the Faithful and Fashionable Audience, for the New York City and Santa Fe Operas have audiences of a more varied kind. These audiences include opera lovers like those at the Metropolitan who want the safe and familiar and grumble at the new and different. But among these audiences are people with a taste for something novel and different. Audiences, if I have not said so earlier, have a way of cutting across any categories one may wish to set up.

Concerts by Soloists: Thousands of communities have their series of concerts by soloists and ensembles. Here, too, offerings, are generally conventional. The reason is the audience — the old, Faithful and Fashionable one.

Festivals: There are famous established ones like the one at Tanglewood, now more than thirty years old, and there are new ones founded in the last few years at Saratoga Springs, N.Y., and Meadow Brook, Michigan. These festivals are centered around major orchestras like the Boston, Philadelphia, and Detroit. They encompass not only symphonic music, but opera and the dance. They offer a predictably safe repertory for the most part and perform it with high standards. They reach much larger audiences than can be held in a concert hall during a winter series. They appeal to some of the people who attend the winter concerts, but they also reach a new and younger audience. The question that might be asked: Is this new audience being trained to be merely a part of the old, Faithful and Fashionable Audience of the future?

It should be added that at some of these festivals an effort is being made to concentrate on new trends and developments in music. At Tanglewood each year a segment of time is devoted to new works, and these programs draw their own audience. But this audience belongs, in my view, to another of my categories, to which a few other festivals on the American scene appeal.

I now come to my third category, which might be called the Intellectual Audience. It is to this audience that the special contemporary events at Tanglewood appeal. It is to this audience that the novel, unusual events and performances are directed. One finds it on a number of university campuses and in a few big cities. It is small in numbers. I used to have the feeling when I circulated among such audiences that its members came if invited on free tickets and that few either had the money or wished to spend it on such events. This audience, nevertheless, is a lively and curious one. Its influence is far beyond its size. It cannot make the Category No. 2 audience accept its views and preferences, but it can stimulate enough discussion and debate to focus some attention on the works it regards as interesting.

The fourth category embraces the Young Audience. I would say this is an audience that follows its own honest bent, indifferent to the established conventions preferred by Category No. 2 and to the claims and pretensions professed by Category No. 3. It is an audience that listens with open mind and ears to the Beatles as well as Ravi Shankar. I welcome this audience for its willingness to be adventurous, but I am not entirely optimistic about it. It has a way of following fads and fashions. It may develop informed tastes of its own.

On the other hand, it may just run from one fad to the next. I would say that the jury is still out on this audience.

Finally, my fifth category, the Very Young Audience. This group, the largest in America, is still in the elementary schools and even in the kindergartens. Thanks to the efforts of the Federal Government, State Governments, and foundations, millions of dollars are being spent on educating this audience. It is being exposed in the schools and other institutions to old and new sounds — orchestras, string quartets, wind ensembles, as well as electronic music. It hears recordings. It is even getting an exposure to music through television, mostly on educational channels. What will happen to it when it grows up? No one can say, but there is a chance that it will be more experienced in music than any other generation and therefore able to make up its own mind more readily. Then it may be that our recording and television industry, which now concentrates so largely on the familiar and conventional, will be able to range further afield. But whatever happens, the basic minimal musical culture of America is rising and reaching a higher plateau of knowledge and sophistication.

Dragotin Cvetko

MUSICOLOGICAL STUDIES IN YUGOSLAVIA

Compared with West European countries, and some Central European ones, musicological studies in Yugoslavia started very late. The reasons for this are several. Yugoslavia emerged as a federated, multi-national state only in 1918. The nationalities that comprised the new state had developed quite independently, and their cultures were in some ways quite disparate as a consequence of historical circumstance. At the time the new state emerged, only two universities existed throughout its entire territory — one in Zagreb and the other in Belgrade. In 1919, the University of Ljubljana was founded. With that, each of the nationalities recognized at that period — Slovenes, Serbs, and Croats — had their own republican university, their highest scientific and educational institution. Not much later, advanced music schools were also founded, but their structures varied in different regions. Nevertheless, between the two world wars, a fairly homogeneous approach to higher music education developed in the centers where universities had already been established. Different names were given to these schools ("conservatory" or "music academy"), but they meant essentially the same thing.

None of the three advanced music schools showed an inclination or sought an opportunity to initiate any sort of musicological activity in the period between the two world wars. They had one goal only, regardless of the region in which they were situated: to train teams of teachers and artists in the areas of musical performance and composition. The history of music was just one of the many minor subjects which a student had to master as a necessary supplemental area of knowledge. The subject was devoid of a deeper meaning or purpose; least of all had it any scholarly aspirations, nor was it intended for training specialists in its own right.

The universities of that period and their Colleges of Arts were never oriented toward musicological studies. Musicology did not exist as an independent discipline, much less as an independent department. Chairs of musicology were simply unknown. Some lectures in the history of music were given, but never as a separate course or as a required subject, as in other fields of study. Even the lectures did not last throughout the period between the two wars, for lecturers were not always available. Lectures were given in Zagreb from 1928 to 1939 (D. Plamenac), in Belgrade from 1925 to 1939 (M. Milojević), and in

Ljubljana from 1921 to 1924 (J. Mantuani). Such inconsistent treatment of the history of music precluded its development as an independent field of academic study (not to speak about musicology as a whole). Little wonder at the scant possibility of educating the necessary teams of experts in musicology at Yugoslav universities. One could not graduate in that specialty, one could not earn a doctor's degree in it, nor did possibilities exist for obtaining employment as a music historian, had one been able to obtain a degree. In the secondary schools of that era, music education was reduced to a minimum; moreover, in the majority of schools, it was not even a required subject.

Taking these factors into account, one can well understand the lack of fertile ground for the development of musicology, both in the music academy as well as in the university. Of course, the lectures in music history — no matter how haphazard their structure — might have served as points of departure for musicological studies, though without prospects for leading to anything concrete in the professional sense.

Obviously, the situation forced those who wanted a musicological education to find other ways, outside of Yugoslavia. Thus, young people went to foreign universities, primarily to Prague, Vienna, and Leipzig, although occasionally to other centers. Once back home, they generally failed to find positions commensurate with their qualifications, so they turned for the most part to pedagogic work, music criticism, and journalism. Possibilities for research tended to be as undistinguished as the results of the occasional attempts. Chances for publication were few, especially if a study happened to be large. Even the shorter studies were published only after great persistence. Periodicals were scarce, and they featured criticism and essays on music rather than musicological studies.

After World War II, the situation began to change fundamentally, though slowly; but in the earliest period, the direction of change was not clearly defined. It is worth noting that the earliest attempts to solve the question of musicological studies were not made in the universities. At that particular moment (i.e., shortly after 1945), no preliminary steps had been taken to justify musicological studies as an academic discipline. Moreover, in that early postwar period, understanding of musicology and its achievements was so slight that the issue of its importance was rarely even raised. Whatever was accomplished at this time depended entirely on the initiative of individual experts who were determined to carry out their own private plans.

Perhaps it should also be added that musicology as a branch of scholarship was poorly known, if not entirely unknown, not only in Yugoslav cultural and academic circles in general, but even among musicians. This may be accounted for not so much by prejudice — or at least not at first — as by stubborn adherence to the tradition that the study of music and music history consisted of nothing more than a general review of facts rather than of a systematic examination and scholarly interpretation of those facts. Moreover, the development of musicological studies in other nations was unknown for the most part, as were the often admirable results of those studies.

In the period under discussion, no interest or opportunity was to be found in the universities for the introduction of musicological studies into that domain, so it appeared necessary to try something else. I am not referring to the folklore institutes, some of which existed earlier, although after World War II they grew in number all over Yugoslavia (Ljubljana, Zagreb, Belgrade, Skopje, Banja Luka); nor am I thinking of the musicological institute in Belgrade or the musicological institute in the Faculty of Theology at Zagreb, which had existed for some time. None of these instituions were intended for the training of musicologists capable of doing research in the various branches of musicology. Their orientation was different, and so were their aims.

At that early period, the music academy was firmly established and well organized, and it might have helped in achieving the goals of musicological studies, at least to some degree. However, its fundamental structure never provided the circumstances for a successful development of such studies. Nevertheless, it was precisely here, in the music academy, that the preliminary work in the organization of musicological studies began. It happened first at the Music Academy in Ljubljana where, in 1945, a so-called "scientific" department was established. This department consisted of three branches: the history of music, music folklore, and music pedagogy. In 1948, a conference of representatives from all the Yugoslav music academies decided that similar departments should be established in all the existing music academies. In keeping with the recommendations of that conference, the "scientific" department in the Ljubljana Music Academy was reorganized into a department of history and folklore — although it functioned primarily as a department of music history, while folklore studies played a decidedly subordinate role. A department of history and folklore was established in the Belgrade Music Academy in 1948, and a similar organization was introduced in Zagreb in 1951, where the departments were designated for "history and theory" and "folklore and theory." These two were combined in 1963 into a single department of music history. When the Sarajevo Music Academy was founded in 1955, it included a department of history and folklore.

From the first, musicology was given more importance in these new departments than had been usual theretofore in the music academies. No doubt, their primary goal was to produce instructors able to teach in the elementary and secondary schools, where a serious shortage of trained music teachers existed. The departments also had some higher ambitions. While their main subjects were music history and folklore, the curricula also included seminars in esthetics, criticism, music education, and sometimes even acoustics. No uniformity in structure or curricula characterized the departments in the several music academies, however. This may be accounted for by the perfectly valid differences in viewpoint found in the several republics.

The importance given to the history of music and music folklore, as well as to other specialized subjects, indicates that the aim of the programs was to prepare graduates who would not be limited to teaching or performance, but who would also be competent to work in criticism, reviewing, and other areas of expert writing about music. The results are now apparent. In all the Yugoslav republics, specialists have appeared who are broad in outlook and capable of perspicacious comment on a legion of problems in several fields — history, esthetics, the sociology of music, music folklore, etc.

Still, something has been missing. Because of their particular orientation and primary interests, the music academies cannot prepare their graduates for systematic research in any of the branches of musicology, at least not to the point where the student might master fully the methodology and the other skills of theory and practice which are indispensable for independent scientific activity.

The music academies have themselves suggested the possibility of a *Treći stepen*, i.e., postgraduate study, in the history of music or music folklore. Still, the problems of such advanced study in a music academy are essentially the same as for the study of those same subjects in the academy at the undergraduate level. Music academies in Yugoslavia and elsewhere, despite the breadth of their general interests, concentrate first on performance. The diverse theoretical, practical, and historical subjects taught in the academy are supplemental to the primary purpose of developing performing artists and teachers of practical music subjects. This orientation cannot offer a truly favorable environment for the education of musicologists.

In response to the need for expanding the possibilities of university education in the humanities, the University Council of the University of Ljubljana moved in 1961 to establish a Department of Musicology within the Philosophy Faculty of the College of Arts. The move was implemented in 1962. When the Department of Musicology actually began to function, the Department of Music History in the Ljubljana Music Academy gradually declined. It was finally closed in 1965.

At present, the Department of Musicology has two chairs: one for the History of Ancient World Music and one for the History of Slavic and Modern World Music. As the number of students increases and technical resources expand, the number of chairs will grow to include other musicological disciplines, among which esthetics, the sociology of music, and music folklore are especially needed.

The Department of Musicology in the university should not be considered a mechanical transfer of the Department of Music History from the Ljubljana Music Academy. It has been organized on a completely new basis. The organization of musicological studies in certain European countries, as well as in some American universities, has been taken into account; additional features have been introduced which seem necessary because of the particular situation in our country.

The usual secondary school diploma is not sufficient for admission into the Department of Musicology. A certain level of accomplishment in practical music is expected: pianistic facility corresponding roughly to the standards of an intermediate music school, a thorough knowledge of music theory, solfeggio, harmony, and counterpoint. All of this must be mastered prior to the beginning of musicological studies if the student is to fulfill the program.

The regular course of study during eight semesters includes all the musicological disciplines, with stress on music history, while acoustics, esthetics, and music folklore follow closely in importance. Besides lecture classes, intensive work in seminars and proseminars is scheduled, with emphasis given to music paleography. In the first four semesters, some practical auxiliary music disciplines are included: harmonic analysis, formal analysis, and keyboard reduction from score. Attention is given to the historical and musicological aspects of all studies.

The course of study follows two lines, one with two major areas, the other with one. A student may take pure musicology (the one-major line), or he can take musicology as the first major (known as "A") and also a second major (known as "B") selected from one of the subjects taught in the College of Arts (e.g., a foreign language, art history, sociology, psychology, pedagogy, etc.). The one-major line – pure musicology – is particularly suited for students who are at the same time studying a practical subject at the music academy, or who have already graduated from it. The two-major line is better suited for those who intend to teach and who have, therefore, the possibility of obtaining a job through their second major. This is a useful security feature, as art instruction, and more particularly music instruction, still has a precarious existence in our secondary schools.

Once graduated, those students who show exceptional ability may continue their studies in two ways, either by applying for an officially advertised opening for a "magisterium," i.e., a postgraduate course of study with obligatory courses, or by announcing their intention to work for the Ph. D. (which means independent research, with no obligatory courses). Either way involves certain basic requirements. Work for the magister's degree requires demonstrable competence in two foreign languages in addition to a marked gift for musicology and research. Work for the doctorate is approved only when a student has already published a number of scholarly works of such quality as to assure his capacity for successfully completing the doctoral dissertation. In either case, the postgraduate work is planned individually under the guidance of an adviser. The candidate is given every opportunity to concentrate on the methodology of scholarly research and on the specific problems of his thesis subject.

Thesis subjects tend to deal with the history of music of the Yugoslav nationalities, but other areas and fields are not excluded. The national histories of music are particularly in vogue, since not much research has been done in this area. Systematic research is needed in national and foreign archives to discover the documents pertinent to our Yugoslav national music histories; monographs are needed on various subjects, past and present. Only in this way can comparisons be made with the development of West European music, so that the musical activity of each nation in Yugoslavia can be properly evaluated historically. Only then might we reasonably expect that the numerous foreign histories of music would devote space to the musical creativity of the Yugoslav nations. Up to now, Yugoslav creativity has been almost completely ignored or else misrepresented.

Since Ljubljana University is the only one in Yugoslavia offering a Ph. D. in musicology, not only Slovenes but other Yugoslavs as well are enrolled. Theses have been written on such national subjects as the musical instruments depicted in the medieval frescoes in Slovenia and Croatia, and the use of sonata form during the period of Serbian romanticism.

I think the value of such dissertations for both national and international musicology is self-evident. These subjects might never have been studied without the possibilities provided in a Department of Musicology. And a Department of Musicology is possible only within the framework of a university, where professional specialists can be trained — the sort of specialists already known and recognized in countries where musicological studies have been a part of university studies for many years. The legitimacy of musicology as a scholarly discipline is borne out by the high level of work done in other countries of the world. Now, Yugoslavia has joined them by establishing musicology as an academic discipline with the ultimate goal of contributing to the achievements of international musicology — not just in the history of music, but in all other branches of musicology as well. Doubtless, other Yugoslav universities will soon follow the lead set in Ljubljana and establish their own departments of musicology in line with their own specific needs. This will inevitably broaden and strengthen musicology within the cultural context of each Yugoslav nation and in the country as a whole.

Miloš Velimirović

MUSICOLOGICAL STUDIES IN THE UNITED STATES

In its broadest sense the term "musicology" embraces the scientific investigation of any conceivable aspect of the Art of Music — its history and theory, its esthetic and social values, its forms and techniques. In subsequent discussion, however, the term "musicology" will be used in a more restricted sense as a synonym for studies in the History of Music, a branch which has achieved the greatest prominence in recent years. Musicology is a term now used almost exclusively as a designation for studies in the history of music.

In comparison to the other branches of science, musicology is a relatively young discipline. The beginnings of musicological studies in the United States of America may be found in those general courses of introduction to music, more often referred to as "Music Appreciation" lectures. A natural place for such instruction was within the confines of professional music schools, a few of which were structured along the lines of the typical European music conservatory. In addition to these, a number of American institutions of higher learning — colleges and universities — introduced courses that viewed the Art of Music as one of the liberal arts and therefore a legitimate part of humanistic education. Within the last forty odd years musicology has achieved a viable status as a part of the standard, humanistically oriented education in most American universities.

The first chair for musicology was founded only in 1930 at Cornell University, with Professor Otto Kinkeldey as its first occupant. Thus, he has been regarded as the dean of American musicological studies. The American Musicological Society was founded in 1934 by only nine scholars. In the intervening thirty-four years, the Society has grown to almost 2,000 members. There has been not only a quantitative growth and rise of interest in musicology, but also a tremendous increase in the quality of studies, and a diversification and branching into nearly every known aspect of the Art of Music. To be sure, as in so many other scientific endeavors, American musicological studies began by emulating the methods and interests of our European predecessors, primarily the Germans, who were the most systematic students of the history of music at the turn of the century. A few events of significance represent landmarks in the growth of American musicology. The Nazi regime in Germany caused a number of scholars to seek refuge in the United States. Men like Curt Sachs, Alfred Einstein, Leo Schrade, and many others, found themselves helping to establish a new, and at the same time a broader base for their research in the United States. Also, a congress of the International Musicological Society took place in September of 1939 in New York. A number of the scholars present at that meeting decided not to return to their war-torn lands. Their presence in the United States in the course of the 1940's instigated the phenomenally rapid expansion of musicological studies, especially after the end of World War II. Many of these scholars secured the opportunity to pursue their work at American universities where new generations of scholars were being trained. It may be helpful, therefore, to outline briefly here some of the features of the American educational system, because in many ways it differs markedly from general European patterns.

No unified curriculum exists in the United States, either for elementary or secondary (high) schools, and there is also no officially prescribed program which requires a certain basic minimum at this stage of a child's education. This means that the quantity as well as quality of knowledge acquired by a young person of eighteen years of age may and indeed does differ considerably from one school to another, from one town to another. Speaking in relative terms, a young person about to begin his studies at a college or university at the age eighteen has acquired less factual knowledge than his European counterpart.

As an undergraduate at a college or university for four years, the average student is usually required in the first two years of his studies to take courses in diverse fields in order to round out his education. By that time it is assumed that he has acquired sufficient interest in some field of studies — in a branch of the humanities, the social sciences or the pure sciences — to devote the last two years in college to a more specialized approach to his chosen field. It should be stressed, however, that even then, the selection of a major field in college does not necessarily mean that he will devote the rest of his life to this particular branch of studies. Due to the peculiarities of American higher education, studies in a School of Medicine, or Law School, can begin only after four years of undergraduate study. Often a student who has chosen music as his major in undergraduate school goes on to study medicine and becomes a physician.

True musicological studies on an advanced level are possible only in a Graduate School to which a candidate is admitted after his four years as an undergraduate. Thus, the average age of students who begin serious work in musicology is about twenty-two. The period of time required for these studies varies again from one university to another. At present, just under forty such institutions of higher learning offer studies leading to the higher degrees of Master of Arts (M.A.) and Doctor of Philosophy (Ph.D.). Not all of the applicants who express their wish to study musicology are admitted, and of those who do undergo the rigorous training and examinations, on the average only one out of three complete their studies and obtain one or both of these advanced degrees. Some students never advance and change professions in midstream. Others, whose abilities do not appear to offer prospects for future development as scholars, are often advised to stop with the M.A. degree. Only the most persevering and talented ones make it to the highest distinction of a Ph.D. degree. In unusual circumstances it has been possible to complete the studies and write the doctoral dissertation in four academic years. More frequently the period of time needed for graduate studies is between six and ten years beyond the undergraduate level.

As in so many other instances, the variety of courses and methods of approach to the training of musicologists may seem strange to foreigners. Basically, the candidate for a higher degree is required to take a minimum number of courses (which varies between eight and twelve full-year courses or their equivalent in one-term courses), and he has to pass a rather strict oral examination. By that time he is supposed to have been able to fill in whatever gaps in his knowledge may have existed, even in areas in which no formal courses of instruction were offered. It goes without saying that a candidate must demonstrate a considerable, though not necessarily exhaustive knowledge of the general history of music and a thorough knowledge of the stylistic period in the history of music in which he intends to work on his dissertation. He is also expected to show some proficiency in the handling of basic research techniques and tools, such as bibliography and musical paleography. A point which is also evaluated is the student's ability for independent thinking as shown in a wish to reappraise some of the traditional points of view, general or detailed, in the history of music.

The requirement that the student must take a certain number of courses and fulfill satisfactorily all the required work in these is helpful, as it provides the opportunity for faculty members to become acquainted with the candidate both as a person and as a potential scholar. By the time of the final oral examination, the teachers already have an idea what they may expect from the candidate, although surprises do happen.

When it comes to dissertation topics, their diversity may serve perhaps as the best barometer of the almost unlimited possibilities in American musicology. It has often been stated that the absence of narrow nationalistic orientation is characteristic of American studies in historical subjects, due to the fact that America is no nation but only an American population of many diverse national origins. In the best scholarly studies this is certainly true. But the opposite may also be encountered. Probably one of the most interesting aspects of American musicological studies has been the fact that, instead of beginning with individual musical compositions or single composers, the earlier studies were directed toward a synthetic approach and attempted to delineate the basic lines in the stylistic evolution of the Art of Music by utilizing the achievements of European musicological studies. This has been reflected most clearly in the publication of several multi-volume series of books, individual volumes of which are devoted to a clearly established stylistic era in the history of music. Once the basic generalizations were made, scholars scrutinized them, and a more detailed examination of individual composers and their works followed. The aim of this kind of approach was to test the validity of the generalizations. Both of these approaches continue to be utilized, mutually cross-fertilizing each other. Needless to say generalizations are constantly being modified and amplified as more details are becoming known. Deepening the knowledge of a single period or of a school of composers or of an individual's works may easily become a dead-end street if it is not incorporated into the mainstream of history, thus helping to outline both the wider as well as the narrower aspects of a given problem. On the whole, it seems that synthetic studies tend to be products of the scholars already established, while dissertations of younger colleagues serve as testing grounds for hypotheses and exploratory studies about more detailed problems. After all, one seldom expects a doctoral dissertation to represent the final statement. It is rather a demonstration and proof of the mastery of the essential research methodology. That is why one may discover esoteric subjects as topics of doctoral dissertations, ranging from studies of an Ancient Greek or Latin musical treatise to studies of a few select contemporary musical compositions.

Because of this predisposition and perhaps, most of all, because of the availability of resources for study of the music of the past — such as manuscripts and archives, and the requisite ability to handle foreign languages — it is not surprising that the largest number of dissertations deal with topics from the history of Italian, German, French, and English music. Regretfully, the study of music in Eastern European countries is sadly neglected at present. It should be kept in mind, of course, that the majority of present day Americans originate from Western Europe, a point which helps to explain the orientation and involvement of American musicology. There are signs, too few at this moment yet hopeful ones nevertheless, that this neglect of East European music is going to be remedied and that a more balanced picture of the history of European music will soon be obtained.

European music, as important as it is, is not the only area to which American musicologists are devoting their attention. With a growing sensitivity towards other parts of the world, ethnomusicology is also rapidly becoming a field of expanding interest, as a special report at this conference has demonstrated. It should also be stated that American scholars have been quite intrigued with the rapid development of many new research tools which modern technology has placed at their disposal. The use of computers transcends the purely speculative and theoretical considerations; currently, projects dealing with medieval and Renaissance music are being studied with the aid of computers.

As sometimes happens in any field of scholarly endeavor, a certain amount of over-specialization may detach the scholar from his own environment and make him believe that only a few elect co-workers can truly understand what he is striving for. Thus far, this kind of separation from the mainstream has affected only a few philosophers of the art of music who require that a new language be learned in order to follow their expository statements. Most scholars have been able to maintain communication among themselves on a fairly comprehensible level. This does not mean that musicologists are purely popularizers of the history of music, although some of them may be for the genuine benefit of the large musical audience in the United States.

Musicologists have at this time reached a point at which some rather basic and deeply probing questions are being asked. By rejecting the theory of constant progress, historians have come to question the theory of evolution and the degree of its application to an art. The point is whether an accumulation of works of art requires the change from quantity into a new quality, or whether quantity may be independent of quality. Is the history of music a single uni-linear concept of evolution? or is it a hierarchial progress from one lull to another blossoming, where one period of progress must be followed by a period of decline; or can a period of progress be followed by still another one, stylistically distinct and different, yet still evolving? One of the serious questions in dealing with problems of tradition and innovation is the role of originality versus extraneous influence in formulating a new musical style and language. What, finally, is "historical objectivity" and how can one achieve it, if it is in fact desirable?

The problem of "objectivity" is especially acute in relation to contemporary music. Many composers, in addition to composing, have become quite eloquent spokesmen for their own music, writing in various journals. The difficulty in dealing with the new music is formulated in the question: When does the present become a subject fit for a historian? A related question is, to what extent do writings on history, with all their contingent attempts at classification, influence and determine the attitudes that shape the expressions of newly created music? This concern leads to the search for a theory of history which, while perhaps useful in our time, will again have to be periodically re-examined.

In sum then, musicological studies in the United States of America offer, at present, a highly diversified picture. On one hand, the quest for acquisition of knowledge continues, with a zeal to clarify and illumine those points that have hitherto remained insufficiently known. At the same time, the transmitted results are being checked and re-evaluated in the light of this growing body of knowledge. On the other hand, a multiplicity of ways exists for disseminating knowledge on various levels, from the elementary school to the most sophisticated graduate school in which a student learns by doing pioneering research work on his own.

Finally, while some aspects of musicological studies are beyond the comprehension of the average laymen, a substantial effort is in progress to communicate the essential concepts of musical historiography (even when its basic premises are being questioned) to the consumer of music — the audience which fills concert halls or listens to music broadcasts. For the time being, it appears, we are faced with a dichotomy in the transmission as well as the reception of musicological results. The main criticisms of musicology as a science can be divided into two groups: one is that musicology deals far too much with "history" and too little with "music." Much more serious is the opposite criticism that musicology is concerned more with the musical rather than the historical aspects of music history. A proof that this latter view is still shared by most people is to be found in the fact that history of music is still allotted the smallest share in the standard, general "histories of mankind." It would seem to me one of the many tasks awaiting American musicology may be found in the area of successfully bridging the gap between musicology and other humanistic studies, so that the treatment of music as an artistic expression of the human spirit receives its fair share in the records of the achievements of man.

Ivan Klemenčić

PROBLEMS OF MUSIC BIBLIOGRAPHY IN YUGOSLAVIA

We may better understand the problems of music bibliography in Yugoslavia by first examining our most characteristic efforts. Three general areas of activity may be considered: (1) the Yugoslav federal and republican bibliographies, which include music, (2) the specialized music bibliographies or bibliographic adjuncts produced within Yugoslavia, and (3) Yugoslav contributions to and participation in international music bibliographic activities.

Prior to 1945, national bibliographies within the various republics were relatively poorly developed. None of the republics has a *complete* index of books and music, much less periodicals and articles, for this period. *Srpska bibliografija,* compiled by Novaković in the nineteenth century, covers Serbian bibliography in the period 1741 to 1867.[1] Croatian books, which were first registered at the beginning of the seventeenth century, are listed up to 1860 in I. Kukuljević's *Bibliografia hrvatska.*[2] The Slovenes are in a somewhat better position, as they started to register their books in the middle of the sixteenth century. F. Simonič compiled a national *Slovenska bibliografija* for the period 1550 to 1900.[3] Moreover, surveys of books and articles by years for the period 1868 to 1912 appear in *Slovenska Matica.*[4] Separate listings of Serbian periodicals in the period 1768 to 1911 and Croatian periodicals in the period 1789 to 1911 are published in *Jugoslovenska štampa*[5]; Slovenian periodicals are listed in detail up to 1936 in Šlebinger's survey *Slovenski časniki in časopisi.*[6] Although the coverage in these works is not always comprehensive, they are invaluable guides to books on music, scores (in the Slovenian and Serbian bibliographies), and, most important, music periodicals (although none lists articles on music). As for the remaining republics in Yugoslavia (e.g., Macedonia and Montenegro), scant systematic effort on a large scale has been expended on bibliography. All, however, have published shorter bibliographic indexes — some of which include music literature — in the periodical press and in collections of articles.

The attempt to establish an all-Yugoslav national bibliography in the period between the two world wars failed. The venture depended on the full co-operation of the various republics that united to form the new state in 1918:

unfortunately, success was thwarted by differing political, economic, and cultural backgrounds, as well as by inexperience and inadequate preparation.

Following World War II, a different set of conditions facilitated the new tasks of bibliography and paved the way to solving the problems unsolved in the past. National libraries in the capital cities of the republics — Belgrade, Zagreb, Ljulbjana, Sarajevo, and Skopje — began systematic work on an index of the entire current press in their respective areas and started to publish yearly national bibliographies.

Two federal bibliographic centers were also organized: the *Bibliografski institut FNRJ* in Belgrade, which was later named the *Jugoslovenski bibliografski institut,* and the *Leksikografski zavod* in Zagreb. The task of the former was preparation of current Yugoslav bibliographies of all published materials, while that of the latter was compilation of a retrospective bibliography up to the year 1945. Each of the two institutes has already published more bibliographic material than was published in Yugoslavia prior to the end of World War II. The *Bibliografija jugoslovenskih bibliografija*[7] alone, covering the period from 1945 to 1955, lists more than a thousand volumes of bibliography, among which are many limited entirely to music. Incidentally, the problem of complete coverage is handled by requiring publishers to provide the various national libraries and the *Jugoslovenski bibliografski institut* with copies of all books, music, periodicals, and journals of any sort.[8]

The *Bibliografija Jugoslavije* began to appear in 1950 in three separate volumes: (1) *Knjige, brošure i muzikalije* (Books, Pamphlets, and Music) is issued twice monthly; (2) *Članci i prilozi u časopisima i listovima* (Articles and Supplements in Journals and Newspapers) appears monthly in three series, the third of which includes articles on music as well as listings of music published in journals; and (3) *Bibliografija jugoslovenske periodike* (Bibliography of Yugoslav Periodicals) is published every three months.[9] Originally, all volumes were printed in both Cyrillic and Latin, but now only the Latin alphabet is used. The entries are organized according to the Yugoslav variant of the Universal Decimal Classification (UDC). At the end of each year, a subject and an author index are published.

Of course, new problems have arisen even as old ones have been solved. For example, although material relating to music can be found fairly easily, it is scattered throughout several different volumes; no Yugoslav bibliography is published in a cumulative annual volume, due to financial considerations.

An unfortunate time lag occurs between the appearance of works and their bibliographic indexing. The volumes of *Bibliografija Jugoslavije* are being issued a half year late; but if we take into account that most of the works indexed were actually published some six months earlier than the time of their registration at the institute, the actual time lag amounts to about a full year. Moreover, some items are not registered until as much as one or even two years after publication.

One of the larger problems in the organization of the federal bibliography derives from the fact that careful distinctions are drawn between authors from the national minority groups, while authors from the major Yugoslav nationalities are listed all together without distinctions. Thus, a great deal of time may be required to determine whether an author is Serbian or Croatian; the problem is compounded in the case of an author from Bosnia-Herzegovina, for Croats, Serbs, and Moslems[10] also live there. Macedonians and Slovenes have their own languages, distinct from Serbo-Croatian, and they would prefer to be able to identify those authors who belong to their cultural milieus. In this regard, it might also be pointed out that listings in languages other than Serbo-Croatian are neither completely reliable nor exhaustive.

The primary aim of the *Bibliografija Jugoslavije* to provide fast and comprehensive bibliographic service has not been helped by the fact that publication of the annual Serbian national bibliographies[11] was discontinued soon after the founding of the *Bibliografski institut FNRJ*. Not much later, the national bibliography in Bosnia and Herzegovina[12] was also discontinued. The annual Croatian national bibliography of books and articles seems to have ground to a halt because of an excessively methodical indexing procedure.[13] In Montenegro, no regular national bibliography has ever existed.[14] Thus, only Macedonia and Slovenia have continued to publish national bibliographies. In Macedonia,[15] biennial bibliographies of books and selected articles have appeared, while in Slovenia, newspapers, magazines, books, music, and articles are indexed in annual bibliographies.[16] A monthly survey of the Slovenian press appears in the magazine *Knjiga*.[17]

In the *Bibliografija Jugoslavije*, the non Serbo-Croatian speaking peoples — both those who already possess a long cultural tradition as well as those who are just now beginning to create such a tradition — are lost among the Serbian, rather the Serbo-Croatian majority. Bibliographic work within the framework of a single nationality could provide a highly valuable service, as it would doubtless be more exhaustive in coverage — due to the ready accessibility and the immediate responsibility — more accurate, and more fully indexed. For example, Slovenian bibliographies index all the books of Slovene authors, inside and outside of Yugoslavia.

The advantage of individual national bibliographies over the federal *Bibliografija Jugoslavije* is especially evident in the coverage given to music books in certain of the national bibliographies as compared to that found in the *Bibliografija Jugoslavije*. Such a comparison provides ample refutation to the objection that the national bibliographies are superfluous and represent a duplication of effort. One is tempted to see behind such allegedly practical reasoning a trend toward "political centralism." Although our political and cultural problems have been solved in principle, this trend nevertheless persists at times. It would seem, however, that despite the process of general integration going on in the world, we are also tending toward a recognition of the autonomy of different nationalities. This tendency should find expression and confirmation in the field of bibliography as well.

Two examples indicate the practicality of the autonomous republican approach to bibliography. First, individual national centers are planning separate retrospective national bibliographies of books, indexed according to unified criteria, from the earliest period up to 1945. Second, the *Leksikografski zavod* in Zagreb has already begun to publish a large retrospective Yugoslav bibliography of publications up to 1945. This bibliography will include music in one of the thirty volumes projected over a ten or fifteen year period of publication. Several large and small bibliographic centers in the country are contributing to this common effort.

Library catalogs, especially those of national and other large libraries, provide bibliographic access to both national and foreign literature. The *Centralni katalog stranih knjiga FNRJ* indexes foreign books, and the *Centralni katalog stranih časopisa* indexes foreign periodicals. The latter contained about 43,000 entries of various foreign journals and reviews ten years ago. Both of these catalogs are connected with the *Jugoslovenski bibliografski institut*.

Music scores and, lately, collections of recorded music are included in libraries, either together with books in the general collection or in separate music sections; some music libraries exist independently in institutes, academies, and such. The material is indexed in an author catalog, a subject catalog organized according to the UDC, or in a combination of the two; the cataloguing procedure follows to a considerable degree the current international practice (e.g., the newer, smaller size catalog card is used to save space, the cards are printed and then distributed to the libraries, the UDC system of classification is followed, etc.).

Prior to the end of World War II, independent music bibliography was virtually nonexistent. No specialized national surveys of past periods were made, nor were retrospective works undertaken. The situation may be explained by the relatively small production of music literature, as well as by the general lack of interest in bibliography. The meager amount of music bibliography that was produced was scattered in journals, yearbooks, monographs, and the like, and it was usually limited to single composers or historical periods, to the listing of music periodical publications, and, occasionally, to annual reviews of music publications.

The picture changed in many respects after World War II. In the post-war Yugoslavia of some twenty million inhabitants, music publication went through an initial period of rapid development, followed by still greater growth, then it leveled off. At the present time, annual publication includes about five to ten music magazines, hundreds of music scores of various types, no fewer compositions published in journals, fifty or more books on music, and probably some thousand odd publications with some musical content — all of this by native authors, for the most part. Still, even this increased production has failed to stimulate work on comprehensive and accurate independent bibliographies, probably because of economic factors.

Zvuk,[18] the official journal of the Union of Yugoslav Composers, has helped to satisfy the need for a more ample, selective music bibliography independently of the *Bibliografija Jugoslavije*. Since 1956, yearly surveys reaching back to 1946 have been published of Yugoslav publications of music, books on music, and articles on music. Unfortunately, these surveys are published with a delay of several years.

The *Muzička enciklopedija*[19] published by the *Leksikografski zavod* provides valuable initial access to composer bibliography as well as bibliography of particular historic periods. A standard encyclopedic work, the individual biographies of Yugoslav composers and musicians include listings of their works and the basic literature about them. Although the bibliographic information in an encyclopedia cannot be extensive, it is highly selective with regard to quality.

Histories of Yugoslav national musics, general histories of music, biographies, and monographs by native Yugoslav authors also provide useful bibliographic surveys and listings of music literature and material.[20]

Similar bibliographic accessories related to Yugoslavia may be found in various international sources. Yugoslavs and Yugoslavia are represented, of course, in a number of the more significant international music encyclopedias, such as *Die Musik in Geschichte und Gegenwart, Grove's Dictionary of Music and Musicians, Enciclopedia della musica* (Ricordi), *Riemann's Musik Lexikon, Encyclopédie de la Musique* (Fasquelle), and others. These works speak about us at times with greater and at times with lesser objectivity and knowledge, depending on the character of the collaboration, but they do make it possible for the foreign reader to get acquainted with what for him may be little known literature and creative activity.

More and more attention is being paid on an international scale to old historical sources. Much precious material of this sort is preserved in Yugoslav monasteries, churches, archives, and other repositories, especially in Dalmatia and Slovenia. Included are manuscripts dating to the tenth century and printed sources dating from the sixteenth century on. Moreover, legacies of foreign musicians from the Middle Ages and later may also be found among them. Some of this material has been listed in Eitner's *Quellen-Lexikon,*[21] some is indexed in as yet unpublished manuscripts, and the rest is scattered in various music, paleographic, and other scientific reviews, annals, etc. An index of a portion of this material has been published recently in Ljubljana by the *Narodna in univerzitetna knjižnica* and its Music Division as a bilingual catalog of old Slovenian manuscripts and publications.[22]

An important stimulus to bibliographic work was provided a few years ago by the international organization *Répertoire International des Sources Musicales* (RISM), which intends to make an index of all the known historical music sources in Europe, America, and the civilized world. Such a comprehensive index is truly indispensable, as many changes have occurred since Eitner's *Quellen-Lexikon*. RISM will encourage a thorough search of the material in our large, highly organized libraries, and it will also promote the exploration of many small, little known, and perhaps even unknown repositories. Professor Dragotin Cvetko of Ljubljana and Professor Josip Andreis of Zagreb have been assigned the task of researching Yugoslav sources for RISM. The initial issues from RISM, *Recueils imprimés, XVIe-XVIIe siècles* (1960) and *Recueils imprimés, XVIIIe siècle* (1964),[23] contain listings of printed collections from fourteen of our libraries and archives. The co-operative project continues, and at present an edition of old printed texts and manuscripts up to the year 1800 is being prepared.

Yugoslavia is participating in still another international project — *Répertoire International de la Littérature Musicale* (RILM). Professor Cvetko sits for Yugoslavia on the international commission of RILM. Two Yugoslav music journals are being abstracted regularly for *RILM Abstracts.*[24] All of the articles from *Muzikološki zbornik*[25] are included, while only selected articles from *Zvuk* are summarized.

In conclusion, a number of questions may be raised for serious consideration in dealing with the practical problems of music bibliography in Yugoslavia. First, should we have only federal national bibliographies, or should we have both federal and independent republican bibliographic projects? Second, should the national bibliographies be of a general comprehensive character only, or should separate, specialized music bibliographies be encouraged? Third, in addition to the international indexes of historical sources such as RISM, should we not also establish Yugoslav national ones as well? Finally, should not national indexes of current literature be maintained along with such current international indexes as RILM?

Work in the fields of general and specialized bibliography, and in national and international bibliographic projects goes on. Already, many people are needed, and the need will continue, not only for those people with a general bibliographic education, but for musicians and musicologists with professional qualifications, if the work in our own country and in co-operation with other countries is to prosper. A harmonious and rational combination of spiritual and material conditions is necessary, if we hope to produce a proper survey of our Yugoslav musical creativity and to fulfill successfully the ever greater international demand for complete information.

NOTES

[1] Stojan Novaković, *Srpska bibliografija za noviju književnośt 1741-1867* [Serbian Bibliography for Modern Literature 1741-1867] (Beograd, 1869).

[2] Ivan Kukuljević, *Bibliografia hrvatska*, Dio I, *Tiskane knjige* [Croatian Bibliography, Part I, Printed Books] (Zagreb, 1860); *Dodatak* [Supplement] (1863).

[3] Franc Simonič, *Slovenska bibliografija*, I del: *Knjige* [Slovenian Bibliography, Part I: Books], 1550-1900 (Ljubljana, 1903-1905).

[4] Bibliographical publications of *Slovenska matica: Letopis* [Annals], 1868-1898; *Zbornik* [Miscellany], 1899-1906; Janko Šlebinger, *Slovenska bibliografija* [Slovenian Bibliography], 1907-1912.

[5] Uroš Džonić, Pavle Stefanović, Dušan Šijački, *Bibliografija srpskih listova* [Bibliography of Serbian Newspapers], 1768-1911, in *Jugoslovenska štampa*, (Beograd, 1911); J. Lakatos, *Hrvatska štampa* [Croatian Press], 1789-1911, in *Jugoslovenska štampa* (Beograd, 1911).

[6] Janko Šlebinger, *Slovenski časniki in časopisi* [Slovenian Periodicals], *Bibliografski pregled od* [Bibliographical survey from] 1797-1936 (Ljubljana, 1937).

[7] *Bibliografija jugoslovenskih bibliografija* [Bibliography of Yugoslav Bibliographies], 1945-1955 (Beograd, 1958).

[8] According to the law, the National Library in each republic must be provided two copies of each work published in the republic. One copy has to be sent to each of the seven national libraries in other republics and autonomous provinces. The tenth copy is sent by the printing house directly to Belgrade to the *Jugoslovenski bibliografski institut*. Some provincial libraries receive only copies of specific kinds of publications within their republic (e.g., only books or periodicals).

[9] *Bibliografija Jugoslavije, Knjige, brošure i muzikalije* [Bibliography of Yugoslavia, Books, Pamphlets, Music] (Beograd, 1950-); *Bibliografija Jugoslavije; Članci i prilozi u časopisima i listovima* [Bibliography of Yugoslavia, Articles and Supplements in Journals and Newspapers]; Serija A: *Društvene nauke;* Serija B: *Prirodne i primenjene nauke;* Serija C: *Filologija, umetnost, sport, književnost, muzikalije* [Series A: Social sciences; Series B: Natural and applied sciences; Series C: Philology, art, sport, fiction, music] (Beograd, 1950-); *Bibliografija jugoslovenske periodike* [Bibliography of Yugoslav Periodicals] (Beograd, 1950-).

[10] In Yugoslavia, the Moslems are treated as an ethnic group. Perhaps a handful of genuine Turks remain among the Yugoslav Moslems, but the large majority are ethnically Yugoslavs (Bosnians) who converted to Islam during the period of the Ottoman Empire.

[11]*Bibliografija Srbije* [Bibliography of Serbia] 1947, 1948 (Beograd, 1948, 1949). The Serbian bibliography divides books into nine groups, regardless of the contents of the material, and periodical publications into newspapers, reviews, periodicals of national minorities as well as those of a federal character, both without indexes. Items are recorded in the Latin or the Cyrillic alphabets, according to the original.

[12]Djordje Pejanović, *Bosansko-hercegovačka bibliografija knjiga i brošura* [Bibliography of Bosnia and Hercegovina, Books and Brochures] 1945-1951 (Sarajevo, 1953); Djordje Pejanović, *Bosansko-hercegovačka bibliografija knjiga za 1952 godinu* [Bibliography of Bosnia and Hercegovina, Books 1952] (Sarajevo, 1954). The Bibliography of Bosnia and Hercegovina contains more useful indexes and more comprehensive listings. In the first edition, books were divided into ten groups that differed from the categories in the UDC; however, in the second edition, certain changes were made in line with UDC classification. The Bibliography is printed in the Latin alphabet, with the material listed in the Cyrillic alphabet. Periodical publications and articles are not listed.

[13]*Bibliografija knjiga, tiskanih u Narodnoj Republici Hrvatskoj* [Bibliography of Books Printed in the People's Republic of Croatia] (Zagreb, 1945-   ). The period up to 1950 has been covered thus far. *Bibliografija rasprava, članaka i književnih radova u časopisima Narodne Republike Hrvatske* [Bibliography of Dissertations, Articles and Literary Works Published in Periodicals in The People's Republic of Croatia] (Zagreb, 1945-   ). The period up to 1952 has been covered thus far.

The index of Croatian books is organized alphabetically by author. It also has a subject index divided into several dozen groups, such as music, and an index of persons, cities, countries, etc. Articles are similarly divided according to the subject, and at the end there are several indexes: author, translator, and subject. The Croats do not have an index of periodical publications.

[14]Montenegro has published bibliographical material without indexes in chronological order. *Pregled štamparsko-izdavačke djelatnosti u Crnoj Gori* [Survey of Publications in Montenegro] 1494-1954 (Cetinje, 1955).

[15]*Makedonska bibliografija, Od osloboduvanjeto do krajot na 1949 godina, I. del.: Knigi, brošuri, muzikalii, albumi. II. del.: Statii od spisanija* [Bibliography of Macedonia, from the Liberation till the End of 1949, Part I: Books, brochures, music. Part II: Articles] (Skopje, 1951): *Makedonska bibliografija za 1950-1951* [Bibliography of Macedonia for 1950-1951] (Skopje, 1952). Biennial surveys have covered the period up to 1961.

The Bibliography of Macedonia is divided into several main groups according to the UDC. Besides books, brochures, and music, it contains also a certain number of articles. It has a name index at the end. This bibliography does not have an index of periodical publications.

[16]*Slovenska bibliografija* [Bibliography of Slovenia] 1945-1947. Edited by Stefka Bulovec (Ljubljana, 1948). The same editor has also made yearly surveys for the next three years.

In 1951 an index of articles was added to the index of books and periodicals: *Slovenska bibliografija, Časopisje in knjige, Članki in leposlovni prispevki v časopisju in zbornikih* [Bibliography of Slovenia, Reviews and Books, Articles and Fiction in Reviews and Yearbooks], 1951, ed J. Logar, Št. Bulovec, A. Posavec (Ljubljana, 1953). Yearly surveys have covered the period up to 1963. The same editors have completed the Slovenian Bibliography with an index of articles for the period 1945-1950: *Slovenska bibliografija. Članki in leposlovje v časopisju in zbornikih 1945-1950* [Bibliography of Slovenia. Articles and fiction in periodicals and annuals], ed. Janez Logar, Štefka Bulovec and Ančka Posavec (Ljubljana, 1963).

Slovenian bibliography is national in the best sense of the word, because it lists Slovenian publications all over the world, as well as the works of Slovenian authors published in other languages. It comprises all kinds of publications, including music and articles. Periodical publications and books are listed in alphabetical order by author, and there is a subject index at the end. Articles are organized according to the UDC. It has a review of collections, an index of editors, critics, and essayists, statistical surveys, and an index of authors of articles.

[17] This bibliography is published by the National and University Library in Ljubljana. Its titles are: *Slovenski tisk* [Slovenian Press]; *Naš tisk* [Our Press]; *Slovenski knjižni trg* [Slovenian Book Market]; *Knjiga* [Book].

[18] *Zvuk*, Jugoslovenska muzička revija [Zvuk, the Yugoslav Music Review] (Beograd, 1955-1966; Sarajevo, 1967-   ).

[19] *Muzička enciklopedija*, Vols. 1-2 (Zagreb, 1958-1963).

[20] Dragotin Cvetko, *Zgodovina glasbene umetnosti na Slovenskem*, 3 vols. [History of Music in Slovenia] (Ljubljana, 1958-1960); Josip Andreis, Dragotin Cvetko, Stana Djurić-Klajn, *Historijski razvoj muzičke kulture u Jugoslaviji* [The Historical Development of Musical Culture in Yugoslavia] (Zagreb, 1962); Josip Andreis, *Historija muzike za visoke i srednje muzičke škole*, 3 vols. [History of Music for the Schools of Music] (Zagreb, 1951-1954); Dragotin Cvetko includes a list of compositions in his *Risto Savin, osebnost in delo* [Risto Savin, His Personality and Work] (Ljubljana, 1949); Petar Konjović provides bibliographical information on the works of Miloje Milojević in his "Miloje Milojević kompozitor i muzički pisac" [Miloje Milojević, Composer and Musicologist], Srpska akademija nauka: *Naučna knjiga*, pp. 268-286; and an important bibliography is contained in Vinko Žganec, "Kuhačeva literarno-muzička zaostavština" [Kuhač's Musicological Legacy], *Muzička revija* (Zagreb), Vol. 1, Nos. 2-3 (1950), pp. 135-48.

[21] Robert Eitner, *Biographisch-Bibliographisches Quellen-Lexikon* (Leipzig, 1900-1904), reprinted (Graz. 1959-1960).

[22] J. Höfler and I. Klemenčić, *Glasbeni rokopisi in tiski na Slovenskem do leta 1800, Katalog* [Music Manuscripts and Printed Music in Slovenia before 1800, Catalog] (Ljubljana, 1967).

[23] *Recueils imprimés*, XVIe-XVIIe siècles (München-Duisburg, 1960); Recueils imprimés, XVIIIe siècle (München-Duisburg, 1964).

[24] *RILM Abstracts* (New York, 1967) [demonstration issue].

[25] *Muzikološki zbornik* [Musicological annual] (Ljubljana, 1965-   ).

Edward N. Waters

PROBLEMS OF MUSIC BIBLIOGRAPHY IN THE UNITED STATES

A major problem of music bibliography can be simply stated: there isn't enough of it! A minor problem of music bibliography — there's too much of it! To dispose of the minor problem first, let me say that here I refer only to so-called bibliographies of questionable utility that are merely lists of background reading material. Recently I examined two American books, produced in 1954 and 1967, treating the relationship between music and philosophy. The earlier one appends a bibliography of 80 titles, 36 of them non-musical, all in English; the later lists 115 titles, 81 non-musical and all in English. While I do not doubt that these two lists can lead one to useful and important literature, I find them woefully inadequate in supporting the weighty subject they are attached to.

Contrast these two books with two more having splendid bibliographies (with titles in many languages) which vastly enhance their authors' successful efforts: Jacques Barzun's *Berlioz and the Romantic Century* (Boston, 1950), which boasts a bibliography of 1,476 items plus an iconography of six pages, and Donald Grout's *A Short History of Opera* (2nd ed.; New York, 1965), which contains a bibliography of over 4,250 items. Such a list of suggested and directed reading, and reference, is well-nigh overwhelming; one wonders how extensive it would have been if the author had written a "long" history of his favorite subject!

Music bibliography is more complicated than most. It must embrace music *per se;* it includes books and periodicals; it stretches importantly into phonorecords, which are avidly sought by amateur, professional, and scholar alike.

It must be admitted that bibliography of music — music *per se* — is not well served in the United States. We have no national bibliography that shows what musical compositions (good or bad, long or short, classical or popular) are appearing. The nearest thing to it is the *Catalog of Copyright Entries, Part 5,* which reports all compositions, published or unpublished, foreign or domestic, registered for copyright. Quantitatively it is impressive — for example:

1962	1963	1964	1965	1966
67,612	72,583	75,256	80,881	76,805

Qualitatively it is not very helpful. Still, from a commercial and sociological, and therefore musicological, point of view it is important. Both Americans and others should learn how to use it. It may be purchased from the Superintendent of Documents, U.S. Government Printing Office, Washington, D.C. 20402.

More useful qualitatively is the *Library of Congress Catalog, Music and Phonorecords,* which presents "a cumulative list of works represented by Library of Congress printed cards." Issued semi-annually, it is sold by the Card Division of the Library of Congress (Building 159, Navy Yard Annex, Washington, D.C. 20541). Including music, books, and discs, these cards are not limited to newly printed or released items, but new publications and products are included in sufficient quantity to indicate the extent and scope of the Library's steady musical growth.

National bibliographies of other countries vary greatly in the extent of their disclosures about music. Best among them are the *Bibliographie de la France* (Paris: Maulde et Renou), the *Deutsche Musikbibliographie* (Leipzig: F. Hofmeister) and *The British Catalogue of Music* (London: The Council of the British National Bibliography, Ltd.; British Museum). Generally speaking, however, universally systematic and comprehensive bibliography in the field of music *per se* is weak, unguided, and uncontrolled.

Conditions are somewhat better with writings *about* music, more commonly known as music literature. Books themselves don't present too much of a problem. Compared with compositions they are infinitesimal in number. Americans do not produce many books on music, a sad fact quickly gleaned from the 1967 edition of *The Bowker Annual of Library and Book Trade Information.* The total American book title output for 1965 was 28,595 which included 20,234 new books and 8,361 new editions of older books. New books on music for that year numbered only 183, new editions 117. In 1966 the total was 30,050, the new books on music amounting to 207, the new editions to 84. Thus, current music literature in book form in the United States presents a situation that is only too manageable. Unfortunately, bibliography and its problems are not limited to books, current or old, or to American publications, or to the English language.

Periodical literature, in journals that are short- or long-lived, academic or popular, offers a very special challenge to scholar and student; down to the present, it has not been well met. The task is too staggering to accomplish much without enormous resources of time, money, and skill — three elements that are, sometimes, virtually interchangeable.

In the Music Division of the Library of Congress there is an unpublished card catalog of music periodical literature, begun early in this century and discontinued near the outbreak of World War II. It is international in scope, highly selective in content, and invaluable as a key to the vast store of information to which the *circa* 150,000 cards can lead. It is a shame that military urgency and resultant economy caused its demise.

Nearly a decade passed before anything similar appeared on the scene. Then in 1949, *The Music Index,* produced by Information Service, Inc., of Detroit, made its bow; through the years it has proven to be a highly useful and slowly expanding tool in guiding researchers through music magazines. Never out of financial difficulties, always in arrears, issued monthly and annually, it has stubbornly persisted and grown in praiseworthy fashion. For its first year the editors analyzed 81 journals (six in foreign languages; two non-musical), and the cumulative volume had 308 pages. The most recent annual (cumulative) volume, for 1963 (published in 1967 by Information Coordinators, Inc., of Detroit), differed considerably: 223 journals were searched (75 in foreign languages; 12 non-musical) to produce a volume of 891 pages. But a full subscription costs $195 per year, and circulation continues to lag.

The firm that produces *The Music Index,* it may be noted, seems to have a real passion for bibliography. Several monographic lists bear its imprint, and they should be mentioned in passing:

1. Nettl, Bruno. *Reference Materials in Ethnomusicology.* 1961. 46 pp.
2. Poladian, Sirvart. *Sir Arthur Sullivan: an Index to the Texts of His Vocal Works.* 1961. 91 pp.
3. MacArdle, Donald. *An Index to Beethoven's Conversation Books.* 1962. 46 pp.
4. Mixter, Keith. *General Bibliography for Music Research.* 1962. 38 pp.
5. Mattfeld, Julius. *A Handbook of American Operatic Premieres, 1731-1962.* 1963. 142 pp.
6. Coover, James, and Richard Colvig. *Medieval and Renaissance Music on Long-Playing Records.* 1964. 122 pp.
7. Mangler, Joyce E. *Rhode Island Music and Musicians, 1733-1850.* 1965. 90 pp.
8. Blum, Fred. *Jean Sibelius; an International Bibliography on the Occasion of the Centennial Celebrations, 1965.* 1965. 114 pp.
9. Hartley, Kenneth R. *Bibliography of Theses and Dissertations in Sacred Music.* 1967. 127 pp.
10. Fruchtman, Caroline S. *Checklist of Vocal Chamber Works by Benedetto Marcello.* 1967. 37 pp.
11. Warner, T. E. *An Annotated Bibliography of Woodwind Instruction Books, 1600-1830.* 1967. 140 pp.

These eleven titles, irrespective of the fields they represent or how well they cover them, afford a glimpse of the infinite task that confronts bibliography as it attempts to unlock an infinite amount of information on a subject as infinite as music.

Music and musical knowledge cannot be expected to stand still. Critical and expository literature grows apace. It is an awesome situation, and the conscientious bibliographer may experience the keenest terror. A modest example will suffice. In 1939 (copyright 1938), Dodd, Mead & Co. published the first edition of *The International Cyclopedia of Music and Musicians*, edited by Oscar Thompson. Fairly popular and useful, and large in format, it ran to 2,287 pages; the final 65 pages provided a general bibliography of music literature. In 1958, the eighth edition came off the press, edited by Nicolas Slonimsky. The book now comprised 2,397 pages, 99 being devoted to the bibliography. Six years later, in 1964, the ninth and most recent edition appeared, its last page was numbered 2,476. The bibliography? There was none! Perhaps this illustrates the greatest problem of all — what price completeness or comprehensiveness?

Bibliography can never be rigid; it must ever be flexible. It should, however, be systematically disciplined — by field, area, subject, personality, period, style, or what not — so that each bibliographical product has a viable unity of some sort. Without repetitiously reporting well-known titles and monuments of the past, I want to offer a few unusual and/or outstanding bibliographies or well-organized lists of titles or materials which may be the solution to a researcher's problems at some given moment.

    1. Briquet, Marie. *La Musique dans les Congrès internationaux, 1835-1939.* Ouvrage publié avec le concours du Centre National de la Recherche scientifique. Paris: Société française de Musicologie, Heugel et Cie., 1961. 124 pp. 8vo.

    2. Karl Gregor, Herzog zu Mecklenburg. *Bibliographie einiger Grenzgebiete der Musikwissenschaft.* Baden-Baden: Verlag Heitz, 1962. 197 pp. 8vo.

I call your attention to the latter, as it is a bibliography disciplined in a very flexible way — by fields *related to* musicology; there are virtually unlimited. The book contains 3,519 titles broadly divided into several areas: 1) Philosophy-ethics-health; 2) Psychology; 3) Ecology and natural phenomena; 4) Sociology; 5) Other arts, physically and aesthetically; 6) Individual personalities.

    3. *Catalog of Published Concert Music by American Composers.* Selected, compiled and prepared by [the] Music Branch, Information Center Service under the direction and supervision of the Music Advisor, United States Information Agency. September 1964. Washington,

D.C.: Superintendent of Documents, U.S. Government Printing Office [1964]. 175 pp. 12mo.

Here one will find 390 American composers, from Stephen Collins Foster to John Cage, from Richard Rodgers to Elliott Carter. The organizational scheme presents works for voice (solo and choral), solo instruments (various instruments), instrumental ensembles (various sizes and types), orchestra, opera, and concert band. It also provides a key to publishers and an index of composers. Thus, despite minor flaws, this little work is useful as a guide to readily available American music of the past 100 years.

A bibliographical problem which is rarely considered — destination and purpose — may be identified by reference to the Catalog discussed above. The work was justified by a need for information, which would be disseminated by the cultural affairs officers in our diplomatic service, concerning American music and its availability overseas. These foreign service officers could scarcely be expected to be familiar with the vast range of American music and its creators. Unfortunately, however, the completed catalog offers scant help in recommending what might be appropriate, applicable, or even feasible in foreign lands. It contains no annotations explaining style, period, or degree of difficulty. A musically unsophisticated user might well be bewildered and confused by it. Therefore, a useful bibliography, one limited to or designed for a specific purpose, must include *all* the necessary data to fulfill that purpose.

4. Chailley, Jacques. *Précis de musicologie;* ouvrage collectif publié sous la direction de Jacques Chailley. Paris: Presses Universitaires de France, 1958. xxi, 431 pp. 12mo.

This interesting volume, essays by several writers, is not a bibliography; but chapter one is entitled "Principes de Bibliographie." Thus our subject is hailed as the foundation stone, so to speak, on which musicology is erected.

5. *A Check List of Thematic Catalogues.* Prepared by a Committee of the Music Library Association. New York: The New York Public Library, 1954. 37 pp. 8vo.

It is astonishing how many thematic indexes were rounded up for this pioneer brochure — not only individual composers (129), but also collections (52), libraries (21), and even publishers (12). A new edition, eagerly awaited, is still in progress.

6. Duckles, Vincent. *Music Reference and Research Materials,* an Annotated Bibliography. Second edition .... New York: The Free Press, 1967. xiii, 385 pp. 8vo.

Here is a solid work of reference, augmenting the author's splendid reputation and leading one far along all the paths of musical knowledge.

> 7. Gerboth, Walter. "Index of Festschriften and Some Similar Publications," pp. 183-307, *in* LaRue, Jan, ed. *Aspects of Medieval and Renaissance Music.* A birthday offering to Gustave Reese. New York: W. W. Norton & Co., Inc., 1966. xvii, 891 pp. 8vo.

Festschriften and the like are not fleeting publications. Yet their distribution is sometimes so limited, their *raison d'être* so local, that obtaining copies for indexing poses serious difficulties. Mr. Gerboth has analyzed 410, listing no less than 2,710 articles, many of which are the *crême de la crême* of musical scholarship.

> 8. Gillis, Frank, and Alan P. Merriam. *Ethnomusicology and Folk Music:* an International Bibliography of Dissertations and Theses. Middletown, Conn.: Published for the Society for Ethnomusicology by the Wesleyan University Press, 1966. 148 pp. 8vo.

Many of the titles in this interesting and informative bibliography are supplied with annotations.

> 9. Haywood, Charles. *A Bibliography of North American Folklore and Folksong.* Second revised edition. New York: Dover Publications, Inc., 1961. 2 vols., xxx, 748 pp.; ix, 749-1301 pp. 8vo.

This is a splendid example, years in the making, of an enormous single-handed achievement. The reprint publisher deserves commendation for his willingness to enlarge upon a first edition.

> 10. Hewitt, Helen. *Doctoral Dissertations in Musicology.* Fourth Edition. Philadelphia: American Musicological Society, 1965. 152 pp. 8vo.

A bibliography of this nature is the surest means of keeping abreast of the musical research being done in America. It may also lead, though indirectly, to other bibliographies without which a dissertation might be incomplete. Incidentally, 1,204 titles are listed in this edition.

> 11. Heyer, Anna Harriet. *Historical Sets, Collected Editions, and Monuments of Music, a Guide to their Contents.* Chicago: American Library Association, 1957. iv, 485 pp. 4to.

Somewhat difficult to use because of its format, this unusual work is a true revelation if examined carefully and used wisely. Miss Heyer has indexed 562 collections, which range from a single volume to a hundred or more, and has also included an index of individual composers. A new edition is in progress.

12. Johnson, H. Earle. *Operas on American Subjects.* New York: Coleman-Ross Co., Inc., 1964. 125 pp. 8vo.

Anyone who consults this slender but fascinating book will be amazed by the number and nationality of composers who have been attracted to the new world for their operatic ventures.

13. Loewenberg, Alfred. *Annals of Opera, 1597-1940.* Second edition, revised and corrected .... Genève: Societas Bibliographica, 1955. 2 vols., xxv pp., 1756 columns. 4to.

Many scholars have surely consulted this magnificent work, which first appeared in 1943. In that first edition, Loewenberg included 3,603 operas; in the second edition, he added three more: Ralph Vaughan Williams' *Riders to the Sea* (1937), Gustav Holst's *The Wandering Scholar* (1938), and Heitor Villa-Lobos' *Izaht* (1940). Nevertheless, indispensable as it is, it may fail to include the very opera that one must investigate tomorrow. Perhaps bibliography's greatest problem is achieving absolute completeness — an unattainable goal.

14. Schaal, Richard. *Verzeichnis deutschsprachiger musikwissenschaftlicher Dissertationen, 1861-1960.* Kassel: Bärenreiter, 1963. 167 pp. 8vo.

The century examined here produced, apparently, 2,819 theses, a figure far behind what the United States will have reached when she reaches her 100th musicological birthday. Even in scholarship we can out-produce everybody, but achievements based on quantity alone may leave something to be desired.

15. Sonneck, Oscar George Theodore. *A Bibliography of Early Secular American Music (18th century).* Revised and enlarged by William Treat Upton. Washington: The Library of Congress, Music Division, 1945. xvi, 617 pp. 8vo.

I am sure that most readers of these lines are familiar with this splendid work which contains 2,876 entries (and about half as many titles). Sonneck's original work came out in 1905 and was the first truly penetrating look at the extent of our early musical life. Mr. Upton broadened and deepened that view tremendously. And it led to a new and mammoth sequel:

16. Wolfe, Richard J. *Secular Music in America 1801-1825.* A bibliography .... New York: The New York Public Library, 1964. 3 vols., xxx, 448 pp.; 449-928 pp.; 929-1238 pp. 8vo.

Well over 10,000 titles are embraced herein, testimony that our forefathers must have been playing and singing much of the time! America not a musical nation? Bibliography alone proves that it was.

17. Watanabe, Ruth T. *Introduction to Music Research.* Englewood Cliffs, N.J.: Prentice Hall, Inc., 1967. viii, 237 pp. 8vo.

The last title to be mentioned in this group is a textbook, and there are four reasons for its inclusion — the titles of four separate chapters: 9. "Bibliography: Books" pp. 77-90; 10. "Bibliography: Periodicals" pp. 91-103; 11. "Bibliography: Music" pp. 104-120; 12. "Discography" pp. 121-128. These chapters present clear, succinct statements on "how to" and "why," and each has a bibliography of its own.

Bibliography can and must be applied to conventional subjects and deserving personalities. But new subjects and unfamiliar persons appear, and new ventures in bibliography must be launched, else the beginning of new knowledge will be irretrievably lost.

Two years ago an enterprising student at the Eastman School of Music earned a Master's degree with the following project as a thesis:

Bahler, Peter Benjamin. *Electronic and Computer Music,* an Annotated Bibliography of Writings in English. August 1966. viii, 128 pp. 4to.

The paper contained 430 entries. Although it was a commendable pioneer venture, it was far surpassed (at least quantitatively) by a Canadian product only a year later:

Cross, Lowell M. *A Bibliography of Electronic Music.* [Toronto]: University of Toronto Press, 1967. ix, 126 pp. 8vo.

Now the entries, in various languages, totaled 1,562. A year from now who can say how extensive the literature will be?

Already a new magazine is in existence which is an important bibliographical entity in its own right and which will supply bibliographical material of prime significance. The title is *Electronic Music Review;* the first number is labeled: No. 1, Jan. 1967; the publisher is the Independent Electronic Music Center, Inc., in Trumansburg, N.Y. Giving it a fair review in the March 1968 issue of *Notes* and pointing out how it can have a long and useful life, Jon Appleton also stressed a new problem which may very well be reflected in bibliographical formation:

> The second issue will take the form of an impressive catalogue of some 7,500 electronic works, including information about the composers and the studios where the works were produced. The catalogue was prepared by Hugh Davies in co-operation with, and as a second edition of, the "Répertoire International des Musiques Expérimentales." It will be made available to the general public through the distribution services of the M.I.T. Press. Only an extended review could describe the manifold difficulties encoun-

tered by the compiler, but an example, demonstrating the complexities which arise with the birth of a new artistic medium, is the question "Who is a composer?" The usual answer is based on aesthetic judgments, but what happens when the "composer" is guided by a "technician"? This catalogue mentions both parties when possible, but concludes that "unfortunately, technicians are not usually credited, although their contribution is often equal to that of the composer." This topic, and the many others that reflect a point of view, are extremely debatable and may be the headaches of musicologists in 2068.[1]

They may also be the headaches of future bibliographers, who must know exactly what and whom they are listing or risk the charge of misleading their dependent readers. Incidentally, the catalog of 7,500 electronic works had not appeared as these lines were being written, so a number of unsolved problems may remain.[2]

Not so new a subject as electronic music, though it has many electric qualities, jazz (with ragtime and popular music) occupies an important niche of its own. In recent years it has not been well served by bibliographers. Perhaps people would rather listen to it and play it, than read about it or list it. The outstanding book in the field is now dated:

> Merriam, Alan P. *A Bibliography of Jazz* .... with the assistance of Robert J. Benford. Philadelphia: The American Folklore Society, 1954. xiii, 145 pp. 8vo.

Herein one finds 3,324 entries, the titles of 113 magazines devoted to jazz, and a complicated but extremely helpful subject index.

Four years later (1958), in England, the jazz lover hailed

> Gammond, Peter, ed. *The Decca Book of Jazz.* Foreward by Milton "Mezz" Mezzrow .... London: Frederick Muller, Ltd., 1958. 431 pp. 8vo.

It includes a selective bibliography filling 79 pages.

Another year later (1959), the New York Public Library issued a 69-page booklet entitled *The Literature of Jazz: a Selective Bibliography.* The compiler was Robert George Reisner, and it listed general books on jazz, background books, magazine articles, and jazz magazines.

The latest sizeable book in this field that I have seen is

> Blesh, Rudi, and Harriet Janis. *They All Played Ragtime,* the True Story of an American Music. Revised and with new additional material, including

scores to 13 never before published ragtime compositions and 26 pages of photographs. New York: Oak Publications, 1966. xxiv, 347, ix pp. 8vo.

Its bibliographical aids include 46 pages listing ragtime and similar compositions, 12 pages of player-piano rolls, and 10 pages of phonograph records.

A very curious book is

Pernet, Robert. *Jazz in Little Belgium.* History (1881-1966), Discography (1895-1966). [Bruxelles: R. Pernet, 1966] 135, 338 pp. 8vo.

In spite of the title-page, the explanatory text is in French. The relatively brief narrative (135 pp.) is followed by an enormous discography (338 pp.), and an index and bibliography fill 28 supplementary pages. Belgium may be a little country, but it produced a large book on a large subject.

Sound recording — cylinder, disc, tape, or whatnot — has greatly complicated and activated the bibliographer's operations. He has had to devise new forms of entry, new terminology, new methods of dating, measuring, and collating. Moreover, he is confronted by new values: When one studies music in the form of "recorded sound," the performer takes on a new dimension, vying in importance with the composer in the eyes (or ears) of the record collector. The "discographer" must reckon with this fact if his bibliographic service is to be fully appreciated.

I shall mention first a few trade journals because of their utility in the complex field of American discography. The *Schwann Long Playing Record Catalog* is issued monthly from Boston; it contains listings of titles currently available on well over five hundred fifty labels, representing virtually all of the commercial recording companies with American distributorships. By comparing its pages year by year — or even month by month — one will discover, sadly, how short the average commercial life of a fine recording may be. The *Phonolog,* produced in Los Angeles, is a loose-leaf accumulation designed to keep the retail dealer abreast of all releases on the most current possible basis. The same publisher issues *List-of-Tapes,* "All in One" Tape Catalog, which provides the same service for open-reel and cartridge-type pre-recorded tapes. A similar loose-leaf trade publication is the *One-Spot Numerical Index,* which comes from Mt. Prospect, Illinois, and features both LP and EP releases. (The EP disc is only an "extended play" 45-rpm record, I am informed by Donald L. Leavitt, my expert colleague in the Library of Congress.)

Before dwelling on discographic literature *per se* (not trade journals), I want to call attention to a recent publication which will certainly have a great effect upon record bibliography. It is

A Preliminary Directory of Sound Recordings Collections in the United States and Canada. Prepared by a Committee of the Association for Recorded Sound Collections. [New York] : The New York Public Library, 1967. 157 pp. 8vo.

ARSC, founded only about two years ago, already has 1,610 members (individuals and institutions) in the United States and 40 in Canada. The *Directory* gives the full name and address of each member, then declares the area of special collecting interest. The Association is not concerned only with recordings of music. It embraces such areas of recorded sound as: piano rolls, personality, country music, jazz, dance bands, interviews, hill-billy, ethnomusicology, psychiatry, public affairs, sexual topics, bawdy songs, American banjo, theater pipe organ, Judaica, gospel songs, spirituals, American humor. A society of this sort may well settle old problems in discography while raising new ones.

Discographical literature seems still to be disorganized and produced at random. A good starting point, however, for an exploration of its possibilities and limitations may be found in "A Bibliography of Discographies" compiled by Carl L. Bruun and John Gray. It appeared in the summer issue, 1962, of *Recorded Sound,* an admirable journal published by the British Institute of Recorded Sound (London). Now dated, it nevertheless retains much of its original usefulness, and it suggests a rational approach to the broad problem of organization. Its eight pages of title listings are divided into: (1) General; (2) Vertical cut (hill and dale) cylinders and discs; (3) Makes of record; (4) Type of material recorded; (5) Individual performers; (6) Individual composers — selected works only, as general discographies of *one* composer are excluded. It will be noticed that performers rank ahead of composers in the scheme.

Many record fans are doubtless familiar with Robert Bauer's *The New Catalogue of Historical Records, 1898-1908/09* (London: Sidgwick and Jackson, Ltd., 1947). Its 494 pages are filled with the choicest recordings of early years, practically every one a collector's item. This leads immediately to consideration of Julian Morton Moses' *Price Guide to Collectors' Records* (second edition; New York: American Record Collectors' Exchange, 1967). The new issue shows the same prices as the one that appeared in 1952, but Mr. Moses includes a "revised value chart" whereby one can calculate augmented values on a percentage basis. He suggests that a record worth $5 in 1952 is worth about $6 in 1967; a $10 record may have risen to about $13; and a $150 rarity may have jumped to $250. It should not be imagined, however, that there is any high degree of stability in record prices.

Young as it is, the record industry has its "early past," and discographers are beginning to explore it in depth. One impressive guide is

> Girard, Victor, and Harold M. Barnes. *Vertical-cut Cylinders and Discs*. A catalogue of all "Hill-&-Dale" recordings of serious worth; made and issued between 1897-1932 circa. London: British Institute of Recorded Sound, 1964. xxxviii, 196 pp. 4to.

Again, the primary entry is by performer, while the sub-divisions include: (1) vocal recordings; (2) declamation (or speech) recordings; (3) instrumental and orchestral recordings; (4) complete operas and plays; (5) anonymous Pathé recordings of vintage 1897-1900. A mine of useful and frequently unsuspected information is contained in the volume.

Fascinating, amusing, and entertaining is

> Murrels, Joseph. *Daily Mail Book of Golden Discs*. The story of every disc that has sold a million copies since 1903. Edited by Norris and Ross McWhirter. Foreword by David Jacobs. London: McWhirter Twins, Ltd., 1966. x, 374 pp. 8vo.

I cannot vouch for the reliability of this survey, which is obviously based almost 100 per cent upon popular music, vocal and instrumental. But the first record in the book and consequently the first one to pass the million mark – can anyone guess what it is? It is the 1903 recording of "Vesti la giubba" sung by Caruso! And the biggest seller of all time – will anyone venture another guess? – is the 1942 recording of "White Christmas" sung by Bing Crosby. The author estimates that sales of this rendition of Irving Berlin's classic have amounted to 25,000,000!

The most impressive and laudable attempt to compile a discography of serious music, with entries by composer instead of by performer, is

> Clough, Francis F., and G. J. Cuming. *The World's Encyclopaedia of Recorded Music*. London: The London Gramophone Corporation, 1952. xvi, 890 pp. 8vo.

Two separately printed supplements followed in 1953 and 1957 (London: Sidgwick and Jackson). Subsequent printings have been forestalled by lack of financing.

It is of more than passing interest that Messrs. Clough and Cuming paid fine tribute to American skill in the foreword to their encyclopedia:

> The principles and procedures of discography were laid down by R. D. Darrell in his *Gramophone Shop Encyclopedia of Recorded Music* (New York, 1936), and have been followed by subsequent compilers; the present

work is planned on similar lines, and we must acknowledge, what is indeed obvious, the inspiration and instruction we have derived from Darell's work. p.v.

The quarterly journal *Notes,* published by the Music Library Association, offers in every issue a unique "Index to Record Reviews" from which one can quickly determine the quality of a vast number of current releases. Composer entry, fortunately, is the guiding principle. Reviews from nearly a score of standard news media are summarized by Kurtz Myers of the Detroit Public Library in terms of "excellent," "adequate," or "inadequate." The usefulness of his labors has been widely acknowledged.

This continuing index has been in operation for many years; in 1956, Kurtz Myers and Richard S. Hill brought it out in book form accumulated to that date. It was called *Record Ratings,* issued by Crown Publishers, Inc., of New York. Large in format, with 440 pages, it was hailed with delight and quickly became a standard reference work. Then bibliography's ever present foe — lack of money — took over, and follow-up volumes, badly needed, never appeared.

Several attempts have been made to compile guides to music history illustrated by sound recordings. The most recent to come to my attention is the attractive French discography:

> Lory, Jacques. *Guide des Disques.* L'aventure de la musique occidentale du chant grégorien à la musique électronique, racontée en 2,500 microsillons. Buchet/Chastel, 1967. xxvii, 434 pp. 12mo.

An interesting connecting narrative and plausible evaluations accompany the listings.

I have commented on the fact that discography to a very large extent favors the performer over the composer. Such an approach seems to be implicit or inherent in the medium, reversible only when a composer happens to be his own interpreter. I want to mention only three outstanding examples of performer-discographies:

> Favia-Artsay, Mrs. Aida. *Caruso on Records.* Pitch, speed and comments for all the published recordings of Enrico Caruso. Valhalla, N.Y.: The Historic Record, 1965. 218 pp. 8vo. (With 2 stroboscopes)

> Moore, Jerrold N. *An Elgar Discography.* Reprinted from *Recorded Sound.* London: British Institute of Recorded Sound, 1963. 48 pp. 8vo.

> Moran, W.R. "Geraldine Farrar..." (In *The Record Collector,* Vol. XIII, No. 9/10 [1961?] ; pp. 196-239; published in Ipswich, England)

The first of these three calls attention to the fact that early recordings were often made at various speeds, with consequent distortions of pitch. The second has a most unusual descriptive feature. Elgar was a composer, of course, and also a conductor. All of his experiences in recording studios are described in great detail in Mr. Moore's intimate and revealing book.

Discographers show an astonishing diligence and perseverance in pursuit of their favorite manifestations. Noteworthy by size alone are several works which can fittingly terminate this section. Two come from England, one from Germany:

Dixon, Robert M. W., and John Godrich. *Blues and Gospel Records, 1902-1942.* Swansea, Wales, 1963. 765 pp. 8vo. (An attempt "to list every distinctive Negroid folk music record made up to the end of 1943.")

Rust, Brian A.L. *Jazz Records A - Z, 1897-1931.* Hatch End, Middlesex, England: The Author, 1962. 736 pp. 8vo.

Rust, Brian A.L. *Jazz Records A - Z, 1932-1942.* Hatch End, Middlesex, England: The Author, n.d. 679 pp. 8vo.

Lange, Horst H. *Die deutsche "78er"-Discographie der Jazz- und Hot-Dance-Musik, 1903-1958.* Berlin: Colloqium Verlag, 1966. 773 pp. 8vo.

Is it not curious that these massive works, devoted as they are to popular music of American origin, have few parallels in the United States?

The best, most comprehensive and most enlightening musico-bibliographical aid in America, and perhaps in the world, is probably *Notes,* the quarterly journal of the Music Library Association. I had the privilege of launching this magazine a quarter of a century ago (1943). Under the brilliant editorship of Richard S. Hill, who poured his heart and soul and money into it, *Notes* quickly won a commanding position in the field of bibliothecal journals. Under the present editorship of Harold E. Samuel (of Cornell University) it is maintaining that position. Look at a recent issue, March 1968, which typifies present policy and coverage: a report on a most important bibliographical development; a series of miscellaneous notes, one of which concerns the current flood of musical reprints; a listing of current dealers', publishers', and record dealers' catalogs; reviews of twenty-six important books criticized by expert reviewers; a list twenty-six pages long of recently published books on music in all languages; a list of forthcoming reprints of music and music literature (published in every other issue); an index to record reviews (thirty pages); reviews of new music publications by expert critics (thirty-one pages); an annual survey of sacred choral octavo music (different subject surveys in different issues); a selective list of music received (new publications, classified according to medium). Not as large and as effective as it might be were it more affluent, it is nevertheless a microcosm of the musical macrocosm, and no serious student of musical life can afford to ignore it.

Notes naturally reports on all major musico-bibliographical undertakings, domestic, foreign, and international; it was very largely responsible for one. The first editor of *Notes,* Richard S. Hill, played a leading role in launching *Répertoire International des Sources Musicales* (RISM) which, when completed, will be a magnificent attempt to identify, list, and locate all music and music literature of the western world from earliest times to ca. 1800. Five volumes have already appeared:

> Husmann, Heinrich. *Tropen- und Sequenzenhandschriften.* München - Duisburg: G. Henle Verlag, 1964. 236 pp. 8vo.
>
> Lesure, François. *Recueils imprimés.* XVIe - XVIIe siècles. I. Liste chronologique. München - Duisburg: G. Henle Verlag, 1960. 639 pp. 8vo.
>
> Lesure, François. *Recueils imprimés.* XVIIIe siècle. München - Duisburg: G. Henle Verlag, 1964. 461 pp. 8vo.
>
> Reaney, Gilbert. *Manuscripts of Polyphonic Music.* 11th - early 14th century. München - Duisburg: G. Henle Verlag, 1966. 876 pp. 8 vo.
>
> Smits van Waesberghe, Joseph, ed. *The Theory of Music.* From the Carolingian era up to 1400. Volume I. With the collaboration of Peter Fischer and Christian Maas. Descriptive catalogue of manuscripts. München − Duisburg: G. Henle Verlag, 1961. 152 pp. 8vo.

It will be years before the project is completed, but the accomplishment so far is noble, perhaps even incredible in view of the obstacles arising from distant collaboration, the searching of new repositories, the instruction of non-music librarians, the cooperation of many institutions, and the uncertainty of continuous financing.

The March 1968 issue of *Notes* carries a report on the newest vast musico-bibliographic enterprise, this one known as RILM, the acronym of *Répertoire International de la Littérature Musicale.* The report is written by the inspirer of the project, the dynamic Barry S. Brook, professor at Queens College in New York City, who is thoroughly justified in estimating the need for RILM and bold enough to devise its *modus operandi*. The first issue of *RILM Abstracts* is dated January-April 1967, and from its masthead we learn

> RILM Abstracts is planned as a quarterly journal publishing abstracts, indexed in depth by computer, of all significant literature in music that has appeared after 1 January 1967. Included are books, articles, essays, reviews, dissertations, catalogues, inconographies etc.

We also learn

> RILM was established in 1966 by the International Musicological Society and the International Association of Music Libraries to attempt to deal with the explosion in musicological documentation by means of international cooperation and modern technology.

It is sponsored by the two societies just named, plus the American Council of Learned Societies, that body of learned associations that so valiantly promotes humanistic studies and values in the United States.

Sponsorship of the ACLS is important to RILM, and RILM has aroused unusual interest within the ACLS. In the *ACLS Newsletter* of December 1967, Thomas J. Condon describes RILM at some length. Explaining the need for abstracting services in the humanities and pointing to their success in science and medicine, he expresses great hopes for RILM and clarifies the promise a venture like this holds for the future of musical learning (and for the future of learning in other disciplines). Mr. Condon says:

> RILM asks journal editors to obtain abstracts from the author of an article they accept and to combine with it full bibliographical data including indexing terms before passing it on to the RILM National Committee for review and forwarding it to the International [RILM] Center. This decentralized mode of data collection insures that those who are most concerned with a scholarly article are involved in the process — a process that might be termed article registration. The data can then be put into machine-readable form. Ideally — and this is the promise of the new technology — this need be done only once. The information can then be retrieved endlessly in whatever form desired: to produce an abstracts journal; to compile a title list that can be published in any journal requesting all works in a specialized field; to produce the index for a cooperating journal; to prepare quarterly, annual, or five year cumulative indexes; to produce specialized topical bibliographies; or to be personally interrogated along with other terms in a data bank by a scholar at a remote terminal when this becomes technologically and economically feasible. Instead of having people type and retype the

same information for different format purposes, the International RILM Center can make it available in the form specified by the individual, group, or institution requesting it. The saving in man-hours and tedium will be enormous. Of course not all of this is available now, nor will it be in five or even ten years; but this kind of flexible control is the goal of RILM.

Obviously a long life is hoped for RILM; may that hope not be frustrated.

The first issue of *RILM Abstracts* is encouraging. Large in format, it runs to 72 pages and presents 497 entries (all with abstracts except reviews, which may be abstracted if they are of special significance). There is an author index and a subject index, the latter still in need of further disciplining. There are clear explanations of the queer signs and symbols that data processing demands. There are instructions (in English, French, German, Italian, Spanish, Russian) on how to prepare abstracts. The inside front and back covers show the countries participating (Yugoslavia comes last, but only for alphabetical reasons); there are 33 nations represented. Periodicals abstracted are in two categories: completely indexed and partially indexed. Of the former there are 71, of the latter 85. Barry S. Brook is the editor; the editorial address is International RILM Center, Queens College of the City University of New York, Flushing, N.Y. 11367.

Problems? Bibliography itself is one massive problem: how to reveal, expose, disclose, often to estimate and evaluate existing sources and bodies of information pertaining to subject areas that command the attention of academic and artistic mankind. A bibliography may be the accidental (incidental is perhaps a better word) by-product of a single individual's research on a single topic. A basic bibliography is a necessity at the outset, and as research progresses it may grow to frightening proportions. A bibliography, or a bibliographic project, may be inspired or demanded by an entire discipline and, under ideal conditions, may flourish as long as that discipline attracts attention. Here more than one person will usually be needed, for the findings can be assimilated and organized only by constant co-operation and co-ordination. A bibliographer can aim at 100 per cent completeness, but he must realize that he will never achieve it. He may wish to avoid the trivial, but he must realize that sometimes trivia provide the missing links in a chain of loosely connected evidence. Carelessness, haste, and superficial examination are enemies of effective bibliography; they exact a heavy toll if one is guilty of them.

Bibliography (including discography) can be tedious and boring as well as heartily satisfying. It is not an end in itself. But it is absolutely indispensable to learning, to knowledge, and to cultural enlightenment and intellectual breadth, whether these qualities come from academic disciplines, the manifestations of art, or the revelations of science. Bibliography is also inexhaustible. Unlike birth rate, it cannot be controlled. A new article, a new book, a new composition, a new recording — some time, somewhere they all belong in a bibliography. Bibliography is a ceaseless struggle to discipline the output of data and theories, even when one eliminates the worthless or the superficial (if these can be determined), and this in itself is a problem of no small magnitude. A person who produces a fine bibliography or administers a project or participates in such an enterprise is contributing to learning in no uncertain way. Major problems are: (1) lack of time; (2) lack of judgment and patience; (3) lack of money. The world of learning and those who support it must realize that these lacks must be remedied if its priceless handmaiden, bibliography, is to flourish and produce and fertilize the soil from which knowledge springs, on which art is nurtured, and in which cultural values take root.

NOTES

[1] *Notes,* March 1968, Volume 24, No. 3, p. 485.

[2] At the very moment of releasing this paper I had the great good fortune of seeing the following curious document, fresh off the press and startling in its novel presentation. Although a part of *Electronic Music Review,* it deserves to be listed under the compiler's name:

> Davies, Hugh, compiler. *Répertoire International des Musiques Électroacoustiques. International Electronic Music Catalog.* A cooperative publication of Le Groupe de Recherches Musicales de l'O.R.T.F.... and The Independent Electronic Music Center, Inc.... distributed by The M.I.T. Press, Massachusetts Institute of Technology, Cambridge, Mass., and London, England. [c1968]. xxx, 330 pp. 8vo. *(Electronic Music Review,* Nos. 2/3, April/July 1967).

The main body of the work (pp. 1-236) — composers and their products — is arranged by country, then by city (for the United States it is by state and city), then by studio, and finally by individual. Sometimes these last two elements are the same, but more frequently not. There are several specialized appendixes, a directory of permanent studios, and an index of composers (occasionally groups, studios, and *anonymi).* Of these there are 909!
In the preface (in English and French) the compiler states:

> The aim of this new catalog is to document all the electronic music ever composed in the almost twenty years since composers first began to work in this medium. Naturally, it could never be possible to reach 100 per cent completeness: many electronic compositions have been produced on a minimal amount of equipment, and much background music, particularly for films, radio, TV and commercials, has been produced anonymously by organizations which have not been traced in the very extensive research undertaken.... The only restriction has been the decision not to include sound effects, such as montages made in school classrooms, for amateur tape recording competitions, mood music, effects for film, radio, and TV, and other similar applications which do not really come under the heading of musical composition.... Nearly 5000 compositions [are] actually listed, the [appended] notes indicate the existence of some 2500 more....

Not only is this bibliography a remarkable achievement in itself, it also shows the expansiveness, the attentiveness, and the expert knowledge the art demands when representing a body of music or musical sound that is new, experimental, and revolutionary.

Milivoj Koerbler

LIGHT AND POPULAR MUSIC IN YUGOSLAVIA

Yugoslav light and popular music reflects in its various branches a number of heterogeneous influences. Our folk and urban song, regional patriotic song, operetta and musical comedy, dance and jazz music, hit song and popular chanson, film and stage music, concert jazz, and light orchestral music — all have been subject to strong foreign influences before they achieved a specifically Yugoslav character. For centuries, the territory of Yugoslavia served as a battle ground for competing powers. The peoples of our territory have absorbed elements from Hungarian, Romanian, and Turco-Islamic folklore, from Byzantine-Greek, Italo-Mediterranean, and Alpine culture, from Gypsy melodies and Russian romances, Czech patriotic songs, and Viennese, French, and Hungarian operetta, from American jazz, the French chanson, the Latin dance, the Mexican song.... These multifarious elements have been incessantly crossed and mixed with the autochthonous folk heritage of different Yugoslav regions and with the individual efforts of composers attempting to write in an original style.

I shall concern myself primarily with the period after World War II, when light and popular music experienced such a spectacular boom as a consequence of developments in mass communication (radio, television, and the recording industry). Nevertheless, some notice must be taken of those composers and performers, both professional and amateur, who paved the way for the boom in the period between the two world wars.

Gjuro Prejac and Vlaho Paljetak composed melodies in the spirit of traditional urban and folk song that gained wide popularity before World War II. In the same period, Miroslav Biro, Myka Polo, Bojan Adamič, Neno Grčević, and Strahov began to write successful dance music and popular songs.

Departing in some degree from the tradition of Viennese operetta, which had several distinguished representatives in Zagreb before World War I (Ivan Zajc, and Srećko Albini, among others), the following composers wrote operettas in the period between the two world wars: Eduard Gloz, Gjuro Prejac, Ziga Hirschler, Rikard Šimaček, Josip Deči, Milan Asić, Alfred Prodes, Radovan Gobec, and Janez Gregorc. The most successful member of this group and the creator of the modern national operetta was Ivo Tijardović *(Mala Floramy* [Little Floramy] and *Splitski akvarel* [Split Aquarelle]).

The earliest champions of contemporary dance and jazz music were amateur and semiprofessional bands: "The Bingo Boys" (Zvonimir Bradić), *"Colibri"* (Krešimir Kovačević), and "The Revelers" (Božidar Mohaček) in Zagreb; Milutin Negode, Ernest Švara and the "Sonny Boys" (S. Dražil) in Ljubljana; and the "Jolly Boys" (Mile Marjanović), the "Singing Boys" and the "Melody Boys" in Belgrade. In the last years before the war, several large jazz bands appeared, among them the "Devils" (Marjam Marjanović and Neno Grčević) and the orchestras of J. Remenar, B. Hohnjec, and the Johan brothers in Zagreb; the "Ronny" (D. Pestotnik) and the orchestras of the Azjc brothers and of Bojan Adamič in Ljubljana; and the Stule-Jovanović orchestra in Belgrade.

During World War II, our activity in the field of music was almost completely curtailed. More than twenty jazz musicians died in the ranks of the Liberation Front in Slovenia alone.

After the end of the war and the liberation of the country, a young generation emerged which approached the creation of modern light music with great seriousness. Of course, the young were joined and encouraged by colleagues who had been active before the war (Bojan Adamič, Marjan Marjanović, Zvonimir Bradić, Bojan Hohnjec, and Ferdo Pomykalo, among others). The experience of these established composers was of great help in the period immediately after the war, since the metier had to be learned and mastered. While trying to achieve high professional standards, the young composers and performers also had to struggle for social acceptance in the new conditions.

The younger generation approached its task seriously. Several large professional and amateur orchestras were formed. Professional orchestras were established by radio stations, and amateur orchestras or bands were organized on the initiative of individual conductors or of groups or organizations. Among the large professional orchestras worth mentioning were the Radio Ljubljana Dance Orchestra (conductors Bojan Adamič, Miha Gunzek, and Mario Rijavec), the Radio Zagreb Dance Orchestra (Zlatko Černjul, Miljenko Prohaska, Milivoj Koerbler, and Miroslav Killer), the Radio Zagreb Entertainment Orchestra [*Zabavni orkestar*] (Ferdo Pomykalo), and the Radio Belgrade Entertainment Orchestra (Mladen Guteša, Ilija Genić, and Vojislav Simić). The most notable among the large amateur ensembles were those of Boris Sorokin, Milivoj Koerbler, Miljenko Prohaska, and Mihajlo Švarc in Zagreb; *"Veseli Berači"* in Ljubljana; and the orchestras of Dušan Vidak, Karlo Takač, and Milan Kotlić in Belgrade. The most important small ensembles at the time were those of Boro Roković, Predrag Ivanović, and Stevan Markičević in Belgrade; the Ljubljana Jazz Band; and the bands of Milivoj Koerbler and Dražen Boić in Zagreb. All the ensembles mentioned here tried to eliminate commercial hits from their repertory. Although American jazz ensembles inevitably exerted a powerful influence, the various Yugoslav groups tried to develop an independent creative direction, especially in their own arrangements. They wanted to acquaint their audiences with a new, contemporary sound, more complex harmonic structures, and modern conceptions of rhythm.

It is interesting to observe how the new generation looked upon the development of jazz. Musicians were enthusiastic about new ways of handling instruments and new possibilities offered by improvisation. They agreed wholeheartedly with Honegger:

> Jazz, real and unique, has entered our life. . . . Jazz certainly is not just a fad, as some short-sighted observers have declared, nor is it an expression of decadence; on the contrary, it represents a return to vital sources of inspiration, because it follows the line of the forgotten tradition of improvisers — minstrels, trouvères, and troubadours. At times, jazz is burlesque, often pathetic, but always fascinating in its rhythm and its mystery; it has a soul, therefore it lives.

Composers strove to destroy stale norms and outmoded molds and to raise popular music to a higher level, which would make the reception of serious contemporary music easier. ("A few years more of such liberties in the harmony of jazz, and the boldest experiments of Igor Stravinsky will become accessible to the man in the street too." A. Copland.) Dancers were enthusiastic about the new rhythms and avidly sought whatever did not resemble the waltz and the tango. Young audiences sensed the possibility of expressing through jazz their aspirations to the new, the contemporary urbanized and industrialized society; jazz thus became at times a kind of protest against outdated operetta music, banal popular "hit tunes," and cheap pseudo-folklore. Officially, however, jazz was severely censured for a long time. Official critics (who, unfortunately, always seem to suffer from a lack of professional qualifications) simply could not grasp that true originality does not necessarily consist in avoiding foreign influences while inflexibly preserving the local status quo, but rather in using foreign stimuli for the enrichment of one's own development and thereby raising the general level of all art. One must, of course, learn from the most highly developed source, and in the case of jazz, America was unquestionably that source. But perhaps the opposition of official critics was inevitable, for as Schopenhauer has said, every new thing must pass through three stages: in the first stage it is considered ridiculous, in the second it provokes opposition, and in the third it is taken for granted.

In the early 1950's, Yugoslav composers and performers in the field of popular music began to organize professional associations, among which the Association of Jazz Musicians in Belgrade and the Association of Composers of Popular Music in Zagreb are particularly prominent. The printing of music, the publication of journals, and the organization of concerts also began about that time. Public organized professional activity dates from the same period. The radio, motion picture, and recording industries sought more native, contemporary popular music. The process of differentiation into jazz, dance, popular, and light orchestral music began. Radio stations began holding competitions to obtain works for their programs; and in 1954, a group of composers established the Zagreb Festival of Popular Music — the first of its kind in our country. Later, the Association of Croatian Composers took over the organization of the festival.

An ever increasing number of composers, conductors, and performers attained high professional qualifications in the music schools of Yugoslavia. That period of learning and mastering the craft of so-called light and popular music and that time of achieving both professional and social affirmation ended about 1958.

Concluding this first era of the postwar development of contemporary Yugoslav popular music, I must name those composers whose work was to continue developing. In Croatia, they include first Neno Grčević, then Marjan Matković (composer of the first review-operetta, *Stvaramo reviju*, in 1955), Ljubo Kuntarić, Miroslav Biro, Milutin Vandekar, Zvonimir Krkljuš, Ivo Koerbler, Ferdo Pomykalo, Miljenko Prohaska, Milivoj Koerbler, Dragiša Dukić, Boris Sorokin, Miroslav Johan, Bojan Hohnjec, Tomica Simović, and Mario Kinel. The most active in Slovenia were Bojan Adamič (dean of Yugoslav popular and film music), Mojmir Sepe, and Mario Rijavec. In Serbia, Milan Kotlić, Dušan Vidak, Dragomir Ristić, Vojislav Simić, Mihajlo Živanović, and Vojislav Djonović must be named.

The year 1958 may be taken as the beginning of the next era. The first Opatija Festival was held then, September 18-20. This festival was a contest for popular music, organized by the Yugoslav Broadcasting System, and it signified "official" recognition of popular music.

The problem of national expression seems to present the greatest difficulty in the case of popular songs. This type of music is most subject to the influences of international dance rhythms and fashions (through the imitation of particular international hits of the moment), so that one can speak of the domination of Italian, Greek, and lately, of "beat" music. However, an unusual situation exists in Yugoslavia in that hit songs are not generally created and presented to the public as part of a larger whole, e. g., a movie or a musical; rather, they usually appear as individual creations, mostly at festivals of popular music.

Radio stations quickly realized that festivals provided an excellent means for selecting and "filtering" the enormous amount of popular music needed for their programs. Professional juries guarantee the necessary minimum creative and professional quality. Moreover, the songs presented at the festivals also pass the demanding test of the audience's taste, thereby guaranteeing the rights of the ultimate consumers.

National and regional festivals play a very important role in Yugoslav popular music (e. g., the Festival of Slovenian Songs in Ljubljana, the Festival of Kajkavian Songs at Krapina, the "Melodies of the Adriatic" in Split, among others). These festivals bring the specific qualities of the dialect, the local milieu, the idiosyncrasies, and the particular taste of a given area to their fullest expression, while at the same time insisting on modern themes and performing media. In this context, a number of tunes have emerged which seem to justify the opinion that soon a truly successful synthesis of national-traditional and international-modern components in the field of popular tunes will be achieved. This opinion seems even more well founded if one considers the success of some pop music composers from Macedonia, Istria, Bosnia and Herzegovina, who have in their music reflected something of their peculiar folk heritages (Aleksandar Džambazov, Petar Pešev, Ljubomir Brangjolica, Dragan Dakonovski, Karlo Milotti, Žarko Roje, Kornelije Kovač, and Julije Marić).

Many newly successful composers of popular tunes came to the fore in this period: Alfons Vučer, Nikica Kalogjera, Stipica Kalogjera, Arsen Dedić, Alfi Kabiljo, Mario Nardeli, Stjepan Mihaljinec, Mario Bogliuni, Marija Radić, Pero Gotovac, Heda Piliš, Drago Diklić, Vili Čaklec, Ivica Krajač, Zdenko Runjic, Zvonko Spišić, Branko Mihaljević, Ivo Robić (the most successful Yugoslav singer of popular music and the winner of several golden records), Deki Srbljenović, and Hrvoje Hegedušić in Croatia; Mirko Šouc, Aleksandar Nećak, Darko Kraljić, Angelo Vlatković, Bogoljub Srebrić, Aleksandar Korać, and Radoslav Graić in Serbia; V. S. Avsenik (three golden records), Jose Privšek, Vladimir Stiasny, Jure Robežnik, Ati Soos, Boris Kovačić, and Borut Lesjak in Slovenia.

Among all the branches of popular music, the greatest international acclaim in this era was earned by Yugoslav jazz. The Radio Belgrade Jazz Band, led by Vojislav Simić, won first place in the European Jazz Festival in Juan-les-Pins (France) in 1960, and the ensemble "Ad hoc" from Ljubljana won a gold medal at the jazz festival in Helsinki in 1962. The international success of the Radio Ljubljana Dance Orchestra (Jože Privšek), the Ljubljana Jazz Band, the Radio Zagreb Dance Orchestra (Miljenko Prohaska), the Zagreb Jazz Quartet

(Predrag Ivanović), and the Yugoslav Jazz Festival (at Bled and Ljubljana), as well as a number of individual musicians, is the result of dedicated efforts in this area for many years. Some orchestras and composers (a notable example is Miljenko Prohaska) have created their own identifiable style which is very personal and original and yet has a distinctive national color, so that we can speak of Yugoslav jazz as a definite and acknowledged category.

Conspicuous results have also been achieved in the field of light orchestral music (symphonic jazz). A number of composers can be mentioned here: Dušan Vidak, Vojislav Simić, and Aleksandar Džambazov received awards at the festival of symphonic jazz in Cava dei Tireni, Italy. Miljenko Prohaska, Bojan Adamič, Milivoj Koerbler, Mihajlo Živanović, Milutin Vandekar, Bojan Hohnjec, and Ferdo Pomykalo have also contributed much to this particular repertory. In this regard, it might be noted that activity in the field of music for the stage has been increasing during the past few years (Stjepan Mihaljinec and Milivoj Koerbler).

At the end of my survey, it is only fair that I mention some of the negative trends in the development of Yugoslav light and popular music. As I have noted, the entire development has been marked by a great seriousness of purpose and attitude of responsibility. The socio-economic situation has in the past been a positive contributing factor in maintaining such a responsible approach, since it did not make commercial considerations an immediate concern. But lately, an increasing number of businessmen have appeared who could seriously jeopardize further development by their reckless commercialism in the recording industry (reflected in an inundation of pseudo-folk banalities), the publishing business, and the press. To some extent, this is an international phenomenon. We can only hope that the dedicated, professionally qualified, and responsible majority of composers and performers will successfully fulfill their commitment to the continuing development of Yugoslav light and popular music in spite of it. To this end, greater attention should be paid to the publication of high quality professional literature and to the truly professional education of composers, with special regard to the needs of the movie industry, the legitimate stage, and radio-television.

Andrej Rijavec

APPLICATIONS OF MODERN TECHNOLOGY IN MUSICOLOGY AND MUSIC THEORY IN YUGOSLAVIA

The subject with which this paper deals has no historical background in Yugoslavia. The organizers of the Seminar have been well aware that they might be criticized for including a topic so unsuited to mutual participation. The United States has an enormous technological advantage over Yugoslavia in this area; important results have already been achieved there through the application of modern technology to various musical problems. Still, the organizers of the Seminar have been equally aware of the significance of this topic for the future development of Yugoslav music; we must make the first step. If our pioneering efforts cannot, in such a short time, lead to equality between the two partners in the discussion, they may at least lead to an active response on the part of the Yugoslav participants. For, after all, the purpose of any international seminar is to share experiences and to stimulate further achievements. Our discussion here will certainly play an inaugural role in the "application of modern technology" to musical problems in Yugoslavia.

The material possibilities in American institutes and universities, the availability of technological aids, especially of computers, is undoubtedly greater than anywhere else in the world. The implications of this technology for music begins to become apparent upon examination of the reports of different universities in *Current Musicology* (No. 5, 1967). A group of American universities has organized computer centers which can be used for projects in music research. Uninformed people might think that in our country, possibilities for any kind of activity of this sort have yet to exist. But this is not so. Computers have been in use for several years in the large Yugoslav university centers, Belgrade, Zagreb, and Ljubljana — from the modest ZUSE–Z–23 to the CAE 90-40 and the IBM 705. More equipment has been acquired quite recently: the University of Skopje has received an IBM 1130, the Mathematical Institute of Belgrade University an IBM 36-44, and the Mathematical Institute of the University of Ljubljana a CDC 3300. The excuse that we have no technological resources for the development of research with computers must thus be dropped, at least from 1968 on.

Perhaps the question may arise why no musical projects have as yet been undertaken, making use of the equipment already available in Yugoslavia. Here we must take into account that musicology in our country is still, despite its achievements, in an early stage of development. The historical constituent of Yugoslav musicology, significant for our musical past and present, has been firmly established. Much less energy has been devoted to the sociology and esthetics of music, and less still to the psychology of music and music theory. We must remember as well that the systematic education of musicologists is a relatively recent occurrence, and that the number of positions which provide for full-time research work is quite limited because the material possibilities for the creation of such positions are also quite limited. In short, the production of Yugoslav musicologists is not such that we might speak of a musicological boom. Musicology is not an area exposed to the immediacies of everyday life. It is not surprising that such a field, relying on a few individuals, has not sensed the need to study more intensely the possibilities of computers in the service of musicological research.

I dare not state that information on technological innovation has not reached us, because music periodical and other scholarly musicological literature from abroad — especially since 1960 — has reported increasingly about applications of modern technological achievements in the field of musicology. But we have received such information with certain prejudices as a result of our belief that musicology is essentially a humanistic discipline which cannot be measured quantitatively and which is therefore unsuited to the mathematical operations performed by computers. Some of us may even have imagined that the "purity" of musicological thought was in danger of mechanization and dehumanization.

Yet, on the other side, the fact remains that in the scholarly interpretation of music we have always used nonmusical means, for we use letters and words, and numbers as well. Indeed, throughout the history of music we see references to the concept of music as a mathematical discipline. The use of computers in music research may therefore represent a novelty in technological development, but not a fundamental change in the historic way of thinking about music.

Rather than protesting emotionally against the machine, we should remind ourselves that a very large part of research work consists of a rather mechanical dissipation of energy, e. g., in tiresome and repetitious processes — the counting of "typical" chords used by a composer, the search for motives in the structure of a large composition, documentation, the preparations of indexes, bibliographies, and the like. Such work often takes many years, and in the end it may turn out to be incomplete or even insignificant, though it will nevertheless be called "scientific" in reward for the author's diligence. Neither the most refined intuition nor the highest intelligence can replace purely quantitative research in musicology. Why, then, should we not use computers, which can do this sort of work with astonishing precision and incomparable speed?

The very precision and speed of a computer's operations open the way for new qualitative insights. For example, it has been found that the main theme of Gallus' motet *Praeparate corda vestra (Opus musicum III,* No. 34) coincides, surprisingly, with the beginning of the Slovenian song *Šel sem, šel čez gmajnico* (Across I went, across the meadow). How did Ludvik Zepič and Dragotin Cvetko arrive at this realization? By mere chance. For no human mind can remember several thousand Slovenian folk songs — not to mention their variants — and compare them with the beginnings of all 455 of Gallus' motets. It could be done systematically by traditional means, of course, but it would require an enormous expenditure of time. A computer could do the job in a minute fraction of the time.

The chance discovery by Zepič and Cvetko poses a genuine question. To his signature, Gallus added the adjective "Carniolus," which means that he was from Carniola, a part of Slovenia. He must have known many Slovenian songs. Is *Šel sem, šel čez gmajnico* the only one he used in his motets? The answer would throw new light on the work of one of the more significant composers of the European musical Renaissance.

But the computer is capable of far more complex operations than those necessary to solve the problem posed above.

Round table conferences at the Seventh Congress of the International Association of Music Libraries in Dijon (1965) dealt with the "Utilization of Data Processing Techniques in Musical Documentation," and from the discussion came the *Répertoire International de la Littérature Musicale* (which both Mr. Waters and Mr. Klemenčić discuss in their respective papers). At the Tenth Congress of the International Musicological Society in Ljubljana (1967), "Computer Aids to Musicology" was the subject of a round table conference scheduled for the first time during a regular session. All of this indicates that use of computers has reached such a stage that the results of past achievements may be evaluated and guidelines set for the future. Some of the questions to be answered and problems to be faced are discussed in a very valuable work only recently published, *Elektronische Datenverarbeitung in der Musikwissenschaft* (Regensburg, 1967); it contains a number of articles and an exhaustive bibliography. This work together with the papers from the Tenth Congress of the IMS represent a starting point for us to begin to catch up with the achievements in computer research.

Obviously, the computer is no substitute for individual creative capacity, in the same way that the latest stereo equipment is no guarantee for the musical taste of its owner. Computers cannot replace man; they can only make his job much easier. This can be observed in the work achieved by our colleagues abroad. If we follow their example, quantitative results provided by the computer will not be our goal, but only the means to achieve new insights, thus musicology and music theory in Yugoslavia will have gained a new and useful tool for research.

Vladimir Ussachevsky

APPLICATIONS OF MODERN TECHNOLOGY IN MUSICOLOGY, MUSIC THEORY, AND COMPOSITION IN THE UNITED STATES

Through all history, interaction between music and technology has been a normal result of man's ability to spread the advances in one field of knowledge to other areas of human activity. Cat-gut was not developed, but adapted, for string instruments; the metal frame of the modern piano, a simple technological adaptation of the existing material, has had a far-reaching effect. The evolution of new musical instruments inevitably brought about the enrichment of musical literature, and, on occasion, caused the emergence of a new musical style.

However, not since the introduction of music printing and, centuries later, of the phonograph, has so great a potential for change been accessible to scholars and composers as exists in the present century. Around 1945, modern technology began to impinge upon the compositional, acoustical, historical, and theoretical areas of music. Composers began immediately to employ the technological aids that became available after World War II. In the ensuing period, numerous electronic music studios were built. Thus, when the idea of using computers for musical production was embryonic, many compositions in the electronic medium already existed. By the time Dr. Max Mathews of Bell Telephone Laboratories had made his first proposals and practical implementations to generate electronic materials with the aid of the computer, concert and radio performances of works by Edgar Varèse, Otto Luening, Luciano Berio, Karlheinz Stockhausen, this author, and, of course, by several members of the *musique concrète* school, were rather common. Musical scholars were largely aloof during this initial period of electronic turmoil, but when the computer possibilities for musical research began to be explored, a respectable number of musicologists, music theorists, and bibliographers swelled the ranks of technologically involved musicians. A glance at the attached list of computer-dependent projects (see Appendix I B) indicates that the areas of exploration already started cannot help but be filled in with many additional undertakings within the next few years. I propose to survey first the area of electronic music.

The production of electronic music, with or without computer, has certain procedures that clearly distinguish it from the preparation of music to be played on conventional instruments. When performers are not involved, the composer addresses himself to the task of communicating directly with the listener by means of his finished product on magnetic tape, or possibly a later version in the form of a disc. Thus, by himself or with the aid of a technician, the composer has to assume total responsibility for generating and shaping his compositional materials. In the working environment of the electronic music studio, this requires various degrees of technological involvement, not only with the apparatus for generating electronic sounds, but also with certain basic electronic units which are employed to control spectrum characteristics.

The central tool is still the tape recorder, which is relatively simple to operate and which, once the sound is recorded on tape, becomes a secondary generator of material. There is a great deal of sound manipulation which can be done with the tape recorder alone, but usually the sound is shaped externally through such devices as filters, reverberation chambers, resonators, and ring modulators. Full acquaintance with the capabilities of these devices must form an essential part of the composer's skill. No less important is the development of a knowledge of experimental procedures – a skill that may become highly individual. One has in particular to take full advantage of the unique feature of working with sound material that can be listened to in all stages of development. (This important possibility is also available on the unique Mark II RCA Electronic Sound Synthesizer, now located at the Columbia-Princeton Electronic Music Center in New York City.)

From the early period of electronic music, and still at the present time, a great deal of work must be done by handicraft methods: treating a magnetic tape as if it were a lump of clay, measuring and cutting it to achieve desired durations of sound, creating certain limited variations in the attack characteristics by varying the angle of the cut, etc. The very real problem of how to overcome the tedium of a note-by-note construction of musical patterns – the first apparent disadvantage of dispensing with conventional instruments – has led to the employment of certain controlling devices, such as typewriter-like keys, punched paper tape, and also the specialized keyboards found in the ingenious Phonogene of *musique concrète* and the Creative Tape Recorder invented by Dr. Hugh LeCaine of Canada. The first comprehensive attempt to combine in one unit versatile electronic sound generating and modifying devices (controlled by binary code instructions punched by attached special keyboard devices on a fifteen-inch wide paper roll) was successfully demonstrated in the RCA Synthesizer Mark I and, subsequently, in the Mark II. The following components of the musical event can thus be controlled: frequency, envelope, spectrum, intensity, duration, and the mode of progression from one event to the following event. The output of the RCA Synthesizer is recorded on magnetic tape. (Similar principles, though varying considerably in the method of execution, are to be found in the synthesizer constructed for the original Siemens Electronic Music Studio in Munich.)

In the past five years, particularly in the United States, several manufacturers, recognizing the need for reducing the manual operation in the production of electronic music, have provided either keyboard-control devices or automatic signal sequencers which can be pre-set to produce a desired succession of pitches at a predetermined rate of speed. Many compatible units for sound generation and sound modification are normally associated with these control devices. The number of such units can be increased at will, and thus a very small or very large studio can be established with the prefabricated and connectable components. The availability of such packaged studios makes it less likely that the future studios will depend on generating and modifying devices of the type common to engineering and acoustical laboratories. It should be noted that the most significant trend is toward voltage-controlled oscillators, filters, and ring modulators. This is important because a conventional electronic studio which has this type of equipment is more readily coupled with computer installations. Small computers (in the $12,000 to $15,000 class) combined with certain specialized inter-facing devices help to eliminate, to a considerable degree, the sound-by-sound shaping necessary in standard manipulation. Thus, the control of sound production is beginning to be transferred to a programmed, punched state. Such small computers also provide a certain amount of memory in which a lot of electronic signals can be stored, to be recalled and shaped by a suitable program. Studios equipped with such small computer installations will serve for a number of years as an intermediate stage to total generation of musical materials on large computers. It should be noted that the various devices for speeding up the process of creating electronic sound paradoxically may have an adverse effect on the quality of sound. A widespread misconception exists that the various steps, taken in the direction of eliminating the tediousness of manual production, automatically assure an increase in volume of production without a loss in quality. This has not proven to be the case, and the very proliferation of studios equipped with packaged electronic devices has resulted, in my opinion, in a considerable decline in quality. Too often a raw product, easily generated by various keyboard or semi-automatic control devices, is left without additional modification. Sometimes even the use of the modulators which form a part of these units seems to be ignored. Many composers no longer trouble themselves with acquiring manual skills. Tedious as it is, the process of separately shaping smaller segments of material usually results in more sophisticated and individual sound, more ingenious envelopes, etc. The decline in craftmanship is even more regrettable because, basically, the raw material produced on these packaged studio units, with little extra manual effort, could be made a great deal more attractive. Part of this apparent indifference can unquestionably be laid to the wide latitude offered by some current "esthetics" and to a general tendency to circumvent disciplined creative processes. Whatever the causes, entirely too many composers appear to be satisfied with hasty productions of "new" electronic materials unimaginatively strung together and utterly delinquent in structural imagination.

Brief mention should be made of a mushrooming family of electronic performing instruments, including conventional instruments with electronic attachments that make it possible to modify electronically the sound quality at the player's will. Some of these have a considerably extended range. One wonders if the emergence of these instruments is due primarily to a wider acceptance of electronically produced sound, resulting in the necessity for conventional performers to participate in the production of electronic music. Prior to this development, there were already many instances in which the performer on a conventional instrument played in combination either with electronic accompaniment or in true duet, trio, etc., with electronic instruments. These new electronic performing instruments differ markedly from the old electronic organ, both in the design of the keyboard and in the number of possibilities for unusual timbre. Nevertheless, in my opinion, they are thus far not so versatile in providing consistently interesting electronic patterns as those produced in electronic studios.

Only a comparatively limited space may be devoted to a description of the production of music by computer. A computer can be programmed to provide an output which can be converted directly into sound successions recordable on an ordinary tape recorder. A different objective, computer composition, requires an entirely different programming to provide an output in the form of printed symbols which are then transcribed into conventional musical notation. The first method is used by the composer for realization of his pre-composed work in actual sound. In the second method, the computer itself is allowed to "compose" according to programmed instructions which may range from the very specific to the essentially random.

Generation of actual sounds by the computer requires a program which first produces a digital representation of the succession of desired sound material in the form of a digital "computer" tape. This tape cannot be "heard" directly, though the information on it can be printed out in numerical form. To obtain the actual sound, digital tape is subjected to the digital-to-analogue conversion process. It is this "analogue output" that is the audible form of the computer synthesized music.

The evolution of this sound-generating program, initiated some ten years ago by Dr. Max Mathews in the Bell Telephone Laboratories, is described in numerous articles (see Appendix I B. 2 for representative samples). The later version of this program, known as Music IV, was adapted with individual modifications by a number of other investigators (see, for example, the projects conducted by J. K. Randall and Godfrey Winham of Princeton University; Gerald Strang of California; and others mentioned in Appendix II). Lately this program has also undergone substantial revision at the Bell Telephone Laboratories, emerging in the form of Music V. A concise description of the basic procedures, which to a considerable extent are derived from the earlier Music IV, is found in Appendix III. (For an excellent and more detailed presentation of Music IV, see the article by composer James Tenney in the *Journal of Music Theory,* listed in Appendix I. Mr. Tenney has worked both at the University of Illinois and at the Bell Telephone Laboratories.) I should like to single out the computer sound-generating program at Princeton University as particularly beneficial, both in increasing the sophistication of the programming and in serving the needs of about twelve faculty and student composers, including some from Columbia University. A marked improvement in the quality of sound and a growing flexibility in structural approach suggest that, like any new tool, the computer requires a thorough knowledge of its capabilities and responds to skillful and imaginative use.

The speed and a certain idiomatic flexibility with which a computer can be made to organize stored information has recently led to another avenue of investigation, namely, to assess its usefulness for sound "regeneration." The final objective is similar to the one described in the paragraph above. But the first step is to employ the reverse of the conversion process already mentioned. A certain limited amount of sound material previously recorded on magnetic tape – the analogue form – is converted to digital tape. The digital computer is then fed with a program which will cause it to extract any portion of the recorded material. The program may also include instructions to transpose any portion of the material up or down scale (with results similar to the well-known effect of tape-speed variation). Elaborate envelopes can be devised to change radically the amplitude characteristics of the extracted sections of the original or of the transposed materials. In other respects, the computer performs the same tasks it would in the case of the ordinary sound generating program. The extracted and reshaped material is organized in time according to instructions; a new digital tape is produced and then converted to analogue form. Thus, the computer potentially offers an opportunity not only to generate programmed compositions electronically, but also to mix electronic sound materials with "concrete" sounds. I have been investigating the possibilities offered by this latter approach since the fall of 1967 at Bell Telephone Laboratories.

Another possibility, already mentioned in the section on electronic music (see pp. 124-25), is to use a computer purely as a controlling device — not to generate the sounds internally, but to cause them to be produced by voltage-controlled external oscillators, connected by several lines to a computer. The computer is programmed to supply voltages through these lines, and the variations in voltage will determine various parameters of the oscillator-generated electronic sounds.

Mention of another important investigation should be made, namely that of using "Graphical Language for the Scores of Computer-Generated Sounds" by Max Mathews and L. Rosler of Bell Telephone Laboratories. I quote from the abstract by the authors:

> Conventional scores are an insufficient and inconvenient way of describing sound sequences to computers. A procedure is described for drawing scores as graphical functions of time, using a light pen on a cathode ray tube attached to a small computer. The information is transmitted digitally to a larger computer, which synthesizes the sound and reproduces it immediately with a loudspeaker. Typically, functions for amplitude, frequency, and duration of a sequence of notes are drawn. An algebra allows combining functions by addition and multiplication. In this way, certain compositional processes may be performed by the computer. For example, the time-varying weighted average between two melodic or rhythmic sequences may be synthesized. The graphical programs provide great flexibility for drawing, copying, erasing and altering functions. Thus it is easy to develop a sound sequence by a succession of trials. Microfilm and punched-card versions of the score are automatically provided. In addition to being compositional tools, the graphical scores are effective representations of the sound to a listener. In many ways, they are easier to follow than conventional scores.

A complete description of this intriguing process has appeared in *Perspectives of New Music,* Vol. 7, No. 1 (Fall-Winter, 1968).

In the realm of music compositions through the computer, the initial substantial efforts go back to 1956, when Professor Lejaren A. Hiller, Jr., and Leonard M. Issacson of the University of Illinois launched an investigation into an evaluation of the rules of counterpoint as formulated by J. J. Fux in the eighteenth century. This investigation was soon broadened to test other kinds of compositional constraints by having the computer compose music in accordance with them. This approach has no connection with generating sounds by the computer. The computer's output was in the form of numbers which then had to be converted externally into musical notation. Compositions thus created were arranged for conventional musical instruments. I published the product of this initial study by Hiller, *Illiac Suite for String Quartet,* in New Music Edition (April, 1957, Vol. 30, No. 3), and it probably remains the first published work of computer music. It has since been recorded on a commercial disc.

One aspect (although by no means a necessary condition) of computer composition present in this original study by Professor Hiller was the use of random-number generation as a partial basis for compositional choice. This factor has been present in almost all studies of computer composition since that time, and it has left, as someone said, "an aura of indetermination around the results which have been accomplished." Be that as it may, it is certain that an increasing number of composers will speculate on the idea of entrusting a computer with decisions in the realm of the compositional process. At the present time, the majority of works which have been so created are performed on conventional musical instruments. Among the numerous mathematically dependent instrumental works of Iannis Xenakis, whose preoccupation with stochastic processes of composition is well documented in his writings (see Appendix I), the compositions *Strategie* and *Eonta* both make some use of a computer. Also in France, the work of Barbaud and Blanchard has been carried on continuously since 1960, and Mr. Barbaud's book *Initiation a la composition musicale automatique* (Paris, 1966) has been reported as a detailed and clear exposition of specific proposals and accomplishments.

New directions are emerging. Mr. Hiller has used a program, as a part of a composition "for Prima Donna, Pitchman, Player Piano, and Percussionist," by which the computer generated a set of markings on a player piano, which, once perforated, could be used to play a mixed selection of nearly a hundred themes from the symphonic literature of the nineteenth century. Also at the University of Illinois, John Cage has produced a composition "HPSCHD" for harpsichord and "harpsichord-like" sounds. The latter were composed and synthesized by the computer and recorded on a number of tapes. A computerized program based on the I-Ching book of changes was to be involved, and pitch levels, deviations from these levels, and durations thus selected. A large number of scales (though not the 12-tone scale) would thereby have been created. Computer-derived analytical data of Mozart's melodic structure and a subsequent generation of patterns on the basis of this data were proposed as the next step. The patterns so generated were to be recorded on magnetic tape. The performance of the work involves combining a multiplicity of these tapes with the actual music of Mozart played on a harpsichord. No one, as far as I know, has yet proposed a computer program for the *critical* evaluation of the results of this type of computer application.

Other musical applications of computers are in the categories of sound analysis, analytical studies in the realm of theory and musicological evaluation, and the storing and sorting of various musical data. It is easy both to underestimate and to overestimate the computer's capabilities in all of the areas which I have listed. The very number of investigations undertaken indicates that scholars turn to the computer because they feel that it facilitates access to information which would require far more research time by traditional methods. It should be clearly understood however, that this facility is not immediately available, but depends on an enormous amount of advance preparation of the data as well as construction of ingenious programs to retrieve information in a form useful to the scholar. The real advantage begins to accrue, of course, when the data, properly prepared, is scanned for the desired information with the super-human rapidity of which the computer is capable. It is likely that for some time the debate will continue as to the use of the computer to analyze musical "style" in such a way as to provide complete information on composing in the style of any given composer. This sort of pursuit is laudable and provides a great deal of information which may, in turn, result in new clues about influences exercised on a composer and by him. It is unlikely, however, that the creation of Beethoven's Tenth Symphony or Brahm's Fifth will be undertaken soon, for many reasons, including economic ones. Of greater concern is the capability of the computer to interpret the data in such a fashion as not to interfere with an intelligent final appraisal by the one seeking the data in the first place.

I should like to quote, from an unpublished article by Hubert S. Howe, Jr., a concise statement on the considerations and procedures attendant on an analytical investigation of music by means of a computer:

> Most projects concerned with the analysis of music by computer proceed in the following stages: (1) a method of representing a musical score as computer input is developed, and the compositions under investigation are translated into this form. Many problems are inherent in formulating this representation, and for this reason some projects have actually not advanced beyond this stage. The main difficulty is that not *all* properties of a score can be represented in any manner short of optical scanning, but then the investigators are not always interested in *all* properties of the music, but usually only those connected with the pitch structure or *text*. (2) A program is written to analyze the music according to the interests of the investigators. If only one problem is under investigation, this stage of development is usually accomplished with little difficulty, but since most investigators either anticipate or discover that the results of their initial investigations lead only to further questions, this stage of development becomes a continuing process. In the most sophisticated program of this kind yet developed, namely the "Musical Information Retrieval" project begun by Michael Kassler in 1963 at

Princeton University under the direction of Professor Lewis Lockwood, the program, rather than being geared to any specific problem, itself is a "language" for formulating questions which can be processed on the music. (3) The results of the investigations in stage (2) are published, usually in tabular form. The fact that the output of these investigations is usually a table of *numbers* indicates a rather basic fact of the projects of this nature: Their main value is in processing large amounts of data accurately and in a short amount of time. No projects have yet arrived at the stage where the computer can output ideas for further investigation. This fact also suggests that the publication of great quantities of statistics about musical compositions without much attention paid to the interpretation of these statistics, is of little value in itself, no matter how impressive large quantities of computer output may seem to the uninformed layman. It must be emphasized that projects whose goal is musical analysis must be distinguished from bibliographical investigations, in which the object of study has little to do with the structure of musical compositions.

In addition to the project mentioned above, scholars active in this area include Professor Lawrence F. Bernstein of The University of Chicago, Dr. George W. Logemann, formerly of New York University, Professor Allen Forte of Yale University, and Professor Roland Jackson of Roosevelt University in Chicago....

Studies which are concerned with the generation and analysis of "pre-compositional" or "speculative theoretical" musical materials, although they may strike one as being "pure theory" more than anything else, have been conducted almost exclusively by composers. In this area significant achievements have been made through the use of computers – achievements which could not have been possible using other methods of investigation. The first study of this nature (of which this author is aware) was conducted in the early 1960s by Professor Hans Jelinek of the Vienna Music Academy. Professor Jelinek was concerned with generating all eleven-interval twelve-tone rows, and from this number extracting those which had various interesting properties. His work was duplicated literally a few years later by Stefan Bauer-Mengelberg and Melvin Ferentz, who published their results in *Perspectives of New Music* (Spring-Summer 1965), apparently unaware of Jelinek's study.

Related and somewhat more sophisticated investigations of this nature have been undertaken by J. K. Randall and H. S. Howe at Princeton University.

I should like to close with a quotation about the composer-technician relationship, which is a significant part of the new conditions of technological involvement. No mention is made of computers, the use of which has created a whole series of new problems. Writing for the Spring 1959 issue of the *Juilliard Review*, I said:

> There are several little-discussed aspects of the new set of working conditions in which a composer finds himself. A composer from any generation, when first confronted with an electronic studio used for composition through tape, needs technical help. In this environment an electrical engineer or a technician may be called upon to realize the composer's intentions, or to translate his musical ideas into technical procedures. A composer-technician collaboration is added to and partly substituted for the traditional composer-performer relationship. But where the composer and the performer speak a common language, the composer's intentions must now be put in terms the engineer can understand. A composer often requests procedures which are at variance with standard recording techniques; a technician must accept the inevitable tendency on the part of the composer to treat the electro-acoustical apparatus in the studio as a new instrument. Hence a period of mutual collaboration requiring a varying degree of acquaintanceship with each other's fields is necessary; but the burden of communication rests upon the composer. A definite choice is present. Depending upon his temperament, prior experience with modern electronic gadgetry, etc., a composer will either learn to manipulate the apparatus and become able to handle all stages of developing the tape material himself, or he will remain wholly or partly dependent upon the technician. Dependence upon the technician so complete that he is transformed into an interpreter is undesirable.

APPENDIX I

Selected Bibliography

A. Electronic Music, Musique Concrète, and Tape Music

In reference to the above three categories, it should be noted that though certain differences in relative stylistic characteristics continue to prevail, the boundaries which originally delimited the electronic music of Cologne, *musique concrète* of Paris, and the tape music of Columbia University in New York are now very fluid, and hence, *electronic music* has become a generic term. The amount of printed material about electronic music is so extensive as to discourage separate listing by authors and titles.

I have selected four bibliographies which include most of the articles and books that have appeared up to early 1968. A special mention must be made of the fifth source, which concerns a comprehensive listing of the existing electronic music studios, electronic compositions, and a discography in the *Electronic Music Review,* Nos. 2 and 3, April and July, 1967. This was a co-operative publication of *Le Groupe de Recherches Musicales de l' ORTF,* the Independent Electronic Music Center, Inc., and the Massachusetts Institute of Technology Press.

Bahler, Peter Benjamin. "Electronic and Computer Music: An Annotated Bibliography of Writings in English." MA thesis, University of Rochester: New York, 1966.
Basart, A. P. *Serial Music: A Classified Bibliography of Writings on Twelve-tone and Electronic Music.* University of California Press: Berkley, California, 1961.
Cross, Lowell Merlin. *A Bibliography of Electronic Music.* University of Toronto Press: Toronto, Ontario, Canada, 1967.
Martin, Vernon. comp. *Bibliography of Writings on Electronic Music.* Columbia-Princeton Electronic Music Center: New York, 1964 (an unpublished survey in ditto form).

Davies, Hugh. comp. "International Electronic Music Catalog," *Electronic Music Review,* Nos. 2/3, April/July, 1967.

APPENDIX I B

B. Computer: Applications in Music

Bibliographical data in the following six categories is fairly representative, but by no means comprehensive. The compilation was drawn primarily from publications in the United States, and in general covers the more recent work.

It will be noted that a number of articles are drawn from an excellent recent publication, *Elektronische Datenverarbeitung in der Musikwissenschaft,* Harald Heckmann, editor, Gustav Bosse, Regensburg. Another useful reference is *Computer Applications in Music,* Gerald Lefkoff, editor, West Virginia University Library, Morgantown, West Virginia, 1967. Additional articles can be found in the recent book, *Computers in Humanistic Research,* Edmund B. Bowles, editor, Prentice-Hall Inc., Englewood Cliffs, New Jersey.

1. Musicological and Theoretical Investigations
2. Sound Generation and Spectrum Analysis
3. Computer Composition
4. Score-drawing Program
5. Printing of Music by Computer
6. Computer Handling of Bibliographical Data

APPENDIX I B. 1

1. Musicological and Theoretical Investigations

Babbitt, Milton. "The use of computers in musicological research," *Perspectives of New Music*. Spring-Summer, 1965.

Baker, R. A. "A statistical analysis of the harmonic practice of the 18th and 19th centuries." Unpublished D. M. A. dissertation, University of Illinois: Urbana, Illinois, 1963.

Bauer-Mengelberg, Stefan, and Melvin Ferentz. "On eleven-interval twelve-tone rows," *Perspectives of New Music*. Spring-Summer, 1965.

Bernstein, Lawrence F., and Joseph P. Olive. "Computers and the 16th-Century Chanson: A Pilot Project at the University of Chicago," *Computers and the Humanities*, Vol. 3, No. 3, January, 1969.

Binkley, Thomas E. "Electronic processing of musical materials," *Elektronische Datenverarbeitung*.

Erickson, Raymond F. "Music Analysis and the Computer: A Report on Some Current Approaches and the Outlook for the Future," *Computers and the Humanities*, Vol. 3, No. 2. November, 1968.

Ferentzy, E. N. "On formal music analysis-synthesis: Its application in music education," *Computational Linguistics*, Vol. 4, No. 107. 1965.

Forte, Allen. "A program for the analytic reading of scores," *Journal of Music Theory*, Vol. 10, No. 2. Winter, 1966.

Forte, Allen. "Music and Computing: The Present Situation," *Computers and the Humanities*, Vol. 2, No. 1. September, 1967.

Gould, Murray. "A keypunchable notation for the *Liber usualis*," *Elektronische Datenverarbeitung*.

Hiller, Lejaren A., and Ramon Fuller. "Structure and information in Webern's Symphony, op. 21," *Journal of Music Theory*, Vol. 11.

Howe, Hubert S., Jr. "Some Combinational Properties of Pitch-Structures," *Perspectives of New Music*, Vol. 4, No. 1. Fall-Winter, 1965.

Kobrin, Edward G., and Theodore H. A. Ashford. "A Solution to the Problems of Vertical Serialization," *Perspectives of New Music*, Vol. 6, No. 2.

La Rue, Jan, and Marian W. Cobin. "The Ruge-Seignelay Catalogue: An exercise in automated entries," *Elektronische Datenverarbeitung*.

Lincoln, Harry B. "Musicology and the computer: The thematic index," *Computers in Humanistic Research*. (mentioned above).

Lincoln, Harry B. "The Thematic Index: A Computer Application to Musicology," *Computers and the Humanities*, Vol. 2, No. 5. May, 1968.

Logemann, George W. "The canons in the Musical Offering of J. S. Bach: An example of computational musicology," *Elektronische Datenverarbeitung*.

Randall, J. K. "Three Lectures to Scientists," *Perspectives of New Music*, Vol. 5, No. 2. Spring-Summer, 1967.

Regener, Eric. "A multiple-pass transcription and a system for music analysis by computer," *Elektronische Datenverarbeitung*.

Rhodes, W. "The use of the computer in the classification of folk tunes," *Studia Musicologica Academiae Scientiarum Hungaricae*, Vol. 7, 1965.

Robinson, Tobias. "IML–MIR: A data-processing system for the analysis of music," *Elektronische Datenverarbeitung*.

Rogers, John. "Some Properties of Non-Duplicating Rotational Arrays," *Perspectives of New Music*, Vol. 7, No. 1. Fall-Winter, 1968.

Rothgeb, John. "Some Ordering Relationships in the Twelve-Tone System," *Journal of Music Theory*, Vol. 11, No. 2. Winter, 1967.

Rothgeb, John. "Some Uses of Mathematical Concepts in Theories of Music," *Journal of Music Theory*, Vol. 10, No. 2. Winter, 1966.

Schiodt, Nanna, and Bjarner Svejgaard. "Application of computer techniques to the analysis of Byzantine Sticherarion melodies," *Elektronische Datenverarbeitung*.

Selleck, John, and Roger Bakeman. "Procedures for the analysis of form: Two computer applications," *Journal of Music Theory*, Vol. 9, No. 2. Winter, 1965.

Winograd, Terry. "Linguistics and the Computer Analysis of Tonal Harmony," *Journal of Music Theory*, Vol. 12, No. 1. Spring, 1968.

APPENDIX I B. 2

2. Sound Generation and Spectrum Analysis

Beauchamp, James W. "A Computer System for Time-Variant Harmonic Analysis and Synthesis of Musical Tones," Technical Report No. 15, *Electrical Engineering Publication* No. 992. Urbana, Illinois: University of Illinois, School of Music Experimental Music Studio, n.d.

Chadabe, Joel. "New Approaches to Analog Studio Design," *Perspectives of New Music*, Vol. 6, No. 1. Fall-Winter, 1967.

Divilbiss, J. L. "Real-time generation of music with a digital computer," *Journal of Music Theory*, Vol. 8. 1964.

Ferretti, Ercolino. "Exploration and organization of sound with the computer," *Journal of the Acoustical Society of America*, Vol. 39. 1966.

Freedman, M. David. "A digital computer for the electronic music studio." *Journal of the Audio Engineering Society*, Vol. 15; "Analysis of musical instrument tones," *Journal of the Acoustical Society of America*, Vol. 41.

Ghent, Emmanuel. "Programmed Signals to Performers: A New Compositional Resource," *Perspectives of New Music*, Vol. 6, No. 1. Fall-Winter, 1967.

Hiller, Lejaren A., Jr. "Analysis and Synthesis of Musical Sounds by Analog and Digital Techniques: An Interim Progress Report to the National Science Foundation." Urbana, Illinois: University of Illinois Press, 1967.

Hiller, Lejaren A., Jr. "Some Comments on Computer Sound Synthesis," *Proceedings of the American Society of University Composers*, Vol. 1. 1968.

Howe, Hubert S., Jr. "Music 4BF: A Fortran Version of Music 4B." Princeton, New Jersey: Princeton University Dept. of Music, n. d.

Mac Innis, Donald. "Sound Synthesis by Computer: MUSIGOL, a Program written entirely in extended ALGOL," *Perspectives of New Music*, Vol. 7, No. 1. Fall-Winter, 1968.

Mathews, M. V. "The Digital Computer as a Musical Instrument," *Science*, Vol. 142, No. 3592. Nov. 1963.

Mathews, M. V. "The Technology of Computer Music." M. I. T. Press: 1969.

Mathews, M. V. and Joan E. Miller. "Music IV Programmer's Mannual." For outside distribution – available on request, from Bell Telephone Laboratories, Murray Hill, N. J.

Mathews, M. V., and J. E. Miller. "Pitch quantizing for computer music," *Journal of the Acoustical Society of America*, Vol. 36. 1965.

Mathews, M. V., Joan E. Miller, J. R. Pierce and J. Tenney. "Computer Study on Violin Tones." For outside distribution – available on request, from Bell Telephone Laboratories, Murray Hill, N. J.

Mathews, M. V., J. R. Pierce, and N. Guttman. "Musical Sounds from Digital Computers," *Gravesaner Blätter*, Vol. 4. 1962.

Pierce, J. R., M. V. Mathews, and J. C. Risset. "Further experiments on the use of the computer in connection with music," *Gravesaner Blätter*, No. 27/28. Nov., 1965.

Randall, J. K., "A report from Princeton," *Perspectives of New Music*. Spring-Summer, 1965.

Rissett, J. C., and M. V. Matthews. "Analysis of Musical Instrument Tones," *Physics Today*.

Tenney, James C. "Sound generation by means of a digital computer," *Journal of Music Theory*, Vol. 7, No. 1. Spring, 1963.

Warfield, Gerald. *Beginner's Manual of Music 4B*. Princeton, New Jersey: Princeton University, Dept. of Music, n. d.

Winham, Godfrey. "How MUSIC 4B generates formants and non-harmonic partials, and improves loudness control and 'quality,'" *Proceedings of the American Society of University Composers*, Vol. 1. April, 1966.

APPENDIX I B. 3

3. Computer Composition

Barbaud, P. "Initiation a la composition musicale automatique." Dunod: Paris, 1966.
Brun, Herbert. "On the conditions under which computers would assist a composer in creating music of contemporary relevance and significance." *Proceedings of the American Society of University Composers.* April, 1968.
Hiller, Lejaren A. "Electronic music at the University of Illinois," *Journal of Music Theory,* Vol. 7, No. 1. Spring, 1963.
Hiller, Lejaren A. "Programming a computer for musical composition," *Computer Applications in Music.*
Hiller, Lejaren A., and Robert A. Baker. "Computer Cantata: A study in compositional method," *Perspectives of New Music.* Fall-Winter, 1964.
Hiller, Lejaren A. and A. Leal. "Revised MUSICOMP manual." Technical report No. 13, University of Illinois Experimental Music Studio, Urbana, Illinois, 1966.
Howe, Hubert S., Jr. "Music and electronics: A report," *Perspectives of New Music.* Spring-Summer, 1966.
Strang, Gerald. "The computer in musical composition," *Computers and automation,* Vol. 15, No. 8. 1966.
Tenney, James. "Musical composition with the computer," *Journal of the Acoustical Society* of America, Vol. 39. 1966.
Xenakis, Y. "Elements of a Stochastic music – I to IV," inclusive, *Gravesaner Blätter,* No. 18, 1960; No. 19/20, 1960; No. 21, 1961; No. 22, 1961; No. 23/24, 1962.

APPENDIX I B. 4

4. Score-drawing Program

Chang, Jih-Jie, and M. V. Mathews. "Score-drawing program," *Journal of the Audio Engineering Society,* 15.
Mathews, M. V., and L. Rosler. "Graphic Language for the Scores of computer generated Sounds," *Perspectives of New Music.* Spring-Summer, 1968, Vol. 6, No. 2.

APPENDIX I B. 5

5. Printing of Music by Computer

Bauer-Mengelberg, Stefan and Melvin Ferentz. "Research project in the utilization of high-speed electronic computing equipment for the preparation of photo-masters for music printing." Interim Report, January 31, 1968. Not published.

APPENDIX I B. 6

6. Computer Handling of Bibliographical Data

Brook, Barry S. "RILM Inaugural Report: January 1967," *Notes,* Vol. 23.
Brook, Barry S. "RILM Repertoire International de la Litterature Musicale," *Computers and the Humanities.*
Brook, Barry S. "Some new paths for music bibliography," *Computers in Humanistic Research.*
Kassler, Michael. "Toward Musical Information Retrieval," *Perspectives of New Music.* Spring-Summer, 1966.

APPENDIX II

Computer-dependent Musical Projects
in the United States
(A Partial List)

The categories of the following projects closely parallel the subdivisions of the bibliographical lists in Appendix I above. With a few notable exceptions (such as the Bell Telephone Laboratories' project) the projects listed below are abstracted from the publication *Computers and the Humanities*. For additional technical information, programming language, information on the availability of the programs, etc., readers are referred to the above-mentioned publication, or should get in direct contact with the investigators. The symbols, M3, M5, etc., serve as reference to *Computers and the Humanities*.

Musicological and Theoretical Investigations

University of Chicago Chanson Project. (M3)
    Principal investigator: Lawrence F. Bernstein, Assistant Professor, Dept. of Music, University of Chicago, 5802 S. Woodlawn Avenue, Chicago, Ill.

    Objective: Automated bibliographic and style-analytical study of the 16th Century chanson. Generation of a "Thematic Concordance" of the repertory: machine extraction of quantitative stylistic data. Scope and method: The entire repertory of the 16th Century French secular polyphonic chanson.
    Type of Computer: IBM 7094. Programming language and level: CLML Programming Language, FAP and Machine language.

Thematic Index of Sixteenth-Century Italian Music. (M5)

    Principal investigator: Harry B. Lincoln, Professor of Music, State University of New York at Binghamton, N. Y.

    Objective: To develop indices of various repertories of music in sixteenth-century Italy for purpose of identifying anonymous works, duplications, and borrowings. Scope and method: Specific areas developed and then various areas merged into total index. Coded interval sequence of incipits (e. g., +2+2+2-3-2+5+2) arranged in numerical order and compared.

    Type of computer: IBM 360/40. Programming language and level: FORTRAN IV.

Computer Music (M7)

    Principal investigator: L. Knopoff, Professor, University of California, Los Angeles, California, 90024. Associates: William Hutchinson, Mantle Hood.

    Objective: Analysis, synthesis, and performance of music.

    Type of computer: IBM 7094. Programming language and level: FORTRAN IV, MAP. Special features: Direct Data Connection (2 channels)

Investigation of Various Compositional Processes (M9)

>Chief investigator: Edward G. Kobrin, School of Music, Northwestern University, Evanston, Illinois, 60201. Associate: T. H. A. Ashford.

>Scope: Investigation of the use of various controls in the writing of music for large ensembles (symph. orch., symph. bands) with special consideration to transposing instruments. Method: 1. Serialize given parameters with emphasis on strict synchronization of vertical and horizontal serialization. 2. Choose instruments for transposition. 3. Re-program for correct pitch of these instruments.

>Type of computer: CDC 6400. Language and level: ALGOL 60

Structure of Atonal Music (M13)

>Chief investigator: Allen Forte, formerly Prof. of Music, Dept. of Humanities, Massachusetts Institute of Technology; now professor of the Theory of Music, Dept. of Music, Yale University, New Haven, Conn.

>Scope: Study structure of atonal compositions.
>Method: The complete score is represented in the input language developed by S. Bauer-Mengelberg. An analytical reading program operates on this representation to provide output subsequently processed at higher analytical levels.

>Computer: IBM 360-50. Language and level: SNOBOL 4.

A Syntax-Directed Compiler to Analyze
Musical Compositions and Text (M14)

>Principal investigator: Eors N. Ferentzy, Assistant Professor, Dept. of Computer Science, University of Toronto, Toronto, Canada. Associate: Jim Gabura.

>Objective: To gather statistics on the strings analyzed. Scope and method: A combination and extension of syntax, directed parsing, and Markovian analysis.

>Type of computer: IBM 360/50, 75, IBM 7094/II. Programming language and level: Specifications written in formula ALGOL, implementation in PL/I.

Harmonic Structure in Variation Movements
by Anton von Webern (M15)

>Principal investigator: Mary E. Fiore, Professor, Dept. of Music, State University College at Buffalo, 1300 Elmwood Ave., Buffalo, New York, 14222.

>Objective: To study harmonic usage as a form-defining element in Webern's movements in variation form and to trace the development of this usage through the composer's sketches for the movements analyzed. Scope and method: Basic procedures are pattern matching and comparisons of data sets. The structuring of data was developed from Allen Forte's "A Program for the Analytic Reading of Scores."

>Type of computer: CDC 6400. Programming language and level: SNOBOL with Ford-Columbia Input Code modified for use with 026 key punch.

Music Information Retrieval (M41 and M17)

Chief investigator: John Selleck, Technical Assistant, Dept. of Music, Princeton University, Princeton, N. J., 08540. Associates: Professor Lewis Lockwood, Professor Arthur Mendel.

Scope: To devise an information retrieval system capable of handling the type of music limited to one note at the time per line. It was designed specifically for choral polyphony of the Renaissance, particularly the works of Josquin.

Type of Computer: IBM 7094. Language and level: Fortran II and BEFAP.

Computer Sound Generation: Two Programs (M2)

Principal investigator: David Cohen, Music Dept., Arizona State University, Tempe, Arizona, 85281.

Objectives: To develop flexible and widely usable computer program(s) for sound generation. To write a non-technical manual which will enable composers with no previous computer experience to use the program(s). Scope and method: The programs are similar to the Bell Laboratories' Music IV Program.

Programming language and level: FORTRAN IV. May also require machine language.

Musical Composition (M4)

Principal investigator: Gerald Strang, Professor, Dept. of Music, California State College, Long Beach, California, 90804. Associate: Leon Knopoff.

Objective: To investigate the possibilities of computer sound synthesis and compositional techniques. Scope and method: Adaptation of Bell Telephone Laboratories' MUSIC IV.

Type of computer: IBM 7094. Programming language and level: FORTRAN IV and MAP. Special features: 2 channel Direct Data connection.

Musigol, An Electronic Music Preprocessor (M10)

Principal investigator: Donald MacInnis, Associate Professor, Dept. of Music, University of Virginia, Charlottesville, Virginia. Associates: William A. Wulf, Paul S. Davis, Donald Bowers, Donald Wright.

Objective: A versatile sound-generating program to study the effects of carefully controlled parameter changes on the perceived sound wave, and as a sound source for original musical compositions. Scope and method: MUSIGOL is a skeleton program which becomes complete when the researcher or composer supplies description of "instruments" with all their parameters, and the "score." MUSIGOL then "plays" the music by creating a magnetic tape with amplitude sample numbers at 20,000/sec.

Type of computer: Burroughs 5500 digital computer, and Ambilog 200 hybrid computer (as converter). Programming language and level: Extended ALGOL. Special features: Includes facilities for a Calcomp plotted graph of the final complex wave.

Computer Sound Generation

This research deals with computer sound generation and processing and the development of a sound generation program and language, namely Music V.
Principal investigator: M. V. Mathews, Director, Bell Telephone Laboratories, Murray Hill, New Jersey. Associates: Joan E. Miller, R. F. Moore, J. C. Risset.

Objectives:
1. Investigate the properties of sound relevant to its artificial synthesis and generation by computer.
2. Develop a language for describing sounds for the purposes of their synthesis.
3. Develop a practical, portable computer program which processes this sound language and generates resultant waveforms in digital samples.
4. Develop systems for efficient digital-to-analogue conversion of these digital samples.
5. Document the computer programs in such a way as to make them generally useful to a wide class of sound investigators, such as musicians, acousticans, speech researchers, psychologists, etc.

Scope and methods:
The Music V program represents a powerful logical system which can produce any sound that can be described in precise detail. This means that the program is potentially applicable to an extremely broad range of problems dealing with sound synthesis. In order to augment the useability of the program, it is coded almost entirely in a high-level language (Fortran IV) which is available on most modern computers.

Type of computer:
1. GE 635, a large multiprogrammed computer with 256 K of one microsecond memory.
2. DDP 224, a small computer with 16 K of two microsecond memory. Programming language: FORTRAN IV (high level) with two small assembly-language subroutines which are to be provided by the computer site.

Computer Sound Generation

Principal investigators: J. K. Randall, Associate Professor, and Godfrey Winham, Research Associate, both of Princeton University, New Jersey, and Assistant Professor Hubert S. Howe of Queens College, Queens, N. Y.

Objectives: Investigation of sound in connection with, and by means of, musical composition.

Scope and Method: Digital simulation, using the Music IV B computer program (a re-written and greatly expanded version of the original Music IV Program written at Bell Laboratories by M. V. Mathews and Joan Miller) by Godfrey Winham and Hubert Howe.

Type of computer: IBM 7094, 360/67, 360/91. Language and level: for the IBM 7094 – Fortran II and BEFAP; for the IBM 360 – Fortran IV.

APPENDIX III

A brief description of Music V program
by R. F. Moore, Bell Telephone Laboratories

Music V is a computer program which is designed to synthesize musical sounds and place them on magnetic tape. Furthermore, it is designed to be used by composers who are familiar with electronic music techniques but not computer programming. A summary of its operation might be as follows:

The composer "designs" the sounds he wishes to produce by specifying on IBM punched cards (a) the wave shapes he wishes to use and (b) computer "instruments" which can "play" these waveforms. The "instruments" are made up of basic and general "unit generators," such as oscillators, filters, reverberation units, etc., which are simulated by the operation of Music V. These basic "unit generators" may be thought of as connected together (in a way specified by the composer) to form an instrument. An example might be an oscillator (symbol: ⟨⟩) connected to a reverberation unit: (symbol: ⟨⟩) to an output sound collector (symbol: ⟨⟩). The oscillator has two inputs controlling amplitude and frequency, and an input telling it which of several previously-defined waveforms (sine, square, or other) to use. The entire instrument looks like this:

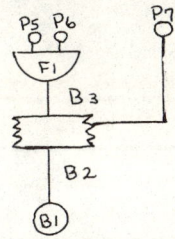

The composer causes Music V to simulate this instrument by typing the following on IBM punched cards:

INSTRUMENT 0 1;   (means define an instrument at time t=0 which we will refer to as instrument No. 1)

	(ampl.)	(freq)	(output)	(function)	(sum)
OSCILLATOR	P5	P6	B3	F1	P 10;

(means the first unit generator in instrument No. 1 is an oscillator. The amplitude of the oscillator is to be controlled by the fifth number (p5) written on a NOTE-playing card; the frequency is controlled by the sixth number; the connection B3 is to be used to connect this to the REVERB unit; function one (F 1) is to be used as the waveshape produced by this oscillator; the sum is special and is not relevant here.)

	(input)	(output)	(time constant)	(special)
REVERBERATOR	B3	B2	P7	B4;

(means the input to the reverberator will come through connecting link B3, the output will go to connecting link B2, and the seventh number on the NOTE-playing card will specify the time constant [reverb. time]).

	(input)	(output)
OUT	B2	B1;	(means take the contents of connecting link B2 and accumulate the sound into B1, which is the main sound output connection.)

END; (means this is the end of the description of instrument No. 1.)

The composer now has an "instrument" which can be "played" upon. He does this by writing "note-playing" instructions on the following IBM cards. Given the above instrument, he might write:

means play a note	starting time of note (in sec.)	instrument no.	duration (in sec.)	amplitude (in Db)	frequency (in HZ)	reverberation time
NOTE	1	1	3	62	440	2.3
P1	P2	P3	P4	P5	P6	P7

The computer would then simulate the operation if instrument number one is controlled by the parameters on the NOTE card.

On the inside, of course, the computer deals exclusively with numbers. The sounds produced are "described" by a long string of numbers which are stored on a computer tape and then converted into sound via a D/A converter.

Cvjetko Rihtman

THE PHILOSOPHY OF FOLK AND TRADITIONAL MUSIC STUDY IN YUGOSLAVIA

The term "folk music" seems a happy one to denote the traditional music practice of the broadest social classes; the expression is used by many people, and I see no need to seek another one. Greater difficulty is met in finding a term for the music practice of the higher social classes of Western urban civilization when trying to define folk music in relation to it. While the problem of designating the musical practice of the masses has been easily and quickly solved, a precise designation for the music of the higher classes has not existed in the past and remains a problem to this day. None of the terms proposed is above criticism: *musique proprement dite,* music in the true sense of the word, *musique savante,* art music, composed music, European music, music of the written European tradition, music of Western Europe . . .

The phrase "music in the true sense of the word" has had the greatest number of adherents, yet it is the least justifiable, chiefly because it is based on the untenable assumption that in addition to "true" music exists another music which is not true. The discussion of this term has led to the question of the essence of music — a question more complex than had been thought — and no one has succeeded in arriving at a definition which could not be applied equally well to both musical practices. Actually, the assumption behind the expression "music in the true sense of the word" derived from the conviction held by cultivated members of nineteenth century higher society that their music was the only "true" tonal art, since it was based on "natural" tonal scales whose qualities and laws of relationship were explained by natural physical phenomena and whose structure followed the logic of "pure" mind. Thus, it was believed, this music was universal and accessible to everybody. By the same token, another music, although it made use of musical sounds, could not correctly be regarded as music because it was in reality only a chaos of impure intervals between "uncultivated" tones. In my estimation, the prejudiced view of the European and his inability to understand the "primitive" peoples is nowhere reflected better than in Berlioz' statement:

> The people of the Indies and the Chinese would have a music like ours if they had a music at all. But, in this respect, they sank into the darkness of deepest barbarity and childlike ignorance, in which one can scarcely distinguish some helpless, lost attempts. What the

Orientals hold as music we would designate as a penetrating sound; for them, as for Macbeth's witches, ugly is beautiful.

Nor is the term *musique savante* a much happier choice, since it implies that in the creative process of this music, a self-conscious, rationally controlled method dominates, as opposed to an intuitive method. But how could a work created according to a rationally controlled method have the emotional effect necessary to a work of art? *Musique savante* is not a convenient term even when applied to a specifically cultivated music practice in contrast to a practice which is not consciously cultivated with the intention of development. The former is sometimes regarded as a mark of the dynamic progress of culture, while the latter is deprecated as an inert heritage transmitted through tradition. *Musique savante* is likewise not the correct term if its definition presupposes that only the professional composer is aware of what he does and operates according to a predetermined scheme which is logically conceived. How naive to assume that the folk artist – a poet, let us say – is not aware of what he does as he creates, but works purely instinctively without plan or else entirely through associations made on the inspiration of the moment.

Whatever term is selected, it must fit the essence of the matter; it can be found, therefore, only after a preliminary consideration of that essence. Examination of a large number of terms can lead to the discovery of a large number of viewpoints. Among the numerous viewpoints or theories, the more popular ones sought for the remnants of a heritage which the common people had adopted from the upper classes. Some researchers thought that the folk did not create (produce) anything, but only re-produced (Hoffman-Krayer); some even thought that as soon as the folk adopted an idea, they spoiled it *("Das Volk zersingt das angenommene Lied."* Naumann). Thus, any artistic value in folk art was denied.

A certain confusion thus exists, which makes it difficult to find a term that not only designates the one type of music practice, but at the same time permits a clearer distinction between the two types. The confusion exists because, while the meaning of that music (i. e., the art music of the higher classes), which as yet has no appropriate name, is not controversial, a serious controversy surrounds the question of what constitutes the essence of that music (i. e., folk music) which is quite suitably designated. However, even this suitable designation has been attacked. One such has been made by the distinguished Yugoslav scholar M. Murko. Although Murko knew well and at first hand the vital music tradition of the Yugoslav nationalities, he has exerted much effort to discredit the "romantic legend" about a "people who sing" and to justify the German theories that the folk do not create, but merely re-create what has already been created by talented individuals of the upper classes:

Il n'y a pas de doute pour moi que la poésie épique populaire actuelle provient, ainsi que la majeure partie de l'art populaire en général, des milieux chrétiens et musulmans les plus élevés. . . .

Ursprünglich war jedoch die Sängerkunst einer der feudalen Überreste des Mittelalters. . . .

If one accepts the belief that the people do not create, the question arises of the beginning of folk art. Some have thought it no older than two hundred years. But no primitive human community known has failed to engage in some sort of artistic activity. Furthermore, it has been convincingly shown that in such primitive communities — where no presumption can be entertained concerning the influence of "upper classes" — artistic activity, even with very limited means for its expression, is more varied in many ways than in highly developed civilizations, particularly with regard to its social function.

A Special Commission of the International Folk Music Council proposed a definition at the conference held in São Paulo, Brazil, in 1954; this definition was accepted by vote of the majority of members present. It stated that folk music is a product of tradition which has evolved through the process of oral transmission. The factors which shape tradition were named as continuity, variation, and selection. It was added that the term "folk music" could be applied both to the music produced by the community from the very beginning, without any influence from "art music," as well as to the music produced by an individual composer, if his music was afterwards accepted into the unwritten tradition of the community. But it cannot be applied to that composed popular music which is received by the community in its finished form and undergoes no subsequent changes, because it is the reshaping and re-creation of the music by the community that gives it the folk flavor.

Commenting on this definition, Charles Seeger observed in 1958 that all musical traditions, and not just that of folk music, are shaped by the factors of continuity, variation, and selection. I would add also that people often accept, and even submit to, outside influences; I see no specific folk practice in this process. Similar practices certainly occur in the creativity of urban civilizations. True, the great creators of civilization consciously seek *new* forms. But these are rare. Minor creators reject new forms in the beginning, but when the forms have achieved social recognition, they accept them readily, imitating them in a way that is occasionally more vulgar than artistic.

The definition of the IFMC Commission has much in common with the "reception theory" as it appears in the modified formulation of Seeger. He maintains that any song, regardless of its origin, can become a folk song if it is accepted by the people and reshaped by them in the spirit of collective poetry.

The Commission's definition is not far also from the "theory of production," according to which certain characteristics, representative of the masses, are inherent in folk song — its content, its language, its emotions, and the ways of thinking it reflects. But a song becomes a song of the community only after it is accepted and passed on by the people.

The traditional repertory is conceived in the IFMC definition as common knowledge in a specific community of undetermined size in which the individual is lost. The content of a repertory equals the sum of those items which are adopted — regardless of their origin. In order to become a part of the traditional repertory, an item must be adopted and, in the course of adoption, undergo certain changes. The question of "folk" in folk tradition is thus reduced to those changes which are imposed on adopted items during the process of their adoption or during their maintenance in the traditional repertory. No mention is made whether these changes affect content or form, nor is their relationship to the traditional forms specified. The forms, which are an essential element of a tradition, are not examined at all.

According to this understanding, improvised works should not be considered a part of the folk tradition if they are not yet adopted and it is not yet ascertained that they will remain in the memory of the people. Thus, for example, such items as a tape-recorded lamentation, improvised singing by the cradle, improprietous teasing during *kolo* dancing, and the like would not belong to the folk tradition; but the poet Aleksa Šantić's poem *Emina,* which is sung in Mostar to a folk tune, would belong. Such a simplified view of what constitutes the "folk" in folk traditions certainly makes the scholar's work easier, because it frees him from his most difficult and responsible duty — the eventual determination of the main features of various traditions which distinguish them from each other as well as those which form their common and distinctive characteristics.

The multiplicity of terms proposed reflects not only the different viewpoints of the various scholars who attempt to define the essence of these traditions, but also their utter disagreement with each other. Thus, it would be vain for us to hope that more comprehensive and systematic research will yield a successful explanation of folk art or fit it into any more predictable patterns. Pulikovski has maintained:

> This is because the scholars, with all their learning and considerable knowledge, are more and more estranged from the people and know their people less and less. Collections are made and catalogued; all kinds of phenomena, principles, perspectives, and similar German scientific concepts are discussed, but at the same time contact with the people is being lost. Judgments are then made *ex cathedra* about

things with which they have not really become acquainted. In no other branch of science has such unprofessionalism and ignorance remained as in that branch devoted to the study of folk song.

As the economy develops, so usually do the means of artistic production, resulting in more complex instruments, more complex instrumental techniques, and more complex forms. As techniques become more complex, the greater capabilities of some individuals are distinguished. Similarly, as the means of expression develops, the original mass of active participants in folk art is reduced, and a new mass of passive spectators forms. We may therefore conclude that the practices of folk art — which are unquestionably older than those of more highly developed social classes — possess some sort of reciprocal relationship in their development to the development of the society in which they exist. The reasons for the various conditions of growth and development of artistic practices may also be, together with general economic conditions, at the basis of varying social relations, of class, religion, etc., within the same or different communities. We cannot talk about folk art as a secondary phenomenon and search for its beginnings apart from the beginnings of musical art *per se*, but we can and should search for the beginnings of divisions and the formation of separate traditions under the changing conditions of their evolution.

The answer to the basic questions about the origin and essence of music should not be sought outside, but within the context in which the creative process of the gifted individual occurs. Likewise, the essential differences between various traditions have to be established through the method of analysis, defining constituent elements, observing relationships, distinguishing common and distinctive characteristics of the traditions, and at the same time observing their evolution in relation to the conditions of development of the society to which they belong.

Thus, it is illusory to seek answers to the questions raised on the basis of such factors as whether the authors are known or unknown, whether a refrain is recorded or not, whether a practice consciously uses a more or less established theory, or knowledge derived from experience, whether that practice is followed by literate and educated professionals or by illiterate amateurs, or whether one practice uses a literary language while another uses a regional dialect. . . . Not one of these or other similar factors, taken separately or together, can define folk music or its "undeveloped" forms; nor can they explain the constitution of its "naive" style, regardless of whether this style has some appeal to the urban ear.

It is a fact that primitive forms are not complex but simple, when observed in certain relationships. In the main, they can be reduced to a very small number of elements which are associated with each other and ordered in a multitude of ways. If such forms appear disconnected, confused, or haphazard, it is because the observer does not perceive the order governing the association of the various elements — the principle that shapes the overall structure. It is precisely that certain order, that principle of structure, which reveals a manner of musical thought, a certain social milieu, this milieu's creative method and the traits which most vividly characterize its tradition and most vividly distinguish it from the traditions of other social communities.

The relationships between elements which determine a form do not exist outside of awareness, but in the individual or collective awareness of all who participate in the music practice — actively or passively, as creators, performers, or listeners. These relationships are consciously in the minds of all members of a certain social milieu in whose traditional artistic practice they have achieved the status of customary, established, esthetic norms.

Even though these relationships manifest themselves in practice with greater or lesser degrees of awareness, like all habits, it does not mean that the relationships were laid down *a priori,* nor that they sprang from some inherited instinct without the participation of the mind and the will. On the contrary, the ability to observe and reproduce the relationships results from a long period of training, which begins in earliest childhood in agreeable conditions, and is not isolated, but rather a part of the particular social milieu.

The folk artist does not seek new means of expression, new forms, or new structural principles. As yet, no new forms have been observed which were created in folk practice. The improvisation of a new verse regularly follows the metric formula already outlined in the existing refrains. Even when speaking of the most recent events, people speak in their accustomed and traditional manner. It is in this way that folk art basically differs from the art of a professional author of high urban culture. The essential difference between folk art and the art of the high urban civilizations of the West lies not in the fact that the former is transmitted orally and the latter in a written form, or that one imitates while the other creates, or that the former is maintained carelessly and instinctively while the latter undergoes a process of careful and conscious cultivation and development. The essential difference lies rather in the fact that the forms — the language of musical thought and the manner in which a people express their emotions and psychic experience — are traditional forms.

Barbara Krader

THE PHILOSOPHY OF FOLK AND TRADITIONAL MUSIC STUDY IN THE UNITED STATES

The study of folk music and the study of Oriental art music or African or American tribal music or even popular music are undertaken, by and large, in the United States by different sets of scholars. Further, folk music studies are diffused, split up into several approaches and divided rather sharply into camps of observers and participants. It will be easier, therefore, to start with the discussion of American points of view in ethnomusicology.

I

Our separate category of ethnomusicology emerged out of despair over the exclusively historical approach of the musicologists and their preoccupation with Western art music. The Society for Ethnomusicology was founded in 1955 by a group including anthropologists and musicologists. The term ethnomusicology, apparently coined by Jaap Kunst in 1940, was adopted in preference to the old term comparative musicology, on the grounds that the discipline was not solely or even predominantly comparative. Willard Rhodes, the first President of the Society, said "the linking of ethnology and musicology in the new name . . . does give fresh emphasis to the symbiotic relationship of the two disciplines here employed."[1] Rhodes also indicated that the difference between the earlier comparative musicology and ethnomusicology was in emphasis: the pioneers in the field had developed methods and theories primarily for the scientific analysis and classification of musical data.[2]

Rhodes, Merriam and McAllester, Waterman and Nettl, Herzog and Seeger were agreed on the importance of learning about man through his music. Charles Seeger had said a few years earlier: "the ultimate task of musicology is to contribute to the general study of man what can be known of man as music-maker and music-user."[3] Merriam's definition of ethnomusicology as "the study of music in culture" became widely known.[4]

In 1958 the Society had another lively discussion about aims and objectives. It was said that "our basic questions . . . revolve around the relation between music and culture. The core of the matter is that we must embrace the subject in its own terms: these may be anthropological, psychological or geographical."[5] Yet objections were raised even when it was suggested that the material be organized by geographical area. Instead it was felt that the study should "start with objective criteria so that expectations of music area do not introduce distortion, and then see if such areas do indeed emerge."[6] Leonard Meyer stated succinctly two points over which there was to be much discussion in later years: "it is not how *we* analyze it, but how *they*, the native speakers and singers, analyze it, that counts." And he suggested the presence in our field of interest of two basic elements: 1) the purely cultural, in which sense the vocabulary of music varies from culture to culture; 2) an overall syntax that may be applied to all music.[7] We shall return to Meyer below, to discuss a later elaboration of his approach.

The anthropologists in ethnomusicology in particular have emphasized the importance of fieldwork. During the same discussion in 1958 David McAllester laid stress upon music in its social context:

> I want to study culture through the avenue of music, to study music as social behavior. Music is essentially a matter of values rather than a matter of notes. With our emphasis on the written word we sometimes confuse speech with writing; it is the same mistake to confuse music with notes. With notes scientific detachment is possible, but not with music as a living part of culture. . . . I would stress the value of field work — you must experience the music in its setting in order to understand it. It is, more than many aspects of culture, one we can participate in. . . . The rewards in rapport and insight are very great.[8]

Alan Merriam has frequently referred to the necessity for the ethnomusicologist of "spending time in the field gathering his material at first hand,"[9] and has gone further to criticize severely those who merely transcribe and analyze without this field experience.

Thus far, the emphasis has been upon the cultural anthropologists' viewpoint. Seeger and Meyer are not anthropologists, it is true, but they are in accord at least with the stress upon the cultural or social or functional dimension, which had been relatively neglected by historical musicologists.

Professor Mantle Hood, a musicologist, represents a different approach to the study of musics outside the Western art tradition. His stress is upon what he calls "bi-musicality."[10] At the University of California in Los Angeles, his Institute of Ethnomusicology, which has the largest number of students of ethnomusicology of any college or university in the United States, emphasizes learning to perform so-called exotic instruments, in particular the gamelan of Java, but Japanese or Iranian instruments may be studied alternatively. When Hood undertook intensive study of the Javanese gamelan, he says "I found that to begin to understand the music I must also seek to understand the people, their ethnic standards, their customs, literature, theatre, art and religion."[11]

And further, addressing the Javanese, he writes: "We Western musicians can learn much from you . . . something from your methods of musical training, from the rhythmic structure of your *gending,* from the function and preservation of a concept like *patet,* from your voice control (intonation) in singing, from your gamelan conductor who is heard but not seen, from your feeling for playing in ensemble, from the impersonal quality of your compositions."[12] Hood believes in the importance of learning the traditional way of performance on musical instruments of non-Western cultures, as a means not only to learn to value a different system but to increase sensitivity to other musical cultures.[13] A splendid example of the prejudices to overcome is his reference to Western perfect pitch, which "in the world of microtonal inflections . . . is in fact an imperfect sense of pitch."[14]

Hood's point of view reflects in part a statement by Charles Seeger in 1952, warning that "the particular musical tradition . . . that the student himself carries . . . does, and must . . . constitute an equal part of the working base of every musicologist's study, alongside of the particular language tradition . . . he carries. For it is quite as much *in their terms* that he may distinguish the present or past of any other music. . . .[15] As he said, "we do *not* start with a *tabula rasa,* on which we put the remote music as in an exhibition case."[16] Elsewhere he noted that "we must learn the critical standards of other peoples and approach their music with their canons, not our own."[17]

At the outset of this paper, there was reference to dissatisfaction with the limited range of interests of the American musicologists. We did not regard ourselves as a small separate branch of musicology; on the contrary, we wanted to broaden musicology. Thus in the 1958 discussion, Seeger made the statement that "we must make our domain world music, including all of Euro-American music, not only folk, popular and tribal music. This includes the fine art. . . ."[18] At the founding of the Society, Rhodes advocated the inclusion of popular music and study of the dance among our fields.[19] Some background on other views of the scope of ethnomusicology is provided by George Herzog, who remarked that Jaap Kunst, Curt Sachs, and he had long taken for granted that the study of folk music of Western civilization was a part of ethnomusicology.[20] It may be said that Herzog certainly did follow the work of European folk music specialists, especially that of Bartók, and wrote on the subject in American scholarly journals. Kunst had collected Dutch folk songs as a young man, and retained interest so much that he was President of the International Folk Music Council in his last years. Sachs once advocated the study of European folk music, but for somewhat limited ends. In practice, however, the Society for Ethnomusicology pays little serious attention to

European folk music. It is more inclined to study popular music than folk music, perhaps because it finds the subject wider and less explored.

Nevertheless one cannot leave unmentioned the outstanding American collections of folk music in Yugoslavia and Greece, by the classic scholars Milman Parry and Albert Lord, and by Professor Notopoulos. While their purpose was to illuminate Homer by investigation of the actual composition of heroic songs, the collections have yet to be used for the study of many other aspects of Yugoslav and Greek folk song tradition, in particular their music.

A further basic problem which occupies our attention is change. Professor Bascom gave an excellent outline of the ways in which anthropologists and musicologists can study stability and change in tradition, in a paper presented in Belgium at the International Folk Music Council Conference in 1958.[21] In the discussion which followed, Dr. Wachsmann remarked that perhaps the central problem of ethnomusicology lay in assessing the significance of the changes that took place. He said it was "difficult to distinguish between deep and radical change and superficial and temporary change."[22] George Herzog then noted the difficulty in studying change without observations at different periods, and indicated that a further difficulty lay "in deciding what should be measured in order to assess the significance of the changes. Different societies had quite different attitudes towards experimentation."[23]

It must occur both to European colleagues in ethnomusicology and American historical musicologists that we pay very little attention to the historical dimension. In a sense this is true. We have, so far as I know, produced only one recent study on origins, by Kolinski, and our research tends to be synchronic, largely because we are eager to use and evolve new methods and techniques. Indeed, such a strong tendency exists to observe music as it is practiced today, that a trend against the study of problems like "authenticity" is apparent. Nevertheless research on American Indian music has not overlooked earlier reports of missionaries, travelers and government officials, and certain studies, in particular Merriam's monograph on the Flathead Indians,[24] devote much space to such accounts, comparing and evaluating them, to provide not only historical depth, but also evidence about change. Also in Professor Nettl's recent articles on the Blackfoot Indian musical culture,[25] he divides his treatment into a section dealing with traditions before and about 1900, one on current traditions, of the 1960's, and one on the music of the songs.

Just as an example of the historical approach we do *not* follow, I cite the title of a paper of 1937 by Professor Curt Sachs: "Towards a Pre-History of Occidental Music."[26] In fact, the paper is valuable for recommending the study of European folk music, but only in terms of establishing chronology with relation to art music. Walter Wiora pursues the history of the world's music in his *Four Ages of Music*[27] and elsewhere, and other Europeans favor this subject of inquiry, but it has not found followers in the United States to my knowledge.

A view quite different from those cited above is maintained by Dr. Mieczyslaw Kolinski, who was a founder of the Society for Ethnomusicology and its second President. Perhaps the most succinct statement of his view is the following: "Only by establishing as clearly as possible both the extent and the limitations of musical universals will we be able to successfully explore the infinite multifariousness of music." [28] Thus he asserts that musical universals exist and that it is of the highest importance to establish what they are. Elsewhere he emphasizes the importance of an awareness of the existing links between the musical languages around the world, and adds that these links are apparently due to "basic similarities in the psycho-physical constitution of mankind."[29] He terms this field of study comparative musicology, using the old term.

In his 1967 article "Recent Trends in Ethnomusicology," Kolinski came out sharply against Merriam, as the spokesman for the cultural approach, on two particular points. He disagreed with Merriam's statement that "while the study of music as a structural form and as an historic phenomenon is of high, and basic importance, in my own view it holds this position primarily as it leads to the study of the broader questions of music in culture."[30] This difference of emphasis is clear from the statements of Kolinski quoted above.

Another fundamental point of disagreement is Merriam's assertion that "music is a . . . phenomenon which exists only in terms of social interaction."[31] Kolinski holds, and indeed believes he has shown "that *musical anthropology* forms an integral part of general anthropology . . . [while] *comparative musicology* forms an integral part of general musicology; therefore the fusion of the two subject matters into one autonomous discipline seems inconceivable."[32] In the view of Kolinski, collection in the field should be made by anthropologists, who are trained in this, and transcription and analysis should be carried out by musicologists, separately. They should work together, of course, each to understand the information and insights provided by the other. But music is to be analyzed *qua* music.

Although Kolinski is somewhat isolated, his influence is not inconsiderable. His transcriptions and analyses of Suriname music are studied as a kind of basic text in method.[33] His classification of tonal structures, his method of analysis of the structure of melodic movement, and his exposition of "tint" as a part of his theory of tonal structure[34] may all come to be used some day. Certainly Kolinski's views coincide with those of Wiora on comparative musicology.[35]

In a 1960 paper, Leonard Meyer noted that once music was regarded as a universal language, and it was believed that absolute laws existed which governed the structure and development of all music. When these laws were not found this "form of monism" went out of fashion. "Then . . . an equally monistic relativism . . . sought to study each culture and each music 'in its own terms' and . . . looked with suspicion upon any search for universal principles."[36] The second approach gathered much valuable data, but its avoidance of cross-cultural questions may have caused it to be relatively fruitless.[37]

Then he makes the useful observation that the data gathered by the descriptive method yield relatively few observable regularities, and adds that "the descriptive method is less than satisfactory . . . because it ignores those psychological concepts which might provide common principles for interpreting and explaining the enormous variety of musical means found in different cultures."[38]

Meyer's reference to two extreme approaches, that of universal laws, and that of description of each culture and music in its own terms, sums up perhaps the isolation of Kolinski, whose view is out of fashion, and the shortcomings of the descriptive approach, which is very much in fashion in the United States.

In the final section of this paper we shall turn to psychological questions in the discussion of Lomax and cantometrics.

Professor Kwabena Nketia of Ghana plays an important role in American ethnomusicology, for he knows his own culture from the inside, in addition to being a master of our tools of investigation. His work with Merriam over many years, and his collaboration with Hood have been of great value to the field in general. He writes as follows on how to study music in culture: "Even to those whose music we investigate a musical tradition consists of 'intrinsic' and 'extrinsic' facts of some sort, of repertoire and the oral traditions associated with it. . . . The importance of an integrated approach in the study of African music does not lie only in the fact that the music is organized as part of the process of living together, but also in the fact that formal structure and contexts of use often interact."[39] Further, he writes "in my experience a 'contextual' technique . . . handles 'music in culture' most adequately. It is principally a perceptive technique and requires both analysis (involving the abstraction of elements from wholes such as culture, situation, event, song, etc.) and synthesis (or the interrelations of such elements to one another and to wholes)."[40]

While American ethnomusicologists are open to the views of specialists from all parts of the world, for their subject is worldwide, it is my opinion that Professor Nketia, for a variety of reasons, carries special weight at the present time.

II

The discussion of American approaches to the study of folk song will be more general. As in the preceding section, however, the emphasis will be upon our thinking since World War II.

Folk song research in the nineteenth and early twentieth centuries focused upon the ballad, stressing the texts and rarely bothering with the music. Professor Child's great five volume collection of English and Scottish ballad texts (with a few tunes), the basic edition of which appeared in 1882-1898, was the work of a scholar who had not engaged, so far as I know, in collecting. The stress on English and Scottish tradition was typical. To this day, the bulk of American folklore studies emanates from university English Departments, thus becoming a branch of literature, and the ballad occupies pride of place, always with due reference and reverence to the Child collection. Yet B. H. Bronson demonstrates that music need not be excluded from the research of English professors, for he has given us three volumes (so far) of tunes to the Child ballads.[41]

A second milestone in folk song research was the collection by the Englishman Cecil Sharp and his assistant Maud Karpeles in the American southern Appalachian mountains in 1916-1918. This time the music was given full attention. They were delighted at finding so many English songs which had seemingly disappeared in England, among them numerous ballads, and modal melodies. The first publication of songs from this collection, issued in 1917, was followed by a greatly expanded posthumous edition, also entitled *English Folk Songs from the Southern Appalachians,* appearing in 1932, edited by Maud Karpeles. It is one of the great American collections.

I will mention only one other collector who began before the 1930's. John A. Lomax made his first field trip in 1904 for Harvard, to study (naturally) American ballads. A Texan, his interests went beyond English ballads to embrace cowboy and Negro songs. His *Cowboy Songs and other Frontier Ballads* (1915) was an early landmark, although it had few tunes. (A second edition contains more melodies.) In June 1933 he with his son Alan began an epoch-making collection of Negro folk songs, recorded on discs, traveling through eleven southern states, and covering 16,000 miles. This collection, sponsored by and deposited at the Library of Congress, was closely related to the development of the Library's Archive of Folk Song. In his autobiography *Adventures of a Ballad Hunter,* John Lomax writes (p. 296) that he and Alan contributed to the Archive of Folk Song more than 10,000 songs recorded "in the fields." David McAllester has published a perceptive essay on the collections of the Lomaxes and their books.[42] With this brief background, we can proceed to discuss what D. K. Wilgus has referred to as the cult of beauty and the cult of the common man.[43]

Cecil Sharp believed the permanent value of folk song lay in its intrinsic artistic qualities.[44] Miss Karpeles remarks: "No one would claim that every folk song is a great work of art. That Cecil Sharp did not do so is shown by the fact that he published for general use only about ten per cent of the songs that he collected."[45] It is precisely this selectivity, and the reasons advanced for it, which are not acceptable today to many American folk song students. In fairness, it must be recalled that Sharp's book *The English Folk Song; Some Conclusions* was published in 1907, as part of the renaissance of interest in English folk songs, of which he was a great leader. His appeal was nationalistic: to restore the fine tradition of English folk music to the nation, that all might be justly proud of it. Part of its value lay in its preservation in the rural tradition, but above all, it was uniquely English.

European folk song specialists will not be surprised by these emphases. The esthetic beauty of Vuk Karadžić's collections of songs impressed Goethe and Grimm, the language of the folk poetry was a fundamental part of the literary language as it became established by Vuk, Njegoš and the Croatian poets, and the originality of the national folk heritage was of great importance.

In the United States, however, a reaction developed to the cult of beauty and Englishness, and some articulate investigators, including the Lomaxes, began to collect and write about the music of the common man, the Negro convicts, the poor people in the Ozarks, the lumbermen, the miners, etc. The expression of the life of the poor was important, and even regarded as the expression of the American people. Probably the less literary the song was, the more avidly it was collected.

In a recent lecture on American "art" music in the 1920's and 1930's, Eric Salzman spoke of the innovations of the 1920's and how this movement ebbed all over the world in the later 1930's and 1940's with the Depression and the War. In the United States he thought this change reflected several pressures or movements, that of leftwing idealism, one of general conservatism, and a middle-of-the-road move to have concert music reach wider audiences. In the field of folk music, the emphasis on study of the music of the common man became apparent in the 1930's and is still very strong today, especially among the urban folk song revivalists and some leftwing people. Another focus of interest to which folk music was attracted along with so-called serious music in the 1930's and 1940's, was nationalism. What was American? The Lomax folk song collections published in 1941 and 1947 were called *Our Singing Country* and *Folk Song: U. S. A.* The poet Carl Sandburg earlier published a collection of folk songs called *The American Songbag,* and he gave recitals of folk songs.

Thus we have the trends of nationalism and the importance of the common man. Within this framework, some lasting and valuable work has been done. George Korson, for example, collected and published folk songs and folk lore of mines in Pennsylvania, from the 1920's onward. Two records of his material have been issued by the Library of Congress Archive of Folk Song. He has left us a wonderful social history of a segment of American industrial society, one which has almost disappeared, with the folk songs the miners sang set like jewels within their context. There is a relatively early account of one singer and the publication of his repertoire in *Negro Folk Songs as Sung by Lead Belly* (1934) by the Lomaxes. George Herzog did the music transcriptions. That Lead Belly was a murderer did not stop the Lomaxes, though it may cause others to question how typical his repertoire might be.[46] There is also the opposite kind of study: that of variants of a single song. Charles Seeger has produced such a special study on our most widespread ballad: Barbara Allen. It was published separately as a commentary to a special record issued by the Archive of Folk Song.[47] There have been more regional collections of folk songs in the last twenty or thirty years, and other special occupational lore has been studied. Herbert Halpert did a vast collection from the backwoods country of New Jersey in the late 1930's, unpublished alas, from which he drew important conclusions about the vitality of oral tradition. He writes, for example, of local songs, such as those about local crimes or disasters, that this group "is more important for understanding the function of folk song in a community than is an infrequently sung or little known older ballad."[48] He also concludes that "the presence or absence of parodies or local songs is a test of the vitality of a folk song tradition."[49] One wonders if this is corroborated in Europe too, or if such questions have been investigated in Yugoslavia.

Limits of space and time require me to dwell only briefly on the urban "folk music" development in the United States, which is partly commercial, partly political and leftwing, partly a genuine part of a genuine protest movement. It is not "folk" in the old sense of oral tradition, but it *is* widely popular, actively sung and spread by records and radio, and people invent their own words and sing what they feel. Cecil Sharp would not have liked it at all. I think it is a significant part of our culture, especially that of our youth, and needs studying. The only study I have seen is *Freedom in the Air; Song Movements of the Sixties* by Josh Dunson (1965), which is engagé, but useful.

There is no doubt that the younger scholars, ethnomusicologists and folklorists, are studying such themes as popular music, commercial hillbilly music, religious revival music.[50] Indeed a splendid serious paper on popular music, defining the subject and giving it a new term "mesomusic" was contributed by the senior musicologist Carlos Vega.[51]

As the final part of my paper, I wish to discuss two computer studies now being made. Benjamin Suchoff, of the Bartók Archives in New York, who has worked intensively with Bartók's melodic classification system while preparing the manuscript of Bartók's *Rumanian Folk Music* for publication,[52] has worked with Bartók's tabulation of Serbo-Croatian material, made for the 1951 collection,[53] but never published. Suchoff took the transcriptions from that collection and made a lexicographical ordering of it by computer. The melodies had been divided into sections by Bartók, and Suchoff used the sections as separate entities for the project. For each one a punchcard was made with a string of characters which reflected the interval sequence in terms of numbers preceded by plus or minus to indicate rising or falling. The machine can then arrange all the strings in numerical order and print them out. Identical strings will be single-spaced apart, while others are double-spaced, so the eye sees the identifications. Suchoff has omitted indications of repeated notes, and rhythmic characteristics, but says they can be programmed. He also notes that Kodály examined his system and felt it was valid, but indicated that the rhythmical aspects would need to be considered when treating Hungarian material.[54] Suchoff's contention is that Bartók's indexing systems can be adapted to data processing, making possible international comparisons of melodic material, eventually of rhythmic material and even perhaps of folk song texts. Bartók completed a rhythmic index of the entire Hungarian folk song collection before he came to the United States. He had also evolved a classification of folk song texts. Suchoff has won financial support for further work along these lines, and several foreign archives will send him musical material to index by computer. This may become an important tool for comparative research.

The other system, which is anthropologically oriented, is Alan Lomax's "cantometrics" study. I shall not describe his 37 points of analysis but concentrate upon the principles involved in the study. The outline is based on his article "Song Structure and Social Structure."[55]

The basic framework of his study is music as a form of human behavior, and the goal is to trace the shapes of musical behavior and to relate the set of behavior to its precise cultural setting. (This refers to the separate cultures or cultural areas distinguished by social anthropologists.) "Then it should be possible to discern the bonds between musical patterns and the socio-psychological traits. . . ."[56]

His major premise is that music expresses emotion, and with that assumption he continues:

> I. Therefore, when a distinctive consistent musical style lives in a culture . . . , one can posit the existence of a distinctive set of emotional needs or drives that are somehow satisfied or evoked by this music.
> II. If such a musical style occurs within only a limited pattern of variation in the similar cultural setting and over a long period of

time, one may assume that a stable expressive and emotional pattern has existed in group A in area B through time T.[57]

In the study he has sought a method which would locate sets of musical phenomena cross-culturally. In 1961, he examined from six to twenty musical examples from each of 250 culture areas. As his analytic technique is designed to look at gross traits rather than the detail of music, the difficulties imposed by having small samples and the lack of absolute certainty that they are representative are mitigated.[58]

Lomax states that his points of analysis or performance profiles show up stylistic patterns so quickly and clearly that even when a large sample is available it has been found unnecessary to analyze more than two or three examples. To summarize the elements analyzed by Lomax, they take into account melody, rhythm, harmony, and interval size in general ways. They also examine the size and structure of the music-making group, the location and role of leadership in the group, the type and degree of integration in the group, further the type and degree of melodic, rhythmic, and vocal embellishment in a sung performance are characterized, along with the qualities of the singing voice normally used in the culture. The generality of the musical characterization can be shown by the fact that melodic shape is analyzed as arched or terraced or undulating or descending. Overall range is rated in five degrees, from a second to two octaves or more. The average width of intervals is rated in five degrees, from dominance of narrow intervals (microtones) to dominance of wide intervals (fourths and fifths).[59] Bosnian polyphonic singing in seconds would belong in the narrowest rating here, presumably.

Lomax indicated several conclusions which appeared to be justified by his evidence, of which I cite three:

> 1) As long as music is considered cross-culturally as a whole and in behavioral terms, it is possible to locate structure comparable to known culture patterns.
> 2) These esthetic structures remain relatively stable through time and space.
> 3) These stable structures correspond to and represent patterns of interpersonal relationship which are fundamental in the various forms of social organization.[60]

One feels some scepticism about this. First, he may base generalizations for large areas on a small sample of music. Also he implies that he has not analyzed all the material available to him in some cases. In fact, there may be a great variety of musical types in one area. Second, his second point appears to be untested, for he lacks evidence of the amount of variation in the cultural setting, and is not studying evidence over a long period of time. Third, some of the judgments required for his performance profiles seem too subjective. He distinguishes five levels in volume of singing from very soft to very loud, but surely no two persons would agree on the middle distinctions. The same might be said of five degrees of nasality in singing.

The most valuable aspect of the cantometrics project, it seems to me, is its scrutiny of social behavior in musical performance in relation to musical characteristics. Furthermore, in its results the patterns of the performance profiles may cast light on the boundaries of cultures or cultural areas for the anthropologists. This too would be a valuable contribution to scholarship.

In conclusion, Americans who study traditional or folk music today want to study it in its social context, want thereby to have contact with and to understand people different from themselves, and they prefer to collect now rather than sit at home and study previous collections. They are sceptical of earlier work, and of comparisons and historical chronologies. Perhaps they are somewhat reluctant to study theories. Professor Nettl has said that ethnomusicology has not contributed new purposes to music research but new techniques and approaches.[61] Although our journal *Ethnomusicology* publishes articles by foreign scholars like Wiora, Schneider and others, and the dissenting views of Kolinski, our interests remain mostly as described above, without much intercourse with European ethnomusicology or current European folk music study.

NOTES

[1]"On the Subject of Ethno-Musicology," *Ethnomusicology Newsletter*, No. 7 (1956), p. 3.

[2]Ibid., p. 5.

[3]"Preface to the Description of a Music," *Report of Fifth Congress of International Society of Musical Reserarch, Utrecht 1952* (Den Haag, 1953), p. 366.

[4]E. g., Alan P. Merriam, "Ethnomusicology; Discussion and Definition of the Field," *Ethnomusicology*, Vol. 4 (1960), pp. 107-114.

[5]"Whither Ethnomusicology?," *Ethnomusicology*, Vol. 3 (1959), p. 100. (Report of two panel discussions at the meetings of the Society, December 29 and 30, 1958.)

[6]Ibid.

[7]Ibid., p. 103.

[8]Ibid.

[9]"Ethnomusicology; Discussion and Definition . . .," loc. cit., p. 113.

[10] "The Challenge of 'Bi-Musicality'," *Ethnomusicology*, Vol. 4 (1960), pp. 55-59.
[11] *The Nuclear Theme as a Determinant of Patet in Javanese Music* (Groningen, Djakarta: J. B. Wolters, 1954), p. vi.
[12] Ibid., p. vii.
[13] "Training and Research Methods in Ethnomusicology," *Ethnomusicology Newsletter*, No. 11 (1957), pp. 2-8.
[14] "The Challenge of 'Bi–Musicality,'" loc. cit., p. 56.
[15] "Preface to the Description of a Music," loc. cit., p. 362.
[16] Ibid., p. 361.
[17] "Whither Ethnomusicology?," loc. cit., p. 102.
[18] Ibid.
[19] Willard Rhodes, "On the Subject of Ethno-Musicology," loc. cit., pp. 3-4.
[20] "Music at the Fifth International Congress of Anthropological and Ethnological Sciences, Philadelphia, U. S. A.," *Journal of the International Folk Music Council*, Vol. 9 (1957), p. 72.
[21] William Bascom, "The Main Problems of Stability and Change in Tradition," *Journal of the International Folk Music Council*, Vol. 11 (1959), pp. 7-12.
[22] Ibid., p. 12.
[23] Ibid.
[24] Merriam, *Ethnomusicology of the Flathead Indians* (New York: Wenner-Gren Foundation, 1967).
[25] Bruno Nettl, "Studies in Blackfoot Indian Musical Culture," Part I, *Ethnomusicology*, Vol. 11 (1967), pp. 141-160; Part II, ibid., pp. 293-309; Part III, *Ethnomusicology*, Vol. 12 (1968), pp. 11-48.
[26] "Towards a Pre-History of Occidental Music," *Papers Read by Members of the American Musicological Society at the Annual Meeting held in Pittsburgh, Pa., December 29 and 30, 1937* (1937), pp. 91-97.
[27] *Die vier Weltalter der Musik* (Stuttgart: W. Kohlhammer, 1961). English: *The Four Ages of Music* (New York: W. W. Norton, 1965).
[28] "Letter to the Editor," *Ethnomusicology*, Vol. 11 (1967), p. 239.
[29] "Ethnomusicology, its Problems and Methods," *Ethnomusicology Newsletter*, No. 10 (1957), p. 6.
[30] "Ethnomusicology; Discussion and Definition . . . ," loc. cit., p. 113.
[31] *The Anthropology of Music* (Evanston, Illinois: Northwestern University Press, 1964), p. 27.
[32] Mieczyslaw Kolinski, "Recent Trends in Ethnomusicology," *Ethnomusicology*, Vol. 11 (1967), p. 5.
[33] "Suriname Music," in Melville J. and Frances S. Herskovits, *Suriname Folklore* (New York: Columbia University Press, 1936), pp. 489-740.
[34] "Recent Trends . . . ," loc. cit., pp. 1-24.
[35] Walter Wiora, "Idee und Methode 'vergleichender' Musikforschung," *Kongressbericht der Internationalen Gesellschaft für Musikwissenschaft, Salzburg 1964*, Band I – Aufsätze zu den Symposia (1964), pp. 3-10.
[36] Leonard B. Meyer, "Universalism and Relativism in the Study of Folk Music," *Ethnomusicology*, Vol. 4 (1960), p. 49.
[37] Ibid., pp. 49-54.
[38] Ibid., p. 51.
[39] J. H. Kwabena Nketia, "The Problem of Meaning in African Music," *Ethnomusicology*, Vol. 6 (1962), p. 3.
[40] Ibid., p. 4.
[41] Bertrand H. Bronson, *The Traditional Tunes of the Child Ballads with their texts according to the extant records of Great Britain and America* (Princeton, New Jersey: Princeton University Press, 1959ff.).
[42] "A Review Essay: Alan Lomax and American Folk Song," *Ethnomusicology*, Vol. 6 (1962), pp. 233-238.
[43] *Anglo-American Folksong Scholarship since 1898* (New Brunswick, New Jersey: Rutgers University Press, 1959), p. xiii.

[44] Cecil J. Sharp, *English Folk Song; Some Conclusions,* 4th revised ed., edited by Maud Karpeles (London: Mercury, 1965), p. xv.
[45] Ibid., p. xviii.
[46] Cf., D. K. Wilgus, *Anglo-American Folksong Scholarship since 1898* (New Brunswick, New Jersey: Rutgers University Press, 1959), pp. 218-219.
[47] "Versions and Variants of the Tunes of 'Barbara Allen' in the Archive of Folk Song of the Library of Congress," *Selected Reports,* No. 1 (Institute of Ethnomusicology, Los Angeles, California, 1967), pp. 120-167.
[48] "Vitality of Tradition and Local Songs," *Journal of the International Folk Music Council,* Vol. 3 (1951), p. 40.
[49] Ibid.
[50] Carl I. Betz, "Popular Music and the Folk Tradition," *Journal of American Folklore,* Vol. 80 (1967), pp. 130-142.
   Robert B. Cantrick, "The Blind Men and the Elephant: Scholars on Popular Music," *Ethnomusicology,* Vol. 9 (1965), pp. 100-114.
   James C. Downey, "Revivalism, the Gospel Songs and Social Reform," *Ethnomusicology,* Vol. 9 (1965), pp. 115-125.
   Neil V. Rosenberg, "From Sound to Style: the Emergence of Bluegrass," *Journal of American Folklore,* Vol. 80 (1967), pp. 143-150.
[51] "Mesomusic: an Essay on the Music of the Masses," *Ethnomusicology,* Vol. 10 (1966), pp. 1-17.
[52] Béla Bartók, *Rumanian Folk Music,* ed. Benjamin Suchoff (Den Haag: Martinus Nijhoff, 1967).
[53] Béla Bartók and Albert B. Lord, *Serbo-Croatian Folk Songs* (New York: Columbia University Press, 1951).
[54] "Computer Applications to Bartók's Serbo-Croatian Material," *Tempo.* No. 80 (1967), pp. 15-19.
[55] "Song Structure and Social Structure," *Ethnology,* Vol. 1 (1962), pp. 425-451.
[56] Ibid., p. 425.
[57] Ibid.
[58] Ibid., pp. 425-426.
[59] Ibid., pp. 427-431.
[60] Ibid., p. 449.
[61] Nettl, "A Technique of Ethnomusicology applied to Western Culture," *Ethnomusicology,* Vol. 7 (1963), p. 222.

ADDITIONAL REFERENCES

Bertrand H. Bronson, "Folk-Song in the United States, 1910-1960; Reflections from a Student's Corner," *Jahrbuch für Volksliedforschung,* Vol. 9 (1964), pp. 1-11.
Josh Dunson, *Freedom in the Air; Song Movements of the Sixties* (New York; International Publishers, 1965).
George Herzog, "Musical Typology in Folksong," *Southern Folklore Quarterly,* Vol. 1 (1937), pp. 49-55.
Maud Karpeles, "Some Reflections on Authenticity in Folk Music," *Journal of the International Folk Music Council,* Vol. 3 (1951), pp. 10-16.
Maud Karpeles, "The Distinction between Folk and Popular Music," *Journal of the International Folk Music Council,* Vol. 20 (1968), pp. 9-12
Mieczyslaw Kolinski, "The Origin of the Indian 22-Tone System," *Studies in Ethnomusicology,* Vol. 1 (1961), pp. 3-18.
Mieczyslaw Kolinski, "Classification of Tonal Structures," *Studies in Ethnomusicology,* Vol. 1 (1961), pp. 38-76.
Mieczyslaw Kolinski, "The Structure of Melodic Movement; a New Method of Analysis (revised version)," *Studies in Ethnomusicology,* Vol. 2 (1965), pp. 95-120.

George G. Korson, *Minstrels of the Mine Patch; Songs and Stories of the Anthracite Industry* (Philadelphia: University of Pennsylvania Press, 1938).
George G. Korson, *Coal Dust on the Fiddle; Songs and Stories of the Bituminous Industry* (Philadelphia; University of Pennsylvania Press, 1943).
George G. Korson, *Pennsylvania Songs and Legends* (Philadelphia: University of Pennsylvania Press, 1949).
Alan Lomax, ed., *Folk Song Style and Culture, a Staff Report on Cantometrics* (Washington, D. C.: American Association for the Advancement of Science, 1968).
David McAllester, *Enemy Way Music; a Study of Social and Esthetic Values as seen in Navajo Music* (Cambridge, Mass., 1954). (Papers of the Peabody Museum of American Archaeology and Ethnology, Harvard University, Vol. 41, No. 3.)
Alan P. Merriam, "Purposes of Ethnomusicology; an Anthropological View," *Ethnomusicology*, Vol. 7 (1963), pp. 206-213.
J. H. Kwabena Nketia, "Changing Traditions of Folk Music in Ghana," *Journal of the International Folk Music Council*, Vol. 11 (1959), pp. 31-36.
J. H. Kwabena Nketia, "Traditional and Contemporary Idioms of African Music," *Journal of the International Folk Music Council*, Vol. 16 (1964), pp. 34-37.
J. H. Kwabena Nketia, "The Interrelations of African Music and Dance," *Journal of the International Folk Music Council*, Vol. 17 (1965), pp. 91-101.
Charles Seeger, "Folk Music as a Source of Social History," in Carolyn F. Ware, ed., *The Cultural Approach to History* (New York, 1940), pp. 316-323.
Charles Seeger, "Systematic Musicology: Viewpoints, Orientations, and Methods,"*Journal of the American Musicological Society*, Vol. 4 (1951), pp. 240-248.
Charles Seeger, "Singing Style," *Western Folklore*, Vol. 17 (1958), pp. 3-11.
Charles Seeger, "Prescriptive and Descriptive Music Writing," *The Musical Quarterly*, Vol. 44 (1958), pp. 184-195.
Charles Seeger, "Semantic, Logical and Political Considerations Bearing upon Research in Ethnomusicology," *Ethnomusicology*, Vol. 5 (1961), pp. 77-80.
Charles Seeger, "Preface to the Critique of Music," *Inter-American Music Bulletin*, No. 49 (Washington, D. C.: Pan American Union, 1965).
Cecil J. Sharp and Maud Karpeles, *English Folk Songs from the Southern Appalachians*, 2nd enlarged ed. (London: Oxford University Press, 1932).
Walter Wiora, "Ethnomusicology and the History of Music," *Journal of the International Folk Music Council*, Vol. 17 (1965), pp. 187-193.

RECORD REFERENCES

George G. Karson, ed., *Songs and Ballads of the Anthracite Miners*, Library of Congress, Music Division, Recording Laboratory, AAFS L16 (1959).
George G. Karson, ed., *Songs and Ballads of the Bituminous Miners*, Library of Congress, Music Division, Recording Laboratory, AFS L60 (1965).
Charles Seeger, ed., *Versions and Variants of Barbara Allen; from the Archive of Folk Song*, Library of Congress, Music Division, Recording Laboratory, AAFS L54 [1964?].

Radmila Petrović

THE PLACE OF ETHNOMUSICOLOGY IN YUGOSLAV MUSIC STUDY

The historic, economic, and social changes that have taken place throughout the centuries in the Balkans — the crossroads of East and West — the wealth, diversity, and dynamism of the ethnic structure, and the cultural characteristics of the varied national and ethnic groups all have contributed to making Yugoslavia an interesting and, understandably, highly complex subject for research from every angle of the social, historical, and humanistic sciences. Thus, Yugoslavia provides an especially fruitful source for ethnomusicological investigation.

Today, ethnomusicology in Yugoslavia is established as a fully independent discipline. The scope of its interest relates it not only to music, but to ethnology, folklore, linquistics, sociology, as well as other disciplines.

Work done in the field for the past hundred years presents a picture of logical and gradual development, from the historical and methodological viewpoint. This period may be divided into several chronological phases, each with its own peculiar characteristics, as stages in the progress from Yugoslav musical ethnography to Yugoslav ethnomusicology.

The oldest recorded Yugoslav folk tunes are found in a sixteenth century source. It contains two songs, one epic and the other lyrical, notated in a late mensural notation and published at the end of a literary work.[1] From this time on for almost two hundred years, folk tunes were recorded only sporadically on the initiative of unknown collectors. Although these records are few in number, they constitute a precious legacy in Yugoslav cultural history, and they testify that already at that early date, some people understood the value of folk music as a cultural phenomenon.

Cultural revolution in the nineteenth century opened a new chapter in the history of Yugoslav music, and folk music occupied an important place in that chapter. The increased interest in folk music, its collection and publication, went hand in hand with a widespread intellectual and political affirmation of national consciousness in the country, even though Yugoslavia was not as yet a political unity.

Thus, folk music contributed directly to a prime cultural need of the time.

Before a distinctive art music tradition might develop and a national school of art music emerge, the folk music tradition had to be studied and assimilated.

A great part of the material collected and published at the beginning of the nineteenth century consisted only of folk song texts.[2] However, folk songs in Yugoslavia were and are sung rather than recited, consequently a considerable number of musically literate people began to collect folk melodies along with the texts. Amateurs, such as teachers and priests, rather than professional musicians, were most closely associated with this activity.

The collections of folk tunes published at that time[3] provide important insight into two aspects of the contemporaneous cultural attitude. They testify, first of all, to a deep interest and initiative in collecting folk music by recording it *in the field*. These collections are the product of organized field trips conducted under the extraordinarily strenuous conditions of the time, without modern technical means and in a largely roadless countryside. They stand as testimony to long, arduous work. Many of them also supply valuable ethnographic material in the collector's notes and remarks, or in his forewords and commentary. These transcriptions in the field thus mark the early progress of musical ethnography in Yugoslavia.

The second insight into the contemporaneous cultural attitude provided by these published folk song collections derives from a recognition of the fact that the melodies were harmonized, mostly in arrangements for voice and piano. Why were they published in precisely this form?

I must stress that the nineteenth century, particularly the second half, witnessed a great leap forward in the cultural development of the Yugoslav peoples. Folk song as a product of collective and anonymous folk creativity was recognized for all its beauty and innate value by the emergent cultural consciousness of the nineteenth century. Their published collections of folk songs represented a fund of musical values that was indispensable for the development of musical nationalism. The harmonization of those folk songs represented the first stage in drawing together the tradition of collective folk creativity and the creative effort of individual composers (the art music tradition). The role of folk song in Yugoslav musical culture has been evolving ever since.

The first period of interest in folk music is thus seen to have developed along two different paths: (1) the transcription and collection in the field of folk melodies — an occupation which started to assume a more scientific character with the first attempts to classify the musical material or to analyze it according to its rhythmic, metric, and tonal peculiarities; and (2) the creative use of folk melodies, in which the stock of folk tunes became a stimulus to and a basis for the composer's artistic work.

Yugoslav musicology became broader and more active during the first half of the twentieth century, but it was still not constituted as an independent discipline, nor were there centers for working systematically on the collecting and study of folk music. Individual efforts were the principal source of advancement in the field. A number of new and significant developments characterized the work of this period. First, the problems of folk music investigation were more completely recognized and studied. Second, research tended to be narrowed down into fields limited ethnically or regionally. Third, a methodology of research began to be formulated.[4]

In this stage, composers conducted most of the ethnomusicological research. They were not ethnomusicologists in the true sense, because they did not dedicate themselves exclusively to the study of folk music; composition constituted their main interest. They realized the significance of the study of musical folklore to the development of an autochthonous Yugoslav musical culture, consequently the scientific character of their work became more pronounced. Nevertheless, it was still a secondary element in the total complex of Yugoslav musical culture.

The need to organize a center which would collect and preserve ethnomusicological material was felt soon after World War I. Božidar Širola established a center for the study of folk music in the Ethnographic Museum in Zagreb in 1921. Kosta Manojlović organized a similar center in the Ethnographic Museum in Belgrade in 1923. The Slovenian Folklore Institute was established in Ljubljana (as a part of *Glazbena matica*) in 1934, on the initiative of France Marolt.

Still, those who were engaged in ethnomusicological activities between the two world wars did not possess especially favorable conditions for their work. Many remained primarily composers. A smaller group gradually abandoned other musical activities to dedicate themselves exclusively to the study of folk music. Both groups, with their individual efforts and initiative, opened the way to a scholarly discipline which was scarcely a half century old. Their contributions laid the foundation of Yugoslav ethnomusicology, which would gain new impetus after World War II through the combined efforts of the pioneer ethnomusicologists and their students of the younger generation.

The most important turning point in ethnomusicological work after World War II in Yugoslavia consisted in establishing centers for the scholarly study of folk music. With the training of professional ethnomusicologists, specially educated for this kind of work, the complete autonomy of ethnomusicology as a discipline was insured.

At this juncture, we must mention the direct influence of foreign scholars who studied the folk music tradition of Yugoslavia in the field or who based their investigation on the collections of Yugoslav folk music already published.[5] As a consequence of their studies, their scientific methods gained considerable influence in the work of many Yugoslav ethnomusicologists.

The small centers for the study of folk music, which had been established between the two world wars within the frame of the ethnographic museums in Zagreb and Belgrade and of the *Glazbena matica* in Ljubljana, became after World War II autonomous institutes with carefully designated and planned research responsibilities. Planning has made possible the formulation of long term programs for the systematic collection of material, its classification, and study. Comparable scholarly institutions with similar goals, but different specific areas of investigation, now exist in the capitals of the five Yugoslav republics: the Music Folklore Institute in Ljubljana (Slovenia), the Institute for Folk Art in Zagreb (Croatia),[6] the Institute for the Study of Folklore in Sarajevo (Bosnia and Herzegovina), which is a department of the State Museum, the Institute for Folklore in Skopje (Macedonia), and the Musicological Institute in Belgrade (Serbia),[7] which is unique in the country in its research topics. The three autonomous institutes (in Zagreb, Sarajevo, and Skopje) divide their areas of research into several categories: (1) folk music, (2) folk dance, (3) folk literature, (4) folk customs, and (5) folk visual arts. The institute in Ljubljana comprises three sections: (1) folk music, (2) folk dance, and (3) folk song texts. The Musicological Institute in Belgrade differs essentially from the other four institutes, in that historical-musicological subjects are included in its three divisions: (1) history of music, (2) theory of music, and (3) folk music and dance.

The study of folk music and dance is organized in a similar fashion in all of the centers, and the research work is remarkably co-ordinated between them. Each institute is dedicated first of all to investigation within the territory of its republic, to the establishment of a regional archive of tape recordings, and to the collection of manuscripts of folk melodies transcribed in earlier periods by enterprising collectors.[8]

Inter-republican co-operation is manifested through the exchange of musical materials and publications. Each year, a Federal Congress of Yugoslav Folklorists provides ethnomusicologists an opportunity to exchange ideas and experiences and to discuss common problems.[9] Foreign ethnomusicologists also participate. A particular problem constitutes the focus of each congress, for example the one held in September of 1968 considered the traditional forms of epic singing in the Balkans.

These observations on Yugoslav ethnomusicology bring us necessarily to the question, "What cultural phenomena expand the perspectives of ethnomusicological research in Yugoslavia today?"

The present phase of Yugoslav folk music represents a very complex cultural phenomenon. Yugoslavia still has a rich treasure of musical folklore, despite the intense industrialization which has brought about such profound economic, social, and cultural change. On the territory of present-day Yugoslavia, Illyrian and Thracian cultures flourished. At its periphery, contact was possible with Hellenic and Roman cultures. These older strata were subsequently assimilated by a Slavic cultural stratum, and the infiltration of Oriental cultures during the Middle Ages created yet another stratum in the already entangled cultural aggregate. When we add to this the mutual influences in contacts with neighbor nations in border regions — Germans in the northwest, Hungarians in the north, Italians along the Adriatic — we get some idea of the depth and variety of cultural strata in Yugoslavia.

Because of the retardation of socio-economic development in the Balkans during the Middle Ages, as a result of the prolonged intrusion of eastern and western militants, many ancient forms of traditional music have been preserved until today. The oldest songs survive in the memory of the older generation in many regions of Yugoslavia. In some regions they also constitute a part of the repertory of the younger generation, especially as a part of the still vital tradition of ritual ceremonies (wedding rituals are particularly important in this respect).

The study of musical tradition in Yugoslavia, with all its stratification and diversity, represents a contribution to general historical-cultural research, to ethnology and folklore, to the basic questions of man's evolution, as well as to specifically musicological problems. We are convinced that our research does not fall into the realm of strictly local interest, but contributes in a far-reaching manner to ethnomusicology as a whole. A determination of what belongs to which musical stratum, what precisely was assimilated and how, and what elements infiltrated Yugoslav folk music, might perhaps facilitate the explanation of those problems still unsolved in other, non-European cultures. The properties of musical folklore are certainly as important as linguistic ones, and a particular manner of singing may frequently serve better than language in solving ethno-genetic questions.

Here are some of the problems faced by Yugoslav ethnomusicologists in the study of the musical materials peculiar to our locale. Their historical-cultural significance clearly surpasses Yugoslav frontiers.

The question of the age of any folk music heritage preoccupies ethnomusicologists everywhere. The debate as to whether the pentatonic system is older than the diatonic prompted a number of Yugoslav ethnomusicologists to study the Yugoslav musical material and to reach the conclusion that a non-tempered, narrow-ranged acoustical structure is characteristic of the

Yugoslav territory, and that it may very well antedate the pentatonic (anhemitonic) structure, which is certainly the product of a far more civilized milieu. [10]

This question is also closely related to the problem of the final tone in folk melodies from a wide area in Yugoslavia (excepting Slovenia, the coastal region of Dalmatia, and some parts of Madeconia). In an overwhelming majority of these folk melodies, vocal as well as instrumental, the *tonus finalis* stands at the second degree of the diatonic scale. This purely musical characteristic exemplifies at the same time an ethnopsychological trait, as it expresses a peculiar type of musical thinking and logic.

An equally peculiar type of two-part polyphony in some Yugoslav music also excites extraordinary scholarly interest. I am referring to the type in which the interval of the second represents the basic vertical sonority between the two voices. In this type, the second is conceived psychologically as a consonance, not a dissonance, and its occurrence is planned for particular moments in a piece.[11]

Many ethnomusicologists, especially Yugoslav and Greek, are engaged in investigating the peculiarities of Macedonian rhythms and the modal properties of their songs. The persuasion is becoming more and more widespread that a penetrating and multilateral study might contribute to a fuller understanding of the many remaining uncertainties about ancient Greek music. The presence of seemingly irrational rhythms throughout several sectors of the territory amidst peoples who are excellent dancers (which is evidence of their innate sense of precise rhythm) suggests the possibility that these complex, irregular rhythms may have been assimilated from a much older musical heritage. The fact that the texts of such songs can be understood only dimly or not at all speaks in favor of such a hypothesis.

One of the most important areas for investigation concerns a feature in Yugoslav folk music which relates it to those Afro-Asian areas where the principle of the *ragā* and the *maqām* is dominant. In a number of regions in Yugoslavia, the term *glas (echos)* is used to denote, only approximately, a type of melodic-poetic form which can be sung with various texts different in content but having the same metrical structure. The *glas* is not always identical or uniform in structure throughout the various regions, but the fact that the several types of *glas* are called by the same name in every region (wedding *glas,* harvest *glas,* long *glas,* short *glas,* old-fashioned *glas,* etc.) suggests that in the distant past, when ethnic differences in this territory were minimal and the process of cultural assimilation and infiltration had yet to occur, the ancient Slavic peoples had created a basic repertory of melody types for different occasions and different needs. In keeping with this practice, but certainly at a much later date, regional characteristics appeared in the various types of *glas,* so that nowadays there are differences in the way of singing even between two adjacent villages. These differences are not pronounced, nor are they readily noticed, even by us; nevertheless, such subtleties may well deserve the serious attention of ethnomusicologists.[12]

The study of Orthodox ecclesiastical chant also belongs among the areas deserving serious investigation. The stratification evident in folk music and in folklore as a whole may be detected in this musical area as well. The tradition of Byzantine ecclesiastical chant modified by the influence of folk music created the distinctive Serbian style of Orthodox ecclesiastical chant. The *glas* or *echos* occur here too as a constant principle of tonal organization in both the variable and the unchanging parts of the liturgy. All of the chants belong to one of the eight ecclesiastical *glas*.[13]

Among contemporary cultural phenomena related to folk music, I might mention the recent practice of creating composed "folk" songs in the spirit of folk music. There are more and more of them, and they enjoy great popularity. The manner in which they are created and performed relates these "folk" songs to the category of light music, and many experts consider them no more than vulgarisms and of passing cultural value. Nevertheless, the study of this phenomenon contributes to an understanding of many sociological problems related to the present-day acculturation of countryside and city.[14]

No separate mention has been made of investigation into the folk dance. This is closely connected with ethnomusicology in subject matter as well as in methodology (except in the area of notating the dances). Besides the general, common problems of studying folk music and folk dance, a separate problem peculiar to the folk dance concerns its presentation on the stage. Solutions depend on individual taste, of course, but they should be based on a multilateral, in-depth study of the folk dance tradition.

In this summary of ethnomusicological activity in Yugoslavia, I have tried to outline both the historical development and thematic structure of the subject. Perhaps the impression has been conveyed that our study of folk music has already attained remarkable depth and breadth, but let me emphasize our awareness of the enormous work yet to be done before we truly understand the musical idioms that characterize and differentiate one ethnic group from another.

Up until about twenty years ago, the collection and study of folk music was closely associated with the creative work of composing. But new directions in the music of our day and a trend toward the abstract have virtually nothing in common with the programmatic character of folk music. Our ancient folk music tradition may well move gradually into our archives, to continue its existence as a piece of museum inventory. The preservation of musical tradition is no easy task; the creation of new, true cultural value is a responsibility no less demanding.

NOTES

[1] Petar Hektorović, *Ribanje i ribarsko prigovaranje* [Fishing and Fishermen's Sayings] (Venice 1568). Facsimile edition (Zagreb, 1953).

[2] Vuk Stefanović-Karadžić, *Srpske narodne pesme* [Serbian Folk Songs], 9 vols. (1814-1902). The second edition of the first volume contains six melodies in notation.

[3] Sima Milutinović, *Pjevanija cernogorska i hercegovačka* [Songs from Montenegro and Hercegovina] (Buda, 1833); Brothers Miladinovci, *Zbornik* [A Collection] (Zagreb, 1861); Valtasar Bogišić, *Narodne pjesme iz starijih najviše primorskih zapisa* [Folk Songs from Ancient Manuscripts, Primarily from the Coastal Regions] (Belgrade, 1878); Karel Štrekelj, *Slovenske narodne pesmi* [Slovenian Folk Songs] (Ljubljana, 1895-1898); *Hrvatske narodne pjesme* [Croatian Folk Songs], 10 vols., published by Matica hrvatska (Zagreb, 1896-1942); Franjo Kuhač, *Južno-slovjenske narodne popievke* [South-Slavic Folk Songs], Vol. 1-4 (Zagreb, 1878-1881), Vol. 5 (1941); Kornelije Stanković, *Srpske narodne pesme* [Serbian Folk Songs], 6 vols. (1851-1863); Ludvik Kuba, *Slovenstvo ve svych zpevech* [The Slavs in Their Songs], Slovenian (1890), Montenegrin (1890), Croatian (1892), and Dalmatian (1893-1895); Ludvik Kuba, *Pjesme i napjevi iz Bosne i Hercegovine* [Songs from Bosnia and Hercegovina] (Sarajevo, 1906-1910); *Makedonski melografi od krajot na XIX vek* [Macedonian Melographs at the End of 19th Century] (Skopje, 1962).

[4] Stevan Mokranjac, *Zapisi narodnih melodija* [Manuscripts of Folk Melodies], a publication of the Musicological Institute (Belgrade, 1966); Todor Bušetić, *Srpske narodne pesme i igre sa melodijama iz Levče* [Serbian Folk Songs and Dances with Melodies from Levča] preface by S. Mokranjac, *Ethnographic Annals,* Srpska kraljevska akademija, Vol. 3 (Belgrade 1902); Vinko Žganec, *Hrvatske pučke popijevke iz Medjumurja* [Croatian Folk Songs from Medjumurje], published by Jugoslavenska akademija znanosti i umjetnosti, 2 vols. (Zagreb, 1924-1925); Ivan Matetić-Ronjgov, *Čakavsko-primorska pjevanka* [Čakavian-Coastal Songs] (1939); Vladimir Djordjević, *Srpske narodne melodije: Južna Srbija* [Serbian Folk Melodies: Southern Serbia] (Skopje, 1928); Vladimir Djordejerić, *Srpske narodne melodije: predratna Srbija* [Serbian Folk Melodies: Pre-War Serbia] (Belgrade, 1931); Miloje Milojević has collected about 1000 melodies from Macedonia, Kosovo, and Metohia, to be published soon. Antun Dobronić, *Ojkanje,* published by Jugoslavenska akademija znanosti i umjetnosti (Zagreb, 1915); Antun Dubronić, *Psihologija naše pučke musike* [Psychology of Our Folk Music], bulletin of the Ethnographic Museum (Zagreb, 1934); Božidar Širola, *Hrvatska narodna glazba* [Croatian Folk Music] (Zagreb, 1940).

[5] Milman Parry, Albert B. Lord, Bela Bartók, Constantin Brailou, among others.

[6] The Yugoslav Academy of Arts and Sciences (the Committee on Folk Life and Customs) also studies folk music in the Republic of Croatia.

[7] The Folklore Department of the Ethnographic Institute of the Serbian Academy of Arts and Sciences also studies folk music.

[8] See the bibliography in R. Petrović, "Ethnomusicology in Yugoslavia," *Zvuk,* 77-78 (Sarajevo, 1967), 30.

[9] See the proceedings of the Congresses of Yugoslav Folklorists: Bjelašnica-Pula (Zagreb, 1958); Cetinje (Cetinje, 1958); Varaždin (Zagreb, 1959); Zaječar-Negotin (Belgrade, 1960); Bled (Ljubljana, 1960); Ohrid (Ohrid, 1964); Titovo Užice (Belgrade, 1961); Mostar-Trebinje (Sarajevo, 1963); Cetinje (Cetinje, 1964); Novi Vinodol (Zagreb, 1966); Celje, Dojran, and Prizren (in press).

[10] Stjepan Stjepanov, "Problem starosti muzičko-folklorne baštine" [The Problems of the Age of the Musical Folklore Heritage], *Rad Kongresa folklorista Jugoslavije VI: Bled, 1959* (Ljubljana, 1960), pp. 285-293; Ivan Matetić Ronjgov, "O istarskoj ljestvici" [On the Istrian Scale], Sveta Cecilija, Vol. 2 (Zagreb, 1925).

[11] Cvjetko Rihtman, "Polifoni oblici u narodnoj muzici Bosne i Hercegovine" [Polyphonic Forms in the Folk Music of Bosnia and Hercegovina], *Bilten za proučavanje folklora* (Sarajevo, 1951); Radmila Petrović, "Narodni melos oblasti Titovog Užica" [Folk Melodies in the Region of Titovo Užica], *Rad Kongresa folklorista Jugoslavije u Titovoum Užicu 1961* (Belgrade, 1961), pp. 95-107; Jerko Bezić, "Neki oblici starinskog otegnutog dvoglasnog pjevanja na sjevero-zapadnim zadarskim otocima" [Some Forms of Ancient Protracted Two-Voice Singing on the North-West Zadar Islands], *Rad Kongresa Folklorista Jugoslavije VI: Bled, 1959* (Ljubljana, 1960), pp. 295-302.

[12] Miodrag Vasiljević, "Funkcije i vrste glasova u srpskom narodnom pjevanju" [Functions and Kinds of Voices in Serbian Folk Singing], *Rad Kongresa folklorista Jugoslavije VII: Ohrid, 1960,* (Ohrid, 1964), pp. 375-380; Radmila Petrović, "Morfološke kategorije melopoetskih struktura u napevima Srbije" [Morphological Categories of Melo-poetic structures in Serbian Songs], published by Srpska Akademija nauka i umetnosti (Belgrade, in press); Cvjetko Rihtman, "Oblici kratkog napjeva u narodnoj tradiciji Bosne i Hercegovine" [Forms of Short Songs in the Folk Tradition of Bosnia and Hercegovina], *Glasnik Zemaljskog muzeja* (Sarajevo, 1963), pp. 61-75.

[13] Dimitrije Stefanović, "The Beginnings of Serbian Chant," *Anfänge der slawischen Musik* (Bratislava, 1966), pp. 55-64; D. Stefanović, "The Serbian Chant from the 15th to the 18th Centuries," *Musica Antiqua Europae Orientalis I* (Warsaw, 1966), pp. 140-163; Miloš Velimirović, "The Influence of the Byzantine Chant on the Music of the Slavic Countries," *Proceedings of the 13th International Congress of Byzantine Studies* (London, 1967), pp. 119-140; Dimitrije Stefanović, *ibid.,* Supplementary papers, pp. 141-147.

[14] Radmila Petrović, "The Concept of Yugoslav Folk Music in the 20th Century," paper for the Conference of the International Folk Music Council, Ostende, 1967 (in press).

Bruno Nettl

ETHNOMUSICOLOGY IN AMERICAN MUSIC EDUCATION

When I began to study ethnomusicology some twenty years ago — under Dr. George Herzog, a professor of partly Croatian origin — even many professional musicians and music educators had never heard of the field. Almost everyone to whom I spoke expressed surprise that peoples such as the American Indians and the natives of Africa had any music at all, to say nothing of the doubts indicated about the value of this music and the usefulness to anyone of studying it. Today, the educated public in the United States has heard the term, for it appears even in such popular journals as *Time Magazine*. Everyone knows what an ethnomusicologist is — everyone, that is, except ethnomusicologists themselves. Ethnomusicology has had a great impact on musical life and particularly on music education in the United States during the last ten years. From a highly specialized field with half a dozen practitioners working in what must be regarded as conventional scholarly method, historical and ethnographic, on problems that seemed to have little relationship to other events in education or research, ethnomusicology has suddenly changed into a discipline whose influence is felt in musicology, music education, and musical life at large, as well as in the social sciences. At the same time, the half dozen scholars — who were doing their research in confidence that they were, if not on the right track, then at least on one that would be accepted as belonging in the framework of standard scholarship — have become several dozen in America and hundreds more elsewhere, all casting about feverishly for an acceptable methodology and theory for their research, and for their proper role in education and in the scheme of scholarly disciplines. The relatively relaxed ivory-tower attitude of the 1930's and '40's has now been replaced by worry and controversy about the role, duties, and public image of the field. Suddenly, ethnomusicologists find themselves no longer a luxury in a few academic institutions. All of this is due, I believe, to the many political and social changes that the world has undergone since World War II.

In the Western world at large, ethnomusicology is regarded as a younger discipline than musicology (in the sense of research in music history); consequently, it is viewed as standing somewhat in the shadow of its older sister-discipline. But the history of American scholarship does not conform to this viewpoint. Here, the study of non-Western and folk music came into its own at least as early as did historical study of Western music and, indeed, the early American contributions to ethnomusicology were generally more distinguished. We need think only of Theodore Baker's pioneering dissertation on North American Indian music, or of the early work in American Indian music of others such as Frances Densmore, Alice Fletcher, and B. I. Gilman, or of the great interest shown by the anthropologist Franz Boas in the role of the arts in culture.[1] It must be admitted, of course, that the earliest contributions to American ethnomusicology came about with precious little influence from the European, mainly German-based discipline of musicology, which had burst upon the academic scene in the 1880's. Thus, while much that was done by the early Americans was imaginative and enlightening, it occasionally lacked methodological perspective. Nevertheless, these early scholars were pretty well agreed on their tasks: (1) the preservation of the non-Western heritage through recording, (2) field work with trained informants in an essentially anthropological frame of reference, (3) the study of music as an aspect of culture, and (4) the development of a methodology for making intercultural comparative studies in music. The world's non-literate cultures and the folk music of the Western world lent themselves best to these tasks; the musics of Asian civilizations were more or less ignored and left for a future generation of scholars who would have a different approach.

The picture today differs considerably. Emphasis is on the music of the Oriental civilizations. The ties with anthropology, at one time extremely close, have been loosened. Stress is no longer placed to such an extent upon collecting materials and making contributions to knowledge, but upon educating the general public, and especially the musician, to an understanding of certain non-Western musical cultures. "Pure" research has not been neglected, but the educational role of the field has expanded greatly. The non-literate and folk cultures have been relegated to a secondary place. Comparative work has suffered to some extent at the expense of specialization.

An important feature of ethnomusicology in contemporary America is the introduction of practical instruction in non-Western performance. Although the idea has been generally held that one type of effective field work may involve learning from informants some of the rudiments of musical performance, the idea of developing such performance to a level of high competence as a main purpose of field work, and of giving such instruction not only in the field but at American institutions, is perhaps the most important single characteristic of ethnomusicology in the United States. The idea came from Europe. It was carried to America by Mantle Hood, who had studied with Jaap Kunst in Amsterdam and who knew of Kunst's work in developing a *gamelan* of Dutch students. Brought to America, the idea was put into effect on a grand scale, to the extent that college students at several institutions, as well as some high school and elementary school students, now participate in this kind of study. A certain amount of controversy has surrounded this work, which attempts to develop bi-musicality in the students. As yet many questions about it cannot be answered. For example, can a Western musician become really proficient in a non-Western musical idiom? If so, is it worth the time he spends, assuming research to be his main goal? Do students benefit from brief and admittedly superficial exposure to non-Western performance, such as participating in a *gamelan* or a Japanese *kabuki* ensemble? Whatever the answers turn out finally to be, this approach has undoubtedly had tremendous impact on the field of ethnomusicology and on American music education in general. People in large numbers are beginning to be aware of the existence and nature of non-Western musics, of their subtleties, and of the sophistication necessary for understanding them. Whether the same amount of money and energy expended otherwise would have accomplished more is another question.

A second main characteristic of ethnomusicology in the United States is its presence in a number of departments of anthropology. In the first half of the twentieth century, anthropology departments tended to nurture the somewhat isolated ethnomusicologists; many individuals in the field of music regarded ethnomusicology as belonging properly to anthropology. Now this attitude has changed for the most part among musicians, but ethnomusicology remains a potent force in the field of anthropology. Evidence of this may be adduced from (1) the considerable number of publications on musical subjects – particularly by Alan Merriam, Alan Lomax, Richard Waterman, and David McAllester – which attempt to make contributions to anthropology, (2) the fact that a small number of American ethnomusicologists are professors of anthropology, and (3) the publication of ethnomusicological material in anthropological periodicals. Here, important parallels can be observed in European countries.

A third characteristic today is the close relationship between research and practice – particularly teaching and performing. An ethnomusicologist at a university is likely to engage in the training of researchers, while at the same time teaching a large introductory course attended mainly by prospective school teachers. He may lead a study group in which students who are not connected with the field of music gain what could be called a "general" musical experience by participating in a non-Western ensemble. He may assume the role of impresario, bringing concerts of Indian, Japanese, Indonesian, and Arabic music to his school. The proliferation of such activities brings with it at times a certain amateurism. But the American humanistic scholar has always felt it part of his duty to be a missionary to the general public. While this has occasionally hindered his own specialized research, it has provided substantial contributions to education at large, usually by those most qualified to make them.

In very general terms, here are some facts about ethnomusicology in American education:

1. Approximately ten universities are training professional ethnomusicologists to the level of the Ph.D.[2] In most cases, this is being done within the framework of musicology curricula; in a few cases, the framework is anthropology; and in at least one case, the program is one of ethnomusicology specifically and alone. Most American scholars believe that ethnomusicology should not be a discipline by itself, but a subdivision of one of the established disciplines. The students in these programs come most frequently from an undergraduate background in music. Particularly numerous are those with a background in music theory and composition; many have been practicing musicians — frequently in jazz or popular music. Those students working within the anthropology framework are most frequently individuals who have had a considerable background in music, possibly undergraduate specialization.

Although the various programs differ greatly, they have in common an almost rigid requirement of a year or more of field work as part of the dissertation project, comprehensive examinations in the domain of ethnomusicology at large, plus specialization in one or two world areas.

2. It is felt by most persons in the field of higher music education that some exposure to ethnomusicology is essential for graduate students. Accordingly, there is course work in ethnomusicology offered at about twenty-five institutions. In many of the graduate musicology curricula, a course in some branch of ethnomusicology is required. It is assumed that some cognizance of non-Western music is essential to a well-rounded musicologist, and that some exposure to the theory and methodology of ethnomusicology will have important effects on music-historical research. Similarly, those training public school teachers believe that some knowledge of non-Western music is an important ingredient in the education of their students if they are to contribute to the awareness of the world that is now expected in our schools. Again, teachers of composition believe that awareness of musical structures found outside Western music can contribute to the kind of imaginative thinking that one wishes to foster among composers.

3. After a period of relative decline, in the 1950's, the importance of the arts in anthropological research is again increasing. Accordingly, students specializing in anthropology are being encouraged to familiarize themselves with ethnomusicology. They are being introduced to this field perhaps in part because of the great current interest in American minority groups, of which several have distinguished themselves through their musical activity. At my university, for

example, an ethnologist recently conducted a seminar on problems of urban Negroes and quite naturally expected his students to become familiar with the literature concerning Negro musical culture.

4. The general student body of many universities is being introduced to non-Western musics — though not necessarily to ethnomusicology — through an ever-increasing number of live concerts under university sponsorship. The present availability of touring Oriental musicians, for instance, far exceeds that of a few years ago. Moreover, the change in emphasis among ethnomusicologists from simple cultures to Oriental civilizations has undoubtedly encouraged a climate of interest.

By far the most prominent of these recently publicized musics is Indian, which has become known to many segments of the population and has developed into an important force in the field of commercial pop-music. At my university, for example, six concerts of North and South Indian music took place within a twelve-month period. Japanese, Persian, Arabic, and occasionally Southeast Asian and Indonesian music is also being heard. About ten years ago, concerts of American folk music — typically white and Negro singers from the Southern United States and Negro blues singers from the large cities — were a common occurrence in universities; now, this type of concert has receded somewhat.

5. There is a trend toward making some non-Western music a part of general introductory courses of the type often labeled "music appreciation." This goes hand in hand with the present trend toward including in such courses some contemporary music, even *avant-garde,* as well as medieval and Renaissance music. Many teachers now believe that the general principles of musical structure and style can be illustrated as readily by non-Western and other less-known musics as by the traditional classic masterworks.

6. Non-Western music — especially that of India, the American Indians, and the folk music of North America — is finding its way into primary and secondary schools, often in the more or less anthropological framework of social studies, rather than in music instruction. The tremendous increase in available recordings and films contributes to this trend. However, only the surface has been touched in this area. Folk music, of course, has long been included in public music education, but to a lesser extent than in Europe.

I believe that a number of questions should be asked of ethnomusicology as it relates to education:

> In a period of "information explosion," and of greater specialization, what should be the role of ethnomusicology in the education of the musicologist?

How can one preserve the field of ethnomusicology as an area of research, while at the same time using its products to introduce the general student to non-Western music?

To what extent should ethnomusicologists attempt to participate in practical musical life? Should they strive to preserve and to keep alive the rapidly changing musical cultures of the non-Western world and of the folk, or should they be content to observe and study what they find, including the processes of change? To what extent should they inject themselves and their work into the active musical life of Western civilization?

The answers to these questions will in large part determine the character of ethnomusicology in American music education for years to come.

NOTES

[1] For a selective bibliography of contributions to the field of ethnomusicology by these scholars see the bibliographies in Alan P. Merriam's *The Anthropology of Music* (Evanston, Ill., 1964), or in my *Music in Primitive Culture* (Cambridge, 1956).

[2] Among the institutions offering professional training in ethnomusicology are: University of Michigan, University of California at Los Angeles, University of Illinois, Indiana University, University of Washington, Wesleyan University, Columbia University, Tulane University, Northwestern University, University of Wisconsin at Madison, University of North Carolina, and University of Hawaii.

Zija Kučukalić

FOLK MUSIC AS AN INFLUENCE ON ART MUSIC IN YUGOSLAVIA

For centuries, the Balkan Peninsula has been the focus of severe political struggles and religious conflicts. The interests of great powers East and West crossed here and clashed with particular intensity. The continual bitter rivalry for power, prestige, and influence deprived the local inhabitants of any self determination. A succession of foreign rulers impeded the socio-economic development of the native peoples, so that the achievements of advanced civilization penetrated Yugoslavia slowly and with difficulty. Certainly the creation of our own culture and art was seriously retarded.

These conditions of Yugoslavia's political and socio-economic development tied the Yugoslav peoples for many centuries to their old patriarchal ways and habits — habits which manifested themselves not only in the material aspects of life, but were deeply rooted in the spiritual as well. For generations, folk traditions represented an essential part of the environment of a man born and raised under such conditions. Indeed, under the extraordinarily repressive conditions of continual foreign domination, a man's folk traditions represented the only proof of his creative power.

Precisely for this reason, the folk art of all of Yugoslavia has preserved the character of antiquity and, since it is still vital today, it represents a rich spiritual treasure inherited from a patriarchal civilization. It is precious compensation for all that was denied to the peoples of Yugoslavia in the past.

Folk music, transmitted from generation to generation for centuries, continually enriching itself through contact with the vital experiences of each age, reflects the great creative energy of the Yugoslav peoples. Anonymous musical creators knew how to give form to a specific, individual spirit, how to express through words and tones the full force of their feelings, and how to realize a creative potential of broad compass.

> From the freshness of bright Slovene songs, the rare beauty of the melodies from Medjimurje, the archaism of Istria's musical folklore, and the Mediterranean warmth of Dalmatian tunes, to the ecstatic Bosnian airs, the novel Serbian dances, the subtle Macedonian rhythms, and the modest Montenegran songs — Yugoslav musical folklore asserts itself everywhere as the characteristic creative activity of the common man.   —Josip Andreis

The power of their musical creativity acquired special importance in those moments when the people sought spiritual identity, for it became the starting point of a creative flowering in art music. The creativity of the people could serve the creative impulse of the individual composer. This is precisely what happened for the first time in the early nineteenth century when Romanticism reached Yugoslavia. Insistence on the value and significance of the people's creative power was characteristic of this philosophic-artistic movement. The distinctive traits of Yugoslav folklore became the source from which a national artistic expression in music might be developed.

Folk music revealed its potentiality for development in a wide range of compositional practices; it showed itself capable of inspiring the most purely individual artistic creativity. Its traits could be reflected in all the musical elements. The thread of a musical idea — melody — might be constructed through an elaboration of motifs which derived from the various types of folk melodic motifs. The rhythm of folk music — its most characteristic element — might endow a musical thought with distinct vitality. Harmony based on the principle of folk polyphony might imbue a musical fabric with a clearly identifiable quality.

The reliance on elements from folk music to create art music tends to follow a certain pattern. In its most primitive stage, the folk material is quoted literally and subjected to simple elaboration (perhaps harmonization and instrumentation). The next stage consists of thoroughly reworking the elements derived from folk sources. Finally, a composer becomes inspired by the psychological characteristics of folk music, so that he uses no particular element yet imbues his creation with the authentic spirit of folk music.

The desire to create a national musical style led to technical problems in composition, because the introduction of new subject matter into the traditional context of Western art music required a corresponding introduction of appropriate new technical procedures. However, the issue of creating a new musical style based on folklore could not be reduced to a mere solving of formal, technical, or esthetic problems, for not even the greatest technical virtuosity can by itself create a work of art. A balance between formal technique and content had to be achieved. The optimum co-ordination of these two has remained a fundamental problem in the creation of a national musical style in Yugoslavia.

The earliest self-conscious, conceptually formulated attempt to create a national musical style on the basis of folk music appeared in Croatia in the fourth decade of the nineteenth century as one manifestation of a cultural movement called the Illyrian Renaissance. Apart from seeing in music a means for awakening and strengthening patriotic feelings, the bearers of this ideology strove to create a national art music based on folk materials. Vatroslav Lisinski

(1819-54) was the most significant composer in the Illyrian movement and was the first of the Yugo-slavs (literally, South Slavs) to write a nationalistic opera, *Ljubav i zloba* (Love and Malice) in 1846. He also composed songs for solo voice with piano. His works represent the earliest results of the assimilation of musical folklore into art music.

Around the middle of the century, Korneli Stanković (1831-65) became active in Serbia. He collected folk songs in addition to composing original music based on folk material. He valued folk music for its own sake, but also made arrangements for voice and piano as well as for chorus. Some of his sets of piano variations are based on folk themes.

In Slovenia too, the first signs of nationalistic musical creation appeared about the middle of the nineteenth century. The association *Glasbena matica* in Ljubljana developed a substantial program for cultivating Slovenian folk music and for fostering nationalistic creative activity. By the beginning of the second half of the century, a number of Slovenian composers were engaged in using folk music in the creation of art music forms — for the most part, vocal forms (solo songs with piano and choral works).

The folk music tradition played a decisive role in the emergence of a national musical culture in Macedonia, Bosnia and Herzegovina, and Montenegro, but here the beginnings of such developments date only from the twentieth century.

The first genuine artistic realization among the Yugoslav peoples of the relation between folklore and free musical creation appeared in the music of Stevan Mokranjac (1856-1914). Through his sure intuition, he was able to create extended polyphonic forms by elaborating and combining the simple elements of musical folklore. Early products of his exploration into the essence of folk music were his *Rukoveti* and his sacred polyphonic compositions. Mokranjac limited his work to choral music, which possesses relatively restricted tonal possibilities. Yet the polyphonic structure of his music clearly demonstrates how extended art forms can generate out of folk motifs. With the powerful and convincing logic of his style, he laid the foundation for a subsequent development which included the creation of more complex instrumental and vocal forms. Through his artistic insight he elevated the musical expression of the folk spirit to a higher level of logic and thus gave it greater esthetic significance.

The Romantic conception of folk creativity never completely clarified who represents the people. Folk art was generally considered the expression of a collective, ideally conceived popular spirit — a cultural product not related *just* to the peasantry, even though it was a product of this group. Little attention was paid to peasant life, and any emphasis on the hardships of this life was carefully avoided. Such was the case in romantic music too. The Yugoslav national style in music in its first, romantic phase, used folk sources without understanding them as living material related to a definite socio-economic formation. Elements from folk music were treated as material to be elaborated according to the existing traditional procedures of composition. This approach changed rather slowly. For a long time, only the external aspect of the folk psyche and its artistic expression were noticed. Typical of this are the exoticisms — augmented seconds, for example, or a certain decorative melodic coloration — which constitute the sole proof of "national" quality in many works by nineteenth century Yugoslav composers. Although Mokranjac did not seek artistic inspiration in the social reality of his time, but rather in folk song *per se,* we can still say that he was the first Yugoslav composer to try to perceive fully the essence of a complex and varied national feeling as realistically as possible.

The end of the domination of the Romantic philosophy in art over Yugoslav music did not signal the end of the influence of folk music on the free creative process in music. On the contrary, folklore shows an intense vitality in our own era. Its fundamental qualities are felt more deeply, and its intrinsic value is recognized more surely. It influences not only vocal music, but instrumental as well, and it is felt in the trends and currents of contemporary music. True, folklore is far from dominant in all facets of contemporary Yugoslav music. Stylistic currents and creative norms which have nothing in common with folk music and its ambience have appeared and developed. Their character is free, and they have an individual structure which is completely indifferent to the folk spirit.

Unlike the romantic-idealistic conceptions of the last century, the conception of folklore as a starting point for the creative artistic process in contemporary music is realistic. The folklore of the Yugoslav peoples is now studied as a cultural configuration of a patriarchal civilization. Its value is asserted without overstatement and with a critical attitude. Composers no longer accept the superficial elements from folk music. They study its constituents, absorb them, live with them, synthesize their peculiarities, and then create a musical language which possesses a national quality because it contains the characteristics of the folk spirit. Nationalism such as this does not represent simply an original colorfulness, but rather the expression in music of a personal understanding of moods and emotions. No significance is attached any longer to decorative and sentimental nationalism. Instead, the study of folk rhythms and melodies, of popular language and declamation, is becoming much more important than the use of folk melodies. The original folk spirit is recreated with all its peculiarities, musical and esthetic. Finally, a more equitable relation between form and content is also being achieved. Thus, folk elements in a native state are being less and less subjected to modification and adaptation according to the established, traditional principles of art music. Instead, new technical procedures are being discovered and new esthetic values sought, derived from the specific nature of the folk style and its esthetic. The difference between the romantic and the realistic conceptions of Yugoslav musical nationalism is therefore manifested in psychological, esthetic, artistic, and technical ways.

The highest peak of artistic transmutation and refinement of folk elements in contemporary Yugoslav music is reached in the works of Josip Slavenski (1896-1955). His music is not superficially national. It springs from the deepest roots of the folk spirit. It is original and personal both in its feeling and in its expression. Slavenski was particularly attracted by the pure and uncorrupted archaic elements in the folk tradition, by ancient motifs which have still not become antiquated. He knew well that a national spirit in music could not be achieved either through literal quotation or arrangement of folk music; therefore, he sought the artistic transformation of the folk materials.

The son of a modest craftsman, Slavenski became acquainted with folk music as a child, liked it, and untiringly listened to folk singing and playing throughout his life. His contact with folklore was direct and immediate. He observed it as a part of life and in the milieu from which it grew. In his mastery of the spirit of folk music, he seemed to carry on beyond where the folk musician had to stop. He continued the song and ennobled it artistically. Pavle Stefanović said that Slavenski differed from the folk musician because he acquired a mastery of expression and thus lost the anonymity of the folk musician.

Slavenski started from folk sources, in which the melodic-rhythmic element is paramount. Emphasizing the linear movement of tones, he wove melodic threads with a freedom inspired by folk polyphony. His free treatment of dissonance, for example, has its roots in the folk music of the South Slavs: parallel seconds occur as non-dissonant sonorities in the music of these people. Accepting this principle, Slavenski treated tonal complexes without regard for the traditional concept of dissonance. Thus we find in his works polytonal clusters and polyphonic textures which constitute dissonances in the traditional view, yet Slavenski often uses them as the foundation for lyric melodic lines which evoke a genuine folk spirit. The intense, tonally dense underlying material helps to emphasize the character of the melody.

Critics have often dealt with the problem of the nationalistic as well as the "anti-nationalistic" or "cosmopolitan" style in Yugoslav music. They have usually departed from extremist positions; some of them apotheosized music based on folk elements, while others underestimated, belittled, or completely negated it. In my opinion, the problem should not be confronted in this fashion.

Nationalism in music does not consist in rigid association with an ethnic milieu; this marks only the starting point of a given musical work. If a work is truly artistic, it exists not only in the sphere formed by a nation, but has international significance as well. The works of Josip Slavenski demonstrate the truth of this.

The goals of music are more than national. Only a profound contact with the most basic nature of a people and a deep understanding of the human psyche can lead to the creation of a truly national art; it will at the same time belong to humanity as a whole.

Juan Orrego-Salas

FOLK AND POPULAR MUSIC AS SOURCES IN THE DEVELOPMENT OF NATIONAL SCHOOLS OF COMPOSITION IN THE AMERICAS

Members of various generations of composers from the Americas have for over one hundred fifty years been trying to find local counterparts to the national music traditions enjoyed by their European contemporaries. Until fairly recently such concern represented the core of our cultural evolution, even considering the fact that it was not shared by all composers, since many have appeared during this period of time as either indifferent or against the idea of searching for a mother tongue in art music.

Those who became engaged in trying to develop such local idioms originally proposed a sort of deliberate music-nationalism, perhaps following at first such sentimental views as those of Massenet, quoted by Louis Elson, as saying that if he had been an American, he would have felt exalted as a composer "by the glories of your scenery, your Niagara, your prairies; . . . the beauty of your American women," adding that, "national surroundings must always inspire national music."[1]

Many European musicians established in our countries during the first half of the nineteenth century shared Massenet's views. Among others the Bohemian composer Anton Philip Heinrich (1781-1861), who came to the United States in 1818, prided himself on being considered an "American composer" when turning out such works as his *The Columbiad* or *Pushmataha,* inspired by his interest in vernacular music. Likewise, the Viennese disciple of Haydn, Sigismond Neukomm (1778-1858), a composer appointed to the Imperial Court of Don Pedro I in Rio de Janeiro, expressed a similar pride when writing his *O Amor Brasileiro* for piano, the first example of erudite music showing the use of a Brazilian popular theme.

Among such composers, the spirit of Nationalism emerged as a genuine by-product of Romanticism. Their recognition of the artistic values of folklore was expressed in a clear desire to dig into the traditions indigenous to the New World. Through the use of folk and popular devices in art composition, they visualized the possibilities of asserting their independence from foreign hegemonies and of achieving a self-identification with the values of a new land and its people. This general spirit was after all, the one that stimulated Chopin, Smetana, Dvořák, Grieg, and Glinka.

The circumstances for the development of this spirit certainly appeared to be quite favorable throughout the Americas by the first decades of the nineteenth century. The several Declarations of Independence, accomplished between 1776 and 1824, brought forth a general exaltation of native values. This provided fertile ground for the rise of national spirit, which for various reasons was not to show its traces in erudite music until much later. One of the reasons for the delay derived from the fact that in the specific orbit of art composition, the composers of the New World met with no traditions of music-making other than those developed in the Colonies along paths purely imitative of European music. Thus, the erudite forms that resulted from the earliest tentative confrontations of European and Indian cultures reflected almost exclusively the European traditions of church music favored in the Spanish and Portuguese colonies or the simpler, though no less European, psalmody favored by the early New England settlers. Neither the understanding and love of music, shown by the Puritans, nor the support and recognition of this art as an important educational tool, manifest by Spaniards and Portuguese, was sufficient to counteract the moralistic principles of the first and the missionary intentions of the latter, which to a large extent prevented the free participation of aboriginal practices in the shaping of the New World's traditions as they stood at the turn of the nineteenth century.

Still, the first sparks of an awakened music-nationalism in the Americas, stimulated by the rise of Independence, were nearly extinguished shortly thereafter by an all-inclusive support given to Romantic European music by the upper classes, as the new leaders of musical life, along with a contempt for those composers who appeared to be recognizing the artistic value of folklore and utilizing devices drawn from its musical product. Consequently, the potential rise of national schools yielded in the United States to German influences and, in Latin America, to Italian opera.

On the other hand, by the beginning of the nineteenth century the New World, after two to three hundred years of steady development, had finally established musical idioms peculiarly characteristic of each country in the fields of folk and popular music. These had matured along two different paths, the Afro-American and the Euro-American traditions. Each originally had its share of survivals, distinctively African and non-African in nature, as well as European and non-European; but as time went by, both of these traditions acquired such pronounced new profiles as to justify their being considered substantially American.

Only when the erudite composer finally met with such trends of folk and popular music, and only when he acquired a real consciousness of their being the strongest traditions so far, reflecting in depth the essence of our culture, were the doors opened toward further developments of vernacular significance in the field of art forms. And this phenomenon did not become apparent before the turn of the twentieth century, when a rising middle-class brought forth a growing participation in musical life from those native sectors of society dependent on the folk and popular arts.

Politically, such sectors stressed the point of their anti-Europeanism and sought for the establishment of a society strongly supported by systems developed along lines akin to our own cultural environment. But, culturally speaking they were essentially European.

Along this dichotomy, the first stages of an American music Nationalism became evident, and the Grand Traditions of fine art music—which throughout the Colonial Period and the nineteenth century had been dependent on imitations of European models—became oriented toward the vernacular.

The mechanics through which this type of nationalism evolved in the Americas changed from country to country. In the United States, Antonin Dvořák must probably be accepted as the original force behind the rise of a national school of composition. As Gilbert Chase expresses it, the significance of his presence in this country does not reside exclusively in his enthusiasm for American folk songs or in his writing of notable works inspired by his experiences in the New World, but in the "over-all liberating influence symbolized by his visit in relation to this particular historical moment in the development of musical culture in the United States."[2]

The *Serie Brasileira,* written in 1891 by Alberto Nepomuceno (1864-1920), became the first example of a symphonic work with a definite nationalistic significance in Brazil. Written in Europe, this composition (and many others of the same nature produced by Nepomuceno and some of his Brazilian contemporaries) is certainly a product of the direct challenge imposed on all composers, including non-European natives, by the nationalistic spirit that prevailed in the Old World throughout the Romantic Period. Such works, in spite of their pioneering nature along the line of a Brazilian national school development, still owed much more to the influx of European traditions and techniques than to an imperative need to attain an integrated relationship between European traditions and the essence of American folk music.

Followers of Dvořák in the United States and Nepomuceno in Brazil, as well as Manuel Ponce (1882-1948) in Mexico and Ignacio Cervantes (1847-1905) in Cuba, along with many other composers from the Americas active by the turn of the century, all had to face the fact that as the establishment of a national music idiom declined, their works remained in an unfavorable position compared to the broad appeal shown by a growing repertory of popular music that owed as much to certain European dance forms as to the American folk traditions. The waltz, the mazurka, the polka, and dozens of other forms had found a place in the vernacular of our countries through their assimilation by the populace and their amalgamation with the New World's folk traditions. Likewise, in the United States, through a fast process of absorption into popular culture, genres such as the blues, rag-time, and jazz came to symbolize the national idiom to such a degree that all other genres were practically excluded. Meanwhile, the forms of art composition still failed to provide examples substantially different from those of Europe, in spite of their external embodiment of folk-popular devices. This proved that a New World variant of the Grand Traditions of European music had yet to develop and that Nationalism had yet to surpass the level of being based on mere quotations of folk themes or on programmatic landscapings of an occasionally rampant patriotism. Indeed, the repertory of fine art music produced by the New World composer of nationalistic aims up to World War I was mainly dependent on imitations of certain characteristic features belonging to the national traditions of each country.

The establishment in the Americas of a truly integrated national idiom, such as that observed in the European masterworks of the nineteenth century, depended on the development of compositional techniques grounded in the vernacular of our peoples' music. This could not be achieved by mere borrowings from folk and popular music. Therefore, truly integrated national idioms had still not been developed by the end of World War I, and it remains to be seen if at present the situation has changed.

Perhaps success in achieving an integrated idiom has not yet been extensive, but many recent contributions to music in our countries have certainly proven that we are on our way. Our failure in arriving at a more steady and widespread establishment of such an idiom has not prevented an incredible growth of musical activity in the American Republics and an ever expanding creative process through which a host of composers of the highest professional stance are developing styles certainly representative of our twentieth century at large.

We have suggested that a truly integrated national idiom in art composition, based on the mingling of an American musical vernacular and the Grand Traditions of the Occidental World, had not yet been reached by the 1920's, and that it remains to be seen if developments in the succeeding decades have at all opened ways toward achieving it.

But before continuing our discussion along the lines of twentieth-century history, it is advisable to explore a little further into the concept of "vernacular" in the New World traditions of music, trying to understand its true significance and to establish its real framework.

What did this vernacular represent in the Americas?

Might it be confined to the traditions of Afro-American or Euro-American folk music or, perhaps, to the tribal Indian music made available by ethnomusicological findings since 1900 or thereabouts?

Certainly, the utilization of these or of other subsidiary traditions of folk music had served as vernacular sources from which many composers had borrowed, or to which they had referred, yet without quite reaching the desired goal. In the United States, Charles Wakefield Cadman (1881-1947), among others, had utilized Indian tribal materials; Henry Franklin Gilbert (1868-1928) had turned to the Negro; and John Powell (1882-1963) had used the Anglo-American folk-music traditions. Even earlier, Edward MacDowell (1861-1908) had employed aboriginal Indian themes within a thoroughly Germanic style. None of them, however, succeeded in creating an idiom substantially different from that employed by their Old World contemporaries or forerunners. The American folk-music features employed in their music only represented additions to an European context and were no more strongly attached to that context than the folk-music features of Spain were to some of the "Spanish" works by Bizet, Rimsky Korsakov, Debussy or than those of the American Negro were to Dvořák's Symphony "From the New World."

The nineteenth-century European heritage of a synthetic Nationalism, based on the incorporation of folk-song elements into art music, had no exact parallel in the achievements of New World composers. The main reason lay, perhaps, in the fact that at the time of the European composer's conscious drive toward Nationalism, he already possessed a sophisticated art music with centuries of background development, while the American composer had yet to develop even a distinctive variant of the European art music tradition, due mainly to the discontinuous line of historical hegemonies in the field of art music in the New World and to the lack of mutual contacts along which the existing art music and folk music traditions had developed. If we accept Charles Seeger's understanding of tradition as "a way of doing something inherited, cultivated and transmitted by successive generations of individual carriers of culture," which as he adds, requires "continuity in the general space-time,"[3] we will face the fact that, for the most part at least, such conditions were lacking in the Americas at the beginning of our century. Pre-Columbian traditions in Latin America were practically banished by the early European settlers. Later, the New World by-product of the European tradition of church music, originally imposed by Spain, lost much of its influence when Independence fostered in musical life and taste an upper-class hegemony with an overwhelming preference for Italian opera and French salon music. Admixtures of folk and art music, though existent from time to time throughout our history, did not spring from a ground swell of steady evolution. Consequently it is difficult to find that "continuity in the general space-time," that Seeger considers a prerequisite for a tradition, unless we search for it in the spheres of folk and popular music.

Still, the main concern of this survey is with fine art music and its creators who, when they became concerned with speaking in a distinctive New World idiom, had to face not only a highly discontinuous evolutionary background, but a virtual disconnection from the folk-music heritage of their own peoples. The folk-music heritage, after all, was not written, and its absorption through study of its oral traditions was not something that could be obtained overnight. Moreover, the cultivated composer of the Americas depended on Europe for his training, and a repertory of European music or native imitations thereof stood as the only base upon which he could build his own experience. Thus, the problem of the composer in the New World up to the 1920's was how to establish the necessary links between the various musical streams in his national environment and thereby fulfill the nationalistic aims which he had adopted from his European colleagues.

As we said, the first step undertaken was that of a conscious incorporation of folk-song elements into art music, which shortly proved to be quite precarious and often led to obvious incongruities of style, due to the fact that the self-contained unities of folk tunes did not lend themselves to successful motivic development in the established major forms of art music. Nevertheless, it was under such conditions that most of the so-called "National Schools" operated in the Americas until long after World War I. Works were produced ranging from those that might be characterized as representing an elegant and erudite popular art, such as *Porgy and Bess* by George Gershwin (1898-1937), to more sophisticated and ambitious undertakings such as those of Charles Ives (1874-1954), Heitor Villa-Lobos (1887-1959), or Silvestre Revueltas (1899-1940). Responding to the quest of Nationalism, native folk-popular tunes or titles describing local dance forms or festivities were often used.

Nevertheless, we may agree that by this date, the United States, as well as the leading countries in Latin America, had produced works considered by many as having a distinctive national character, in spite of the fact of their appearing virtually removed from the type of folklorism that prevailed prior to the 1930's. Many such examples can be quoted from the works of Aaron Copland (1900-), Henry Cowell (1897-1965), and Roy Harris (1898-) or from those of Carlos Chávez (1899-), Camargo Guarnieri (1907-), Juan José Castro (1895-), and Domingo Santa Cruz (1899-), among others. In this group we meet with distinctive local flavors emerging from the individual achievements of each of its members. They appear to have established standards, which are acknowledged as embodying definite national traits, and characteristic devices, which other composers might borrow as expressions peculiar to an individual culture. From the practice of such gifted and original composers, a repertory of music began to be built, which in retrospect is now considered to reflect the peculiarities of national schools with a growing international significance.

Thus, not before the fine art composer of the Americas stood at the end of a more extended line of evolution in his own field could he discover how to create a musical vernacular valid for the level of his interests. This evolutionary line comprised all the styles of European music (each carrying its own national vernacular) that the New World composer had imitated throughout the nineteenth century. It included the various local sources of folk music deliberately incorporated during the early decades of our century. It also included jazz. And it absorbed the hybrid consequence of mingling our popular music traditions with the forms of European salon dances sponsored by the aristocracy. Somewhat later, it embraced the various cosmopolitan methods of composition ranging from Neo-Classicism to total serialization, as well as electronic and aleatoric procedures. The whole ensemble of such sources converging into the path of erudite music represents, perhaps, the true American vernacular to which composers of the New World are becoming attached today. By following this, their own path, they are shaping a New World variant of the European Grand Tradition. They are succeeding in our several countries in developing a characteristic manner of music-making, the norms and archetypes of which are defined in certain outstanding examples of music that due to their individuality establish a new, distinctive, and identifiable creative orbit.

Clearly, the Americas could reach this point of true significance in national musical development only after composers appeared who were capable of handling creatively the entire bundle of past traditions from our countries, together with the "international" techniques of contemporary music. Alfred Einstein has observed that national characteristics are a consequence of the work of great masters. [4] A similar viewpoint has been advanced by Manfred Bukofzer, who asserted that what passes as typically French or Finnish in Debussy or Sibelius is, in fact, the individual achievement of artists who were strong enough to create the standards and clichés of what we now consider as national traits in the music of their respective countries. [5] So we have begun to sense in the works of either Charles Ives, Silvestre Revueltas or Heitor Villa-Lobos, of Aaron Copland, Henry Cowell, Virgil Thomson (1896-   ) or Carlos Chávez, certain norms which are quite different from those found in the music of our European contemporaries written along similar esthetic lines. During the stages following their early experiences, these New World composers have produced works through which substantial links are established with their own cultural environments, without necessarily borrowing directly from folk or popular music. Their occasional use of folk tunes is largely immaterial, as it is mainly the personal style of each composer that defines the several national expressions; these are not only different, if confronted one with the other, but constitute a distinctive group within the scope of world music.

The succeeding generation of American composers has enjoyed a similar freedom of thought and appears even more concerned with capturing the essence of their several traditions, rather than with quoting from or making references to the external by-products (e.g., folk or popular tunes) of those traditions. Moreover, as members of a much more integrated international world of culture whose musical lives are considerably more open to all the contemporary advancements of science, their minds appear increasingly alert to absorb without delay whatever new lines of thought emerge in the sphere of music. Consequently the speed with which changes take place in their individual evolution is considerably faster than it was among their predecessors. This accelerated evolutionary pace is evident in the work of such prominent composers as Alberto Ginastera (1916-   ) or Mario Davidowsky (1934-   ) from Argentina, Claudio Santoro (1919-   ) from Brazil, Roque Cordero (1917-   ) from Panama, Hector Tosar (1923-   ) from Uruguay, Gustavo Becerra (1925-   ) from Chile, Aurelio de la Vega (1925-   ) from Cuba, Gunther Schuller (1925-   ), Lukas Foss (1922-   ), Milton Babbitt (1916-   ), or Elliott Carter (1908-   ) from the United States, among many others, bear testimony to this. Most of them have undergone (in a space of time hardly exceeding twenty years) an evolution that started either from various forms of folklorism or from Neo-Classicism and has now reached the most advanced methods of composition, covering the entire spectrum of techniques ranging from total serialization to aleatoric and electronic music. No traces of a self-conscious Nationalism remain among these composers. Nevertheless, they owe a great deal to what at present can be visualized as a subtle but pervasive course of influences emerging from our folk and popular idioms along a continued and rich line of events and developments involving jazz, the Brazilian *bossa nova*, a variety of urban admixtures of popular forms with more sophisticated genres, re-interpretations of primitive Indian rituals, and so on. These composers have succeeded in producing technically up-to-date works of international significance, precisely because they are no longer tied to the type of "nativism" that, even fifty years ago, acted as a generally recessive factor in composition.

At present, we may still meet in the Americas composers who use folk music as a source for borrowing or imitation; but they belong to a minority who turn out products of a skin-deep Nationalism most often attached to styles that belong to the backwash of the Romantic Era. They certainly do not represent our present day cultural evolution. The work of such composers does not affect the broad panorama of twentieth century music in the Americas. That panorama encompasses the same trends of style-changes one finds in Europe, swinging between opposite polarities, from the complex to the simple, from the Neo-Classical to the ultra-romantic, from the abstract to the programmatic, from the aleatoric to the most laboriously controlled electronic and computerized product.

This course of antagonistic, hence dynamic events appears to be sustained by a backbone of creative achievement which has become a significant source for subsequent development. In other words, a creative continuity has been established that naturally fosters tradition.

No one can deny that such a creative continuity has already emerged from the contributions of Aaron Copland or Milton Babbitt in the United States, Heitor Villa-Lobos in Brazil, Carlos Chávez in Mexico, Alberto Ginastera in Argentina and others in other Latin American countries. This is the continuity we can recognize in the works of our younger composers, sometimes quite clearly, sometimes quite subtly, and certainly not always within stylistic frameworks or compositional methods correspondent to established archetypes; but a sense of creative continuity within American national traditions has, without question, evolved at last.

NOTES

[1]Louis C. Elson, *The History of American Music,* revised by A. Elson (New York, 1925), p. 337.
[2]Gilbert Chase, *America's Music* (New York, 1955), p. 391.
[3]Charles Seeger, "Music as a Tradition of Communication, Discipline, and Play," *Ethnomusicology,* Vol. 4 (1963), pp. 156-163.
[4]Alfred Einstein, *Greatness in Music* (New York, 1941), pp. 130, 137.
[5]Manfred Bukofzer, "The New Nationalism," *Modern Music,* Vol. 23 (1946), p. 245.

Krešimir Kovačević

NATIONALISM IN TEXTBOOKS, ARTICLES AND GENERAL STUDIES IN THE HISTORY OF MUSIC IN YUGOSLAVIA

The phenomenon of an emergent self-conscious nationalism in music characterized Yugoslav Romanticism no less than European Romanticism in general. Although the national renaissance at the turn of the century was channeled in the Yugoslav nations primarily toward the creation of a literary language, its scope included musical life as well. Indeed, the two tendencies actually coincided in the early stages of the Slovene and Croatian Renaissance. For example, Jacob Zupan (1734-1810) composed the first Slovene opera, *Belin* (1780 or '82; the score has not survived) on an original Slovene libretto by Janez Damascen Dev; the Slovene Janez B. Novak (1756-1833) wrote the musical score for Anton Tomaž Linhart's humorous play *A Merry Day, or Maticek is Getting Married* and called it *Figaro* (1790). The Croat Vatroslav Lisinski (1819-54) composed *Love and Malice* (1846), the first extant work of its kind by a South Slav. In Serbia, a native musical-theatrical form known as the "folk play with singing" (inspired by the Singspiel) appeared somewhat later.

The search among the Yugoslav peoples for a unique national musical expression continued throughout the nineteenth and well into the twentieth centuries. The principal lines of development are traced by Mr. Zija Kučukalić in his paper "Folk Music as an Influence on Art Music in Yugoslavia," published in the present volume, and I shall not attempt to improve on his historical survey here. Suffice it to say that the situation in Yugoslav music during this period was reflected very accurately in the works of historians and writers on music—all the more since many of them were composers as well.

The first important contributor to music literature was certainly Franjo Kuhač (1834-1911), ethnomusicologist, historian, theoretician, and composer. Kuhač was the founder of Croatian musicology and produced many works significant for the history of Croatian national art music. Apart from the major collection of folk tunes entitled *Juzno-slovjenske narodne popijevke* [Folk Tunes of the South Slavs], published in five volumes (1878-82, 1941), which contains some 2,000 tunes from various parts of Croatia and other South Slav countries, Kuhač also published two historical treatises. These are *Prilog povijesti glazbe južnoslavjanske* [A Contribution to the History of South Slav Music]

(1877-82), which contains descriptions and history of folk music instruments from the earliest period to his own time, and the sizeable comparative study *Osebine narodne glazbe, naročito hrvatske* [The Properties of Folk Music, Particularly That of the Croats] (1905-09). In the latter, he established the characteristic features of Croatian folk music with regard to intervals, performance practice, and formal structure, and compared Croatian folk music with that of the neighboring countries. His outstanding historical works include *Vatroslav Lisinski i njegovo doba* [Vatroslav Lisinski and His Times] (1877; 2nd ed. 1890) and *Ilirski glazbenici* [Illyrian Musicians] (1893). He tried to develop a Croatian musical terminology in his *Katekizam glazbe* [The Catechism of Music] (1875; 2nd ed. 1890), which was actually a translation of J. Chr. Lobe's *Katechismus der Musik* (1851).

A sincere patriot, Kuhač was sometimes carried away by nationalistic enthusiasm. While he correctly pointed out elements of Croatian folk melodies in the works of Haydn and Beethoven, his hypothesis on Haydn's Croat origin *(Josip Haydn i hrvatske narodna popievke* [Joseph Haydn and Croatian Folk Tunes], Vienac, 1880) was later found to have been entirely without foundation. Equally incorrect were his claims for the Croatian descent of Giuseppe Tartini *(Josip Tartini i hrvatska pučka glazba* [Giuseppe Tartini and Croatian Folk Music], Prosvjeta, 1898) and Franz Liszt *(Uspomene na dra Franju Liszta* [Memories of Dr. Franz Liszt], Hrvatsko kolo, 1908).

An important Slovene musicologist, Josip Mantuani (1860-1933), emerged at the turn of the century. He was the first to collect and study systematically materials related to the history of Slovene music. He made an especially thorough study of the life and, to some extent, the work of Jakob Gallus *(Jakob Gallus,* Crkveni glasbenik, 1891; *Jakob Gallus-Petelin,* Dom in svet, 1919; *Über die Messen des Jacob Handl,* Musica divina, 1913). He also published valuable studies on Jurij Slatkonja, a Slovene musician who lived and worked in Vienna at the turn of the sixteenth century (Crkveni glasbenik, 1905; Dom in svet, 1907) and the nineteenth century Slovene composer Jurij Mihevec (Nova muzika, 1929).

While Mantuani was concerned with the Slovene musical past, composer and musicologist Gojmir Krek (1875-1942) was preoccupied with the future and thus greatly influenced the Slovene music of his time. As the editor of the music review *Novi akordi* (1901-14), he rallied around it the best musical creators of the period to promote Slovene music. In an effort to modernize Slovene music and bring it abreast of contemporary international developments, Krek wrote numerous articles of an ideological and historical nature advocating the new trends in music. As a composer of technically accomplished pieces in the neo-romanticist style, he also set an example for his contemporaries.

A similar role was played in Croatia by Antun Dobronić (1878-1955). He emerged at a crucial moment in the recent history of Croatian music, when Croatian artists were implementing the ideas of the Illyrian Renaissance as elaborated by Vatroslav Lisinski in the nineteenth century. Dobronić, "a critical and analytic mind, managed to work out an ideological program for what his predecessors and contemporaries created, deliberately or casually, namely [art] music based on the elements of folk music" (P. Markovac). His radical approach to the ideology of Zajc's period, expressed in his polemic articles, won him the sympathy of the younger generation who rallied to his cause. Thus, he became an ideological leader of the generation of progressive composers who were to create, principally in the period between the two world wars, highly valuable pieces in the nationalist style. Dobronić's activities were not confined to the domain of theory; being also a composer, he contributed many fine works to the repertory of Croatian music.

Musical nationalism was also advocated in Croatia by Božidar Širola (1889-1956), a composer and musicologist of international renown and the founder of Croatian music historiography. Širola studied folk music and collected materials for a history of Croatian music. His works include ethnomusicological treatises on individual folk instruments, *Pregled povijesti hrvatske muzike* [A Historical Survey of Croatian Music] (1922), *Hrvatska narodna glazbaa* [Croatian Folk Music] (1940), and *Hrvatska umjetnička glazba* [Croatian Art Music] (1942). The main object of his musicological works was to establish the territorial characteristics of folk music. In addition, he investigated the origins, historical development, and territorial spread of folk tunes and music instruments, particularly the latter. In that field, he achieved results of considerable significance to ethnomusicology. As a music historian, he was a data collector rather than a critic; nevertheless, his *Pregled povijesti hrvatske muzike* was the first comprehensive book of its kind in Croatia and contains much valuable data. He also left a legacy of several outstanding compositions, mainly oratorios and vocal pieces.

A central part in the development of Serbian nationalist music was played by the composers and music scholars Miloje Milojević and Petar Konjović. A long-time music critic, Miloje Milojević (1884-1946) was guided by consistently exacting criteria and was consequently recognized as "a man who regulated musical life in a period of transition from primitive creation to a larger, broader, and more comprehensive movement on an European level" (B. Dragutinović). Milojević was not content to be a mere chronicler. He tried to deal with the problems of Yugoslav music by analyzing the basic esthetic principles of nationalism in music. A connoisseur of Serbian musical creation, he re-examined the values of music creators in the history of Serbian music and took stands on phenomena and movements in contemporary European music. His treatises and articles were published in three volumes under the title *Muzički članci i studije* [Articles and Studies in Music] (1926-53).

The prominent Serbian composer Petar Konjović (b. 1883) has never hesitated to pick up his pen and present verbally the problems with which he is preoccupied. In his writings, he has generally concentrated on nationalist music, as in the collection *Ličnosti* [Personalities] (1920) and *Knjiga o muzici* [Book on Music] (1947) and in the monographs on Miloje Milojević (1954) and Stevan Mokranjac (1956).

The musicologists Pavao Markovac and Vojislav Vučković occupy a particularly prominent place among musical scholars active between the two world wars. Both were dialectical materialists, and both were killed by the Nazis. Markovac (1903-41) devoted most of his work to elevating the musical life of the working class and to combating the corrupt elements in Croatian musical life. A book of his works, *Izabrani članci i eseji* [Selected Articles and Essays], was published in 1957.

A representative of progressive Serbian art ideology and a partisan of free social development, Vojislav Vučković (1910-42) founded many artist groups. In addition to his talents as an organizer, he was a gifted music scholar. His best treatises are *Materijalistička filozofija umetnosti* [The Materialist Philosophy of Art] (1935), *Muzicki realizam Stevana Mokranjca* [The Musical Realism of Stevan Mokranjac] (1940), and some articles reprinted in *Izboru eseja* [Selected Essays] (1955). He was also a highly accomplished composer.

Josip Andreis, Dragotin Cvetko, and Stana Djurić-Klajn jointly produced the first comprehensive and scholarly contribution to the history of Yugoslav music — *Historijski razvoj muzičke kulture u Jugoslaviji* [The Historical Development of Musical Culture in Yugoslavia] (1962). The abundance of factual data and the meticulously developed chapters on the nationalistic trend and its protagonists are a reliable source of information for anyone interested in the subject.

The most outstanding representative of present-day Slovenian musicology, Dragotin Cvetko (b. 1911), has achieved international recognition for his scholarship. His most important works include *Odmevi glasbene klasike na Slovenskem* [The Echoes of Musical Classicism in Slovenia] (1955), *Zgodovina glasbene umetnosti na Slovenskem* [The History of Music in Slovenia] in three volumes (1958-60), *Academia Philharmonicorum Labacensis* (1962), *Stoletja slovenske glasbe* [Centuries of Slovenian Music] (1964), and *Histoire de la musique slovène* (1967), as well as monographs on Risto Savin (1949), Davorin Jenko (1952), and Jakob Gallus (1965).

The Croatian music historian Josip Andreis (b. 1909) has published a number of significant works, including the substantial *Historija muzike* in three volumes (1951-54; 2nd ed. in 2 volumes, 1966), a monograph on Jakov Gotovac (1957) and the studies *Rezultati i zadaci muzičke nauke u Hrvatskoj* [Achievements and Tasks of Musical Science in Croatia] (1965) and "Music in Croatia Down to the End of the Nineteenth Century" [in English] *(Zvuk,* No. 77-78, 1967).

Stana Djurić-Klajn, the author of the first history of Serbian music, has published a collection of essays entitled *Muzika i muzičari* [Music and Musicians] (1956), as well as many studies, articles, and papers for international musicological congresses. Among them are *Dvadeset Godina Muzičke Akademije u Beogradu* [Twenty Years of the Belgrade Music Academy] (1958), and essays on Josef Schlesinger (Jevrejski Almanah, 1961) and Petar Konjović (Pozorišni život, 1963).

Nationalism in music is the main area of research for Krešimir Kovačević (b. 1913), who has written *Hrvatski kompozitori i njihova djela* [Croatian Composers and Their Works] (1960) and *Muzičko stavaralaštvo u Hrvatskoj 1945-1965* [Musical Creation in Croatia 1945-1965] (1966), as well as the article *"Die kroatische Musik des XVII und XVIII Jahrhunderts" (Musica antiqua Europae orientalis,* Bydgoszcz, 1966), *"Die kroatische Musik des XX. Jahrhunderts" (Zvuk,* No. 77-78, 1967) and *"Dix siècles de la musique croate" (The Bridge,* Zagreb, 1968).

The subject of nationalism in music has also preoccupied Zija Kučukalić (b. 1929), whose contributions to the subject include *Likovi savremenih bosansko-hercegovačkih kompozitora* [Profiles of Contemporary Bosnian-Herzegovinian Composers] (1961), *Dvadeset godina Sarajevske opere* [Twenty Years of the Sarajevo Opera] (1966), *The Development of Musical Culture in Bosnia and Herzegovina* (1967) and the article *"Die Tonkunst Bosniens und der Herzegowina in Vergangenheit und Gegenwart" (Zvuk,* No. 77-78, 1967).

No mention has been made here of the numerous Yugoslav ethnomusicologists and folklorists whose work (collecting folk songs and writing analytical studies of them) has also had an influence, though indirect, on the development of nationalistic music. Also omitted are many other musicologists and music scholars whose works have not been concerned with the music peculiar to Yugoslavia. Further information on them, and on the writers mentioned in the course of this article, may be found in the *Muzicka enciklopedija* Vols. 1 and 2, published by the *Leksikografski zavod* (Zagreb, 1958-63).

H. Wiley Hitchcock

NATIONALISM AND ANTI-NATIONALISM IN AMERICAN MUSIC HISTORIES

The title of this paper may be interpreted as meaning "How American Music Historians Have Viewed American Music," and several subtitles are possible: "A Bird's-Eye View of American-music Historiography"; "Changing Attitudes of American Music Historians toward American Music"; or "American Music History's Neglected Child: American Music."

What I should like to attempt is, first, to discuss the place of American music in general histories of music written by Americans; second, to discuss some specialized studies in American music; finally, to discuss the histories of American music that have been written by my compatriots. I shall be concerned more with the *attitudes* of American music historians than with the contents of their product: the latter can best be gleaned from the actual works I shall cite, and besides, discussion of how Americans have *felt* about their own music will prove quite adequate for our purposes. I should also like to make clear that by "American" I mean "of the United States," with apologies to other nations of the Americas for my provincial (but hopefully not arrogant) use of that hemispheric term to refer only to my own country.

I

How have American authors of general music histories viewed American music?

American musical historiography is almost exactly a century old: our first history of music, published between 1870 and 1874, was the *History of Music* by the Alsatian, Frédéric Louis Ritter. It need not detain us: Ritter, who did not come to America until the age of twenty-seven and who was concerned with instructing the young ladies of Vassar College in the music of Europe's past, did not even mention American music. (He was, however, to publish later the first history of American music.)

Much more startling than Ritter's failure to include American music in his history is the fact that not for seventy years after his book would an American author's general history of music include any discussion of American music. Paul Henry Lang's *Music in Western Civilization* (1941) was a monumental and masterly account of music in its social and cultural contexts; translated into

(199)

several European languages, it was America's first significant contribution to international music historiography. In his book of some 1100 pages, covering the giant span of Western civilization from ancient Greece to the twentieth century, Lang did mention American music—just barely, with a total of seventeen pages.

The next full-length history of music by an American, and the one read universally now in the U.S.A., was Donald Grout's *A History of Western Music* (1960), a work of about 750 pages which also begins with the music of ancient Greece. In his last two chapters, Professor Grout includes a few paragraphs on American music: two pages in a discussion of late nineteenth-century nationalist trends; one-half page on jazz; and two and one-half pages on twentieth-century American music.

Statistically speaking, Professor Lang devoted 1.50 per cent of his book, Professor Grout 0.67 per cent of his, to American music. Nationalism in American music history? One might better speak of *anti*-nationalism. Our view of American music has been exactly the opposite of that of other nationals concerning the position of their own music in history: In Italy, a late nineteenth-century *Compendio della storia della musica* (1866) by Abramo Basevi concluded modestly that "in science and the arts our country surpasses all other nations"; the music history adopted for the city schools of Paris in 1930 *(Histoire de la musique* by Alice Gabeaud) remarks that "French music continues to hold her place as *éducatrice du monde*"; German music histories at least since Hans Joachim Moser's lecture of 1914, "Der Durgedanke als kulturgeschichtliches Problem," have tended to view German music as the "guiding star" of musical development in the Western world (the term appears explicitly in Max Chop's *Führer durch die Musikgeschichte* of 1922). In contrast to such views, American music historians have tended either to omit entirely any discussion of American music in their "histories," to deny that it shared at all in the general development of Western music, or to damn American music with faint praise, including comments on it within the general framework of Western music history as a kind of reluctant afterthought.

To understand this virtual exclusion of their own country's music from their own music histories, one must understand the degree to which Americans of the nineteenth century submitted to domination by Romantic and Transatlantic ideas about music—ideas which have continued to dominate them virtually to the present.

Early America was basically a product of British colonization. The thirteen original states had all been settled mainly by British, and it was against England that they fought a Revolutionary War for autonomy, following their Declaration of Independence in 1776. Early American culture, then, including our music, was predominantly British in character. Early in the nineteenth century, however, a vast change in American musical attitudes began to take place. One influential American composer and educator, Thomas Hastings (1784-1872), hinted at this change when he wrote in 1822, in *A Dissertation on Musical Taste:*

> We are the decided admirers of German music. We delight to study and to listen to it. The science, genius, the taste, that everywhere pervade it, are truly captivating to those who have learned to appreciate it: but such, we presume, are not yet the majority of American or English auditors or executants.

Hastings was writing as one of the first spokesmen for a new tradition in American music, one that I have elsewhere[1] called the "cultivated tradition," as opposed to an American "vernacular tradition." Terms like "science," "genius," and "taste" bespeak special standards, not for all music, but for the *art* of music; not for music as a utilitarian part of everyday life or a pleasant diversion on the surface of life, but as an art whose holy mission was to edify and uplift. "Appreciation" of such music required *cultivation.*

With the early nineteenth century restoration of diplomatic, commercial, social, and cultural relations with western Europe, Americans – particularly those in the old established Atlantic seaboard centers – turned to Europe for cultural models: they sought selfconsciously and un-selfconfidently to cultivate an artistic taste. Western Europe at the time was just approaching the climax of the Romantic movement. Romanticism had had its earliest and strongest flourishing in Germany and, although springing initially from poets and novelists, it found its highest expression and made its greatest impact through German music and musicians. Hardly any European nation escaped this impact – nor did the United States. With the revolutions of 1848, moreover, a wave of Germans emigrated to America, further encouraging the Germanicization of America's cultivated tradition of art-music. The American pianist Louis Moreau Gottschalk commented in his diary in 1863 that "all the musicians in the United States are Germans." A year earlier, with the same kind of exaggeration but also the same perceptive acknowledgment of an America wholly under Germanic musical influence, Gottschalk had written: "It is remarkable that almost all the Russians in America are counts, just as almost all the musicians who abound in the United States are nephews of Spohr and Mendelssohn."[2]

This situation affected in at least three ways American ideas about America's place in the "history of music" and about the history of American music itself: First, Americans rejected their musical *past,* dominated as it had been not only by popular, "unscientific" music but by British backgrounds.[3] In the nineteenth century this rejection of America's past meant a rejection of America's past music as a basis for the new "scientific" music of the cultivated tradition. Early America had indeed a musical tradition; but in the nineteenth century that tradition, founded on Anglo-American psalmody and hymnody and on the great reservoir of Anglo-American song, was scorned completely by composers of the cultivated tradition. Second, Americans rejected the American *present* as a source of either topical or musical subject-matter: the very aspects of nineteenth-century America and its music that were unique had by definition no models in Europe; they got no celebration in American music. Thus no echo of the fantastic American landscape, or of pioneering (despite its being "the Romantic movement in action," as Lewis Mumford has said[4]), or of American industry and science was heard in nineteenth-century American music of the cultivated tradition. Similarly, no echo was heard of the many kinds of vernacular-tradition music of the time — folk hymns, Negro music, minstrel-show songs and dances, popular marches and dances, folksongs of many sorts. That composers of genteel, cultivated art-music were actually ashamed of American vernacular-tradition music is suggested by the career of Stephen Foster (1826-1864), well-known songwriter. Having begun as a composer of genteel "household" songs of sentiment, Foster decided to compose also for the more plebeian, earthy, vernacular medium of the blackface minstrel-show. Ashamed at first to be associated with that medium, Foster sold songs to the minstrel-troupe leader E. P. Christy: thus his most successful song by far, *Old Folks at Home* (1851), was originally presented and published as the work of Christy. Ultimately, attracted by the financial gain promised by the publication of minstrel-show songs, Foster wrote to Christy requesting his "name" back and saying with a fine (but defensive) show of resolution, "I have concluded ... to pursue the Ethiopian business without fear or shame and ... to establish my name as the best Ethiopian songwriter."[5]

The third result of the split between vernacular and cultivated American music traditions was, of course, to throw American cultivated music into direct competition, so to speak, with the European music it sought to emulate. Needless to say, American music was inferior. A Beethoven, a Schumann, a Wagner emerges as the crest of a wave of musical tradition that has been gathering for virtually centuries; America could hardly throw up such a wave-crest in a few decades.

Viewed in this light, it is perhaps no wonder that American writers on the history of Western music have unanimously neglected American music in their books; no wonder that theirs has been a basically anti-nationalist attitude. So long as our music historians concerned themselves only with the great Western tradition of fine-art music — with the "cultivated" tradition — they saw American music, at least of the nineteenth century and earlier, as distinctly second-class: the competition was far, far too keen.

II

What about specialized studies of isolated aspects of American music? What has been done? and what has *not* been done? In relation to "nationalism" what has been or is the attitude of the American scholarly community toward American-music studies?

The first great scholar to make detailed studies of any aspect of American music was O.G.T. Sonneck (1873-1928). Chief of the Music Division of the Library of Congress in Washington, Sonneck, who was born in America but educated in Germany, published many monographs on American music. His most extensive studies were *Early Concert-Life in America (1907) and Early Opera in America* (1915). These, along with his monumental *Bibliography of Early Secular American Music: 18th Century* (1905), provided models of exacting scholarship and exhaustive detail. Today, a half-century later, they have been neither superseded nor matched, for in general American music has continued to be neglected by American musicologists.

American musicology is not yet a century old: our first scholarly journal, *The Musical Quarterly*, appeared only in 1915. Its approach to music history, and one that still predominates among American musical scholars, was based on the principles enunciated by the Viennese musicologist Guido Adler in a famous article of 1885, "Umfang, Methode und Ziel der Musikwissenschaft" *(Vierteljahrsschrift für Musikwissenschaft,* Vol. 1, p. 1). Adler emphasized analytic and style-critical studies of musical "monuments" as the primary responsibility of musicologists; he minimized the importance of studies of the social or cultural uses of music; he was concerned with masterworks by master composers. American musicologists of the 1920's and 1930's almost unanimously accepted those principles. Furthermore, confirmed in their European orientation by the arrival in America during the Nazi era of many fine European scholars, American musicologists focused their attention not on American music but on European. It is a remarkable fact that although American scholars have contributed to many *Denkmäler, Monumenta,* and *Gesamtausgaben* of music by European composers, there is not yet in print a complete edition of the works of a single American composer, and the closest we have come to a volume of *Denkmäler* is a single modest historical anthology of American music including some 130 compositions or excerpts. [6]

The attitude toward American-music studies of a majority of American musicologists was summed up accurately, I am afraid, in a now-notorious colloquialism by Joseph Kerman, in his keynote paper at the 1964 meetings of the American Musicological Society. Suggesting "A Profile for American Musicology," Professor Kerman dismissed studies of American composers' music as a futile exercise: he said we can be interested in the music of, for example,

Marenzio or Couperin because that music can be brought to life and made a vital part of our contemporary experience, but as for Francis Hopkinson, Lowell Mason, or Theodore Chanler (and here Professor Kerman cited American composers from the eighteenth, nineteenth, and twentieth centuries), "Man, they are dead."

Despite the general lack of interest in American music among the American musicological community, a few scholars have made notable contributions. Sonneck's early models of meticulous scholarship, many of them bibliographical studies, have been followed in such a work as Richard Wolfe's monumental three-volume bibliography, *Secular Music in America 1801-1825* (New York Public Library, 1964). Irving Lowens and Allen Britton, working singly and as a team, have explored especially the late eighteenth-century choral music of New England; one among its several genres is treated definitively in Ralph Daniel's *The Anthem in New England before 1800* (Pi Kappa Lambda Studies in American Music, Vol. 1; Evanston, 1966). Donald McCorkle has written extensively about, and edited music by, the German-speaking communities of Moravian brethren in eighteenth- and early nineteenth-century America. Important contributions have been made by scholar-librarians at the Library of Congress and the New York Public Library. Robert Stevenson has concentrated on Spanish music in Latin America, but has also recently completed a careful survey of *Protestant Church Music in America* (New York, 1966). Few professional musicologists have concerned themselves with jazz or related music, but the late Marshall Stearns (a Chaucer specialist!) has written the most objective and well-documented history, *The Story of Jazz* (New York, 1956); Rudi Blesh and Harriet Janis have surveyed a related music in *They All Played Ragtime* (New York, 1959); Charles Keil has written a splendid account of *Urban Blues* (Chicago, 1966); and the composer Gunther Schuller has published *Early Jazz* (New York, 1967), the first serious style-critical study of the subject. Few critical biographies of American composers have appeared; among those that observe high standards of scholarship and are also critically perceptive are Henry and Sidney Cowell's *Charles Ives and His Music* (New York, 1955), John Tasker Howard's *Stephen Foster, America's Troubadour* (revised edition; New York, 1962), and Kathleen Hoover and John Cage's *Virgil Thomson: His Life and Music* (New York, 1959). In a class by itself, a remarkable demonstration of the potential riches for American music history in what I have called our vernacular-tradition music, is Hans Nathan's study of *Dan Emmett and the Rise of Early Negro Minstrelsy* (Norman, Oklahoma, 1962). Among successful broader studies one might single out John Mueller's sociologically oriented account of *The American Symphony Orchestra* (Bloomington, Indiana, 1951) and Arthur Loesser's lively social history, *Men, Women and Pianos* (New York,

1954). By now a number of Ph.D. dissertations have been written on American music. For the most part, these have been style-studies, along Adlerian lines, of the works of single composers. Since it is exceptional for American dissertations to achieve publication, the results of these studies have not been widely disseminated.

The list of specialized studies in American music of which we may be proud (in a scholarly sense) is actually rather small. However, the past twenty-five or thirty years have seen an increase in its rate of growth. This increase was brought about partly by the populist trend of the 1930's, which saw Americans newly interested in their own past; partly by the nationalist sentiments evoked by World War II; and finally by a more liberal view of what historical musicology — especially in a fluid, diverse, and democratic society like that of the United States — could or should concern itself with.

Charles Seeger (born 1886) has been the most eloquent spokesman for this new view of the proper attitude for American musicologists to take *vis à vis* their own music. Seeger asserted bluntly that "the majority of musicologists are not primarily interested in music, but in the literature of the European fine art of music, its grammar and syntax (harmony and counterpoint)."[7] Pointing out that fine-art music is but one of four main traditional idioms in world culture — (1) primitive, (2) fine-art, (3) folk, and (4) popular — and that in a dynamic, nascent culture like that of the United States the fine-art idiom may well be the weakest or at any rate the least universal or representative of the culture, Seeger claimed:

> It will be readily understood, therefore, that the character of music activity in the Americas up to 1900 compels an approach in many ways different from that conventionally in use by historico-musicology. It must perforce be almost exclusively ethno-musicological, quantitative, rather than qualitative, more concerned with tradition than with only the outstanding carriers of tradition, and with all four idioms. . . .[8]

Seeger's point of view was not that of a nationalist but of a cultural historian interested in all levels of culture. Rejecting the older, exclusive concern with a cultivated tradition, an educated culture, an elite art — the best that has been thought and said by the few in a civilization, as Matthew Arnold once put it — Seeger believed we ought to be concerned also with the vernacular tradition, popular culture, mass art — "the run of what is thought, felt, and liked by the many," as Max Lerner has said.[9] But if it was not a nationalistic impulse that led Seeger to his views, his ideas made room for a new interest in American music by American music historians, for they offered new standards of scholarly value and opened up areas of investigation different from those emphasized by the traditional European historical musicology in which for so long American music historians had been schooled. Essentially, what Seeger challenged us to do was to write about the history of *music* rather than the history of *a* music, i.e., the history of musical culture rather than the history of a single musical tradition.

Before suggesting how this challenge has been taken up by some scholars, let me outline briefly the history of American-music histories.

III

The first attempt at a history of American music was by that same Frédéric Ritter I mentioned earlier as the first American author of a general history of music. Ritter's *Music in America* (1883) was concerned exclusively with the cultivated tradition in American music, was if anything anti-nationalist, and measured our music critically by the standards of European fine-art music. Ritter went so far as to claim that "the people's song . . . is not to be found among the American people" — thus relieving himself of any responsibility to discuss our vernacular music tradition. Louis Elson's *History of American Music* (1904) shared Ritter's orientation.

Oscar Sonneck, whom I have mentioned as a peerless pioneer in American-music scholarship, hinted in a lecture of 1916 titled "The History of Music in America" that perhaps American music historians had been too narrowly restrictive in their viewpoint. "Our books," said Sonneck, "deal more with the history of music and musicians *in America* than with the history of *American* musical life." Sonneck himself, however, did not develop this idea into a full-scale history, nor was his hint acted upon by the next historian of our country's music, John Tasker Howard.

Howard's *Our American Music,* far more extensive than any earlier survey, was first published in 1931. Within the next fifteen years so much new research had been done — reflecting the newly awakened interest of Americans in their own past, which I have mentioned as characteristics of the 1930's and 1940's — that Howard had to revise his book twice (2nd ed., 1939; 3rd ed., 1946). Nevertheless, he did not change his basic viewpoint, which was dominated by European fine-art music ideals and which saw American music as having engaged in a long, arduous struggle to rise to European levels of musical excellence. Howard divided American music history into three periods, and the titles of the three sections of his book reveal his attitude: Part I — 1620-1800 — Euterpe in the Wilderness; Part II — 1800-1860 — Euterpe Clears the Forest; Part III — 1860 to the present — Euterpe Builds Her American Home.

The next history of American music, and the first to adopt the multilateral, mutli-level approach urged by Charles Seeger, was *America's Music* by Gilbert Chase (New York, 1955). Reacting violently against what I have called the "anti-nationalism" of earlier American-music historians (which we have seen to be really an exclusive orientation to the fine-art idiom of Euro-America), Chase belligerently introduced his book by saying, "My own approach to America's music is not at all respectable—my bête noire is the genteel tradition." He proudly pointed out that "in this book, some fifteen chapters [of thirty-one] deal, in whole or in part, with various phases of American folk, primitive, and popular music." [10] And he went so far as to say that in his opinion "important" American music *was* important to the degree that it was "different from European music." This sounds suspiciously like a nationalistic viewpoint, and, in a way, Chase was being nationalistic — but only in the sense of downgrading any American music that smacked of European models, and then only if it belonged to the World War I period of American music.

Rather than viewing Chase as being an ardent nationalist, I view him as attempting to redress the balance in American-music historiography between concern for the tradition of fine-art music — virtually the only tradition dealt with by earlier writers — and the traditions of primitive, folk, and popular music. Admitting that primitive music (e.g., of the American Indian) has had almost no rôle in the general culture of the United States,[11] he recognized that in American democratic society, which has lacked the clear-cut cultural stratification of western Europe's older, more autocratic societies, the popular-music tradition — or what I prefer to call the vernacular tradition, since it has drawn on various elements of the folk, the popular, and the once-elite idioms — has been extraordinarily important in relation to the other idioms of folk and fine-art music.

Insisting on this point, which, against the background of earlier American-music histories, was somewhat revolutionary, Chase acted like any good revolutionary: he denied any virtues in the old regime; he devalued American fine-art music (of the nineteenth and early twentieth centuries, at least) to the point of bankruptcy, suggesting that a single popular song by Stephen Foster was worth any number of concertos by Edward MacDowell. In sum, Chase was not writing a chauvinistically nationalist history, he was simply shifting the criteria of significance for American music history — by about 180 degrees!

In my own *Music in the United States: A Historical Introduction,* I have attempted to be more moderate. I see no virtue, nor historical truth, in denigrating American music of the cultivated tradition simply because it aped European music; that is what one segment of our nineteenth-century culture was all about, and as a historian I must accept it. On the other hand, I owe much to Gilbert Chase and Charles Seeger in my recognition of the vitality, the honesty, the "American-ness," and indeed the beauty of our vernacular tradition. That tradition is discussed at length in my book.

IV

Nationalism *per se* has been totally foreign to American music-historical writings. Our historians were first, for a long time continued to be, and to some degree are still, anti-nationalist. The shift of attitude that is now visible has not been, however, in the direction of nationalism. It has been toward a "pan-culturalism," toward an acceptance of not merely one idiom, one tradition, or one mode of musical expression as the proper concern of music-historical study, but of all the kinds of music that America has made, used, sung and played.

NOTES

[1] *Music in the United States: A Historical Introduction* (Englewood Cliffs, New Jersey, 1969).

[2] Louis Moreau Gottschalk, *Notes of a Pianist,* ed. Jeanne Behrend (New York, 1964), pp. 127, 102.

[3] We can observe this rejection as recently as 1963, in an American history of music published in that year: in their *History of Music and Musical Style* (New York, 1963), Homer Ulrich and Paul Pisk soberly declare, in a statement that is palpable nonsense, "For two centuries after the first settlements were established on the American continent a tradition of American music did not exist" (p. 663).

[4] *The Golden Day* (2nd ed., Boston, 1957), p. 20.

[5] "Ethiopian" here means Negro (i.e., blackface) minstrel-show. The entire text of this interesting letter is given in Gilbert Chase (ed.), *The American Composer Speaks* (Baton Rouge, Louisiana, 1966), p. 57.

[6] W. Thomas Marrocco and Harold Gleason, *Music in America . . . 1620-1865* (New York, 1964).

[7] "Oral Tradition in Music," *Standard Dictionary of Folklore, Mythology, and Legend* (New York, 1949-50), Vol. 2 (1950), p. 825.

[8] "The Cultivation of Various European Traditions in the Americas," *Report of the Eighth Congress of the International Musicological Society, New York 1961,* Vol. 1–Papers (Basel, 1961), p. 366.

[9] *America as a Civilization* (New York, 1957), p. 780

[10] *America's Music,* 1st edition, pp. xvii, xix.

[11] In the second edition of *America's Music* (1966) Chase admitted this (reluctantly): his earlier chapter on Indian tribal music was eliminated to make room for a new one on music in the 1960's.